Radical Hamilton

Radical Hamilton

*Economic Lessons from a
Misunderstood Founder*

Christian Parenti

VERSO
London • New York

First published by Verso 2020
© Christian Parenti 2020

1 3 5 7 9 10 8 6 4 2

Verso
UK: 6 Meard Street, London W1F 0EG
US: 20 Jay Street, Suite 1010, Brooklyn, NY 11201
versobooks.com

Verso is the imprint of New Left Books

ISBN-13: 978-1-78663-392-7
ISBN-13: 978-1-78663-393-4 (US EBK)
ISBN-13: 978-1-78663-391-0 (UK EBK)

British Library Cataloguing in Publication Data
A catalogue record for this book is available from the British Library

Library of Congress Cataloging-in-Publication Data

Names: Parenti, Christian, author.
Title: Radical Hamilton : economic lessons from a misunderstood founder /
  Christian Parenti.
Other titles: Economic lessons from a misunderstood founder
Description: First edition hardback. | London ; Brooklyn : Verso Books,
  [2020] | Includes bibliographical references and index. | Summary: "This
  book explains Hamilton's radical ideas in the context of his
  revolutionary times and in contrast to other revolutionaries, such as
  Thomas Jefferson, who emerges as the epitome of rural, slave-owning,
  anti-statist thinkers. This is a book of scholarship, with hundreds of
  notes and explanations of early American economics and history, but
  written in a stylish, accessible, narrative style befitting a leading,
  longtime journalist"— Provided by publisher.
Identifiers: LCCN 2020008282 (print) | LCCN 2020008283 (ebook) | ISBN
  9781786633927 (hardback) | ISBN 9781786633934 (ebk)
Subjects: LCSH: Hamilton, Alexander, 1757–1804. | United States—Politics
  and government—1783–1809. | United States—Economic conditions—To
  1865. | Hamilton, Alexander, 1757–1804. Report on the subject of
  manufactures. | Statesmen—United States—Biography.
Classification: LCC E302.6.H2 P265 2020 (print) | LCC E302.6.H2 (ebook) |
  DDC 973.4092 [B]—dc23
LC record available at https://lccn.loc.gov/2020008282
LC ebook record available at https://lccn.loc.gov/2020008283

Typeset in Sabon by MJ&N Gavan, Truro, Cornwall
Printed in the UK by CPI Group (UK) Lrd, Croydon CR0 4YY

Dedicated to my father, Michael Parenti.

The bit of truth behind all this one so eagerly denied is that men are not gentle, friendly creatures wishing for love, who simply defend themselves if they are attacked, but that a powerful measure of desire for aggression has to be reckoned as part of their instinctual endowment. The result is that their neighbour is to them not only a possible helper or sexual object, but also a temptation to them to gratify their aggressiveness on him, to exploit his capacity for work without recompense, to use him sexually without his consent, to seize his possessions, to humiliate him, to cause him pain, to torture and kill him.

Sigmund Freud, *Civilization and Its Discontents*, Chapter 5

And now, I think, the meaning of the evolution of civilization is no longer obscure to us. It must present the struggle between Eros and Death, between the instinct of life and the instinct of destruction, as it works itself out in the human species. This struggle is what all life essentially consists of, and the evolution of civilization may therefore be simply described as the struggle for life of the human species.

Sigmund Freud, *Civilization and Its Discontents*, Chapter 6

Contents

1

Do We Know Hamilton?

The modern United States has a strange relationship with Alexander Hamilton. Sometimes he is seen as the bad boy of the founding fathers, because of his authoritarian political tendencies. He is portrayed as the patron saint of bankers, because he saw the importance of banks and created our financial system. As a person he was a contradictory mix: a tough soldier, austere workaholic, exacting bureaucrat, yet also a sexual libertine who probably had at least one male lover, and a glory-obsessed romantic with pronounced suicidal tendencies. For much of the twentieth century, Hamilton was out of fashion, while his rival Thomas Jefferson, the patrician democrat and slave owner who feared government overreach, was claimed by all. But more recently, Hamilton has become hip.

Yet Americans still ignore Hamilton's dirigiste economic theory. We take our Hamilton *à la carte*. We recognize him as the architect of our financial system, but we ignore what he wrote about the real economy in which goods and services are actually produced and consumed. We recognize him as a key author of the American Constitution and thus of the modern American state, but we never connect his theory of state to his full theory of economic development.

In particular, Hamilton's magnum opus, his 1791 *Report on the Subject of Manufactures*, a central focus of this book, is almost totally ignored by economists, historians, development specialists, and biographers. Hamilton's statist political economy is all there in print, yet most recent literature on Hamilton shies away from addressing his profoundly statist economic ideas. The *Report* is occasionally name-checked but almost never read, taught in college courses, or publicly discussed in any detail.

In his otherwise highly readable biography of Hamilton, Ron Chernow devotes only four pages to the *Report*. Chernow's lines feel correct to the modern ear: "In the best of all possible worlds, Hamilton preferred free trade, open markets, and Adam Smith's 'invisible hand.'" Hamilton was, he says, "reluctant to tinker with markets." But that is not correct.

In reality, Hamilton sought to create a national market from thirteen semi-integrated pieces and then transition that national economy from a lopsided dependence on export agriculture to a balanced and diversified economy centered on manufacturing. In the *Report* Hamilton lists, in meticulous detail, exactly how government should not merely "tinker with" but fundamentally overhaul, and create from the ground up, whole markets. His set of tools was labeled with a phrase that should be famous: "the Means proper." These included carefully targeted state subsidies; protective tariffs; strategic exemptions from the same tariffs; selective export bans of strategic raw materials; quality-control standards and inspections; public investment in infrastructure; research and development; recruitment of skilled labor, and other measures that are detailed later. Hamilton's means proper were the tools of economic planning, and their presentation in the *Report on Manufactures* was not merely a list, but also a blueprint for the orchestration and execution of a grand national plan aimed at nothing less than fundamental economic transformation. Asserting, as many do, that Hamilton was deep down a free marketeer serves to elide the progressive and immediately useful elements in Hamilton's thinking.[1]

Similarly, Richard Brookshire, an editor at *National Review*, in his recent Hamilton biography spends only six pages on the *Report*, during which he mostly ignores Hamilton's advocacy of government intervention. Instead, he focuses on those portions of the *Report* that defend manufacturing as more productive than agriculture.[2] The PBS *American Experience* documentary on Hamilton devotes one line, or about six seconds out of an hour and a half, to Hamilton's statist and developmentalist policies. Even then the documentary dismisses as sinister and strange Hamilton's flirtation with the idea of public ownership.

One of the most famous books on American economic history, Douglas C. North's *The Economic Growth of the United States, 1790–1860*, mentions Hamilton once in a footnote and then again briefly in the text to name him as the person who created the nation's financial system. North says nothing about the *Report* and Hamilton's role in fostering manufacturing, nor anything about Hamilton's statist ideas in revolutionizing transportation, even though transportation costs are central to North's argument.[3] More recently, Andrew Shankman, who is typically a careful and precise historian, bizarrely minimizes and misrepresents the *Report*. Shankman casts Hamilton as hostile to protective taxes on imports, claiming that Hamilton only "gave protective tariffs 126 words" out of the *Report*'s total of about 40,000.[4] In reality, Hamilton did not use the word "tariff" in the *Report* but did write extensively of "taxes" and "protecting duties" and devoted almost half the *Report* to an explicit and at times painfully detailed discussion of exactly which sorts of duties should be laid on all manner of imports, ranging from iron, lead, and copper to coal, wood, cotton, and grain; to flax and hemp; to printed books; to alcohol, refined sugar, chocolate, and more. By my count, the *Report* uses the word "duty" or "duties" a total of 89 times. Shankman also interprets Hamilton as relatively ignorant of, and hostile to, manufacturing. All this, it would seem, is part of an admirable effort to draw our attention to class struggle and the forgotten interests of the artisans and small farmers.[5]

A few older histories do address the *Report* in a serious fashion, most notably John C. Miller's very fine biography.[6] But that book, published in the 1950s, is fading into the rear view. A smattering of scholars writing in other disciplines have also given a place of honor to Hamilton's dirigiste ideas. The development economist Ha-Joon Chang traces his critique of laissez-faire economics through the experience of South Korean industrialization back to Hamiltonian origins in U.S. history.[7] The economic sociologist Fred Block, who has done stellar work documenting and theorizing America's actually existing, though never named, developmentalist state, also gives Hamilton and the *Report* proper recognition. However, being focused on current political economy, both their discussions of the *Report* are necessarily limited.[8]

The reason for the more general elision of the *Report* is simple. Hamilton's economic ideas contradict, and directly attack, the prevailing orthodoxy of extreme laissez-faire, the market-*über-alles* fundamentalism that is the leitmotif of Wall Street, big business, politicians, academia, and the vast majority of America's center-right pundits. *The Report on the Subject of Manufactures* is ignored because, by today's narrow standards, it is heretical. Its real message, served up in dense, convoluted, and tedious prose, is ignored and thus misunderstood.

The *Report*'s opening paragraphs smash holes in Adam Smith's core argument about the supposedly self-regulating market. Further in, the *Report* outlines a set of policy tools for government intervention in the economy—Hamilton called these "the Means proper." They include: tariffs, subsidies, public investment, and even imply a legitimate place for public ownership. America's real political economy, our real economic history, has been built around these tools, yet we remain in denial. Many years ago the economist Michael Hudson, researching the intellectual history of American protectionism—which is to say the history of those who followed in Hamilton's footsteps—found that: "Not even ostensibly encyclopedic studies of American economic thought paid much attention to [economic nationalists], treating them patronizingly as anomalies rather than the men who designed the nation's rise to industrial supremacy."[9]

Even if we do not acknowledge the role of protectionism and planning in our intellectual histories, their impacts have been central to the history of America's actual economic development.

Impacts and Reverberations

Hamilton's ideas would be called the "American School." Then, in the 1820s under the leadership of the Kentuckian Henry Clay, they came to be known as the "American System." Taken up by Friedrich List and brought to Germany, they morphed into the "National System." These ideas—the "means proper" of 1791—helped shape the late-nineteenth-century industrialization of Germany and then Japan, and a century later the industrialization of South Korea, Hong Kong, and Taiwan. Today, these ideas guide the world-transforming rise of China. Indeed, the *Report* is the basic policy blueprint followed by most other successfully industrialized countries.

Hamilton's defensive developmentalism, though in no way socialist, nonetheless had an anti-imperialist or at least postcolonial tinge, and in that regard anticipated some of the challenges later faced by the socialist experiments in the twentieth century. A more symmetrical comparison can be drawn between Hamilton's project and that of Simón Bolívar. Like Hamilton, Bolívar was a liberal nationalist with a political vision of continental scale, rooted in the quest for development, sovereignty, and a strong central government.[10] As Joshua Simon put it "Bolívar's constitutional thought, especially his views on the separation of powers and on the role of the executive in a republic ... compare well with those of the early American republic's High Federalists, especially Alexander Hamilton."[11] Bolívar's project fragmented, and in Latin America economic development was delayed and distorted by outside powers.

There is a perception, a latent, often unspoken assumption, that the United States was *inevitably* bound for high standards of living and political stability, while the states of Latin America were always and only destined for instability and underdevelopment. That perception not only smacks of racism, it is wrong on both counts. There was nothing inevitable about the formation of the United States. The pessimistic warnings of *The Federalist Papers* could have become reality.

This book treats the modern state and capitalism as historically contingent and politically produced. My aim in this book is not to "side with" Hamilton, but rather to explore parts of his life and context so as to unpack early American state formation and economic development. The book examines the context in which Alexander Hamilton arrived at his ideas about the role of government in economic development.

Hamilton's dirigiste economic theories emerge first from his experiences in the Revolutionary War. As part of Washington's staff Hamilton got a bird's-eye view of the new nation's poverty, corruption, and near-catastrophic disorganization. Then during the "Critical Period," the postwar economic slump and political crisis of the 1780s, Hamilton saw the new nation sliding toward civil war, fragmentation, foreign invasion, and re-colonization. In telling this story, I draw on parts of Hamilton's writing that address the nature of state power.

Relative Autonomy

What drove Hamilton? Charles Beard's 1913 classic, *An Economic Interpretation of the Constitution*, detailed the financial interests of all the framers and the ways in which each of them directly benefited from or was directly assisted by the document. Importantly, Beard exempts Hamilton from such charges: "That Hamilton himself made any money in stocks which he held personally has never been proved by reference to any authentic evidence." And Beard calls "highly improbable" the idea that Hamilton had "ever held any considerable sum in securities."[12] Instead of chasing personal benefit directly, Hamilton did it indirectly. As a man of the state—soldier, politician, then bureaucrat—he was materially bound to it and thus worked to create a political structure that tied various economic interests to the new government. His fortune was linked to that of the state: call him *homo publicus*. National survival was his desideratum.

Hamilton's ultimate allegiance was to the project of state formation. In this regard he embodies what later social scientists would refer to as "the relative autonomy of the state."[13] For Hamilton, a secure future depended on a strong and activist government, powerful military, and robust, nationally integrated economy based on manufacturing. In place of Smith's "invisible hand," Hamilton saw the hand of government. The economy would not, in fact, develop all on its own "as if guided by an invisible hand." Rather, it had to be actually and deliberately guided.

The tripartite circuitry of Hamilton's nationalism cast sovereignty as dependent on national defense. National defense was dependent on the capacities of a professional standing army, which was, in turn, dependent on the wealth and technological sophistication of a manufacturing-based national economy. And that sort of economy, which did not yet exist in 1790, could only be created with the active guidance and support of a powerful central state. Thus, the state was both means and ends. A weak state, in this logic, is the path toward economic underdevelopment and permanent dependence.

Or as Hamilton put it in *Federalist* 11: "If we continue united, we may counteract a policy so unfriendly to our prosperity in a variety of ways. By prohibitory regulations, extending, at the same time, throughout the States, we may oblige foreign countries to bid against each other, for the privileges of our markets." Here, Hamilton illustrates the essence of economic nationalism: the state does not merely react to economic conditions; it creates them. Hamilton's political economy was a defense against European imperialism, a form of postcolonial pragmatism. The young nation's choice was to either build a strong manufacturing-based economy or face disintegration. The mission was, in short, development or death.

Climate Hamilton?

American history is not merely interesting; it is also useful. Although our current world bears little resemblance to the eighteenth century, some parallels exist. After the Revolution the new nation slipped into a dangerous, multifaceted crisis. Political and economic collapse seemed imminent. Yet the framers managed to produce significant political and economic transformations that stabilized the situation, and the early republic avoided social break-down, political fragmentation, and foreign domination. The society produced by the U.S. Constitution and the developmentalist state it empowered was never fair, or just, or ideal. But it was relatively stable and capable. If its mission was expansionist, racist, exploit-ative, its methods were at least functional and effective in their own terms. Many states are born of hierarchical and bigoted agendas. But not all succeed.[14]

Like that first generation of Americans, we contemporary Amer-icans also face crisis. Ours takes the form of anthropogenic climate change and the inability of laissez-faire ideology to address it. Modern civilization must mitigate the causes of global warming and adapt to its effects. Failure to face this reality will mean almost certain violent social breakdown. Addressing climate change hinges upon, among other things, a total transformation of the world's energy sector. We must euthanize the fossil fuel industry and build out clean energy technologies and infrastructure. This means a project of fossil fuel sector *deindustrialization* coupled with a simultaneous *green re-industrialization*.

In short, we must execute a radical and sweeping economic transformation. In facing that task, we could do worse than to consult our own economic history. Hamilton's *Report on the Subject of Manufactures*, born in the shadow of an impending crisis, was, after all, a plan for radical and rapid economic transi-tion. If we must re-industrialize, then let us consider how America first industrialized. What forces drove the transition from an agrar-ian to a manufacturing economy? The actual historical record reveals surprising facts, central among these the very active role of government in driving economic change. Indeed, the develop-mental state begins to appear not as something new and foreign, but rather as something old and indigenous.

Reading the developmental state back into American eco-nomic history forces one to transcend economic orthodoxy and its fixation on laissez-faire and the crackpot notion of a "self-regulating market." The laissez-faire creed, born in Britain in the late eighteenth century, has in recent decades returned to intel-lectual supremacy as neoliberalism. This ideology, regardless of the economic malady, always calls for the bloodletting medicine of deregulation, privatization, and austerity. Even when initially successful, laissez-faire economics inevitably leads to crises. For example, repeal of the Glass-Steagall Act in 1999 significantly deregulated banking and led directly to the crash of 2008 and the Great Recession. These crises, in turn, demand a return of the state with its subsidies and regulations. Thus, the crash of 2008 begets the extremely interventionist macroeconomic triage of the Troubled Asset Relief Program and the largest single stimulus bill ever passed—until the coronavirus emergency spending bill of 2020.[15]

On the inevitability of modern planning, Karl Polanyi is essential. Polanyi showed that while all societies have embedded within them material processes that we would call "economic activity" and many include markets, no society, not even our own, has been totally governed by the rules of the market. As Polanyi put it in *The Great Transformation*, "the idea of a self-adjusting market implied a stark Utopia. Such an institution could not exist for any length of time without annihilating the human and natural substance of society; it would have physically destroyed man and transformed his surroundings into a wilderness."[16] (To update that for the climate crisis, just replace "wilderness" with "wasteland of flooded coastal cities and desiccated agrarian interior.")

According to Polanyi:

> There was nothing natural about laissez-faire; free markets could never have come into being merely by allowing things to take their course. Just as cotton manufactures—the leading free trade industry—were created by the help of protective tariffs, export bounties, and indirect wage subsidies, laissez-faire itself was enforced by the state. ... The road to the free market was opened and kept open by an enormous increase in continuous, centrally organized and controlled interventionism. ... [T]he introduction of free markets, far from doing away with the need for control, regulation, and intervention, enormously increased their range.

Polanyi argued that the transition to capitalism was so brutal and socially destabilizing that mitigating counteractions started immediately and organically. Thus he wrote that while the "laissez-faire economy was the product of deliberate State action, subsequent restrictions on laissez-faire started in a spontaneous way. Laissez-faire was planned; planning was not." Or, at least, planning was not always planned.

Democracy as Fetish, Slavery as Fact

From the very beginning, Hamilton's big-government program for economic development faced considerable opposition. Significant among his opponents were Southern agrarian elites like Thomas Jefferson and James Madison. This Virginian scene was the natal terrain of that sensibility and political economy that became known as "the Slave Power."

In 1791 the nation's economy was largely agrarian and highly dependent on manufactured imports; an arrangement that worked well for Southern gentlemen like Jefferson. Thus the *Report* bends over backward to placate Southern agrarian interests, or as the *Report* puts it, "respectable patrons of opinions, unfriendly to the encouragement of manufactures." Hamilton notes how a manufacturing base in the United States would increase markets for Southern agricultural and extractive products. And then, in a direct and touching appeal for sectional unity, he argues for a common economic purpose: "The Northern & southern regions are sometimes represented as having adverse interests ... [t]hose are called Manufacturing, these Agricultural states; and a species of opposition is imagined to subsist between the Manufacturing and Agricultural interests." Against this he argued, "the *aggregate* prosperity of manufactures, and the *aggregate* prosperity of Agriculture are intimately connected ... to the steady pursuit of one great common cause, and to the perfect harmony of all the parts."

Republicans in Congress feared the Federalist agenda of building a strong central state. This was particularly true of Southern Republicans, who even in 1791 correctly saw the national government as a threat to their "peculiar institution." But slavery was rarely mentioned. Instead, the ideology of states' rights was their defense. Lurking just beneath the surface of states' rights are, of course, plantation rights. Those plantations, places like Monticello, were America's equivalent of feudal manors. On the plantation, economic, legal, and military power were all bound up together and located in the private household of the planter. Virginia planters were the original *localistas*. Southern elites did not want Yankees telling them what to do; how to treat their slaves, how to organize their towns, how to run their elections, how to treat the environment—none of that! Historically, localism and democracy in the South meant that white elites were "free"—free to push Black people around, free to feed racist fantasies to poorer whites.

Fourteen years after Hamilton's death, Congressman Nathaniel Macon of North Carolina summed up the contradiction: "If Congress can make canals, they can with more propriety emancipate."[17] Like many slaveholding Southerners, Macon feared that a strong central government would eventually act against slavery.

At a deep economic level, this is the central and ironic difference between Hamilton and Jefferson. For Jefferson, institutional power in the form of inherited political connections, slaves, land, and a luxurious mountaintop manor allowed for illusions of independence. At Monticello he was omnipotent; his wealth and freedom from drudgery allowed him to pursue fantasies of omniscience by collecting books, scientific instruments, artifacts; he was free to correspond with the great men of the day or write abstracted paeans to the yeoman farmer. No wonder Jefferson fetishized individual agency—he had copious amounts of it.

Hamilton, on the other hand, operated with an acute sense of vulnerability. This helped him see power as operating collectively through institutions. In his meteoric political rise, Hamilton navigated by way of social organizations, communal structures, groups, and hierarchies. From a small island to the mainland, from poor student to pamphleteer and soldier, from soldier to political operative, politician, and state builder—every phase was an object lesson in the *social* and *institutional* nature of power.

Throughout this book, I rely on historians who are sometimes referred to as part of a "neo-progressive renaissance." While sharing their broadly progressive politics, I find myself unsatisfied with their suggestion that local government is necessarily more democratic than national government. Many progressive forces have come from the local level. But local sensibilities and power structures have also nurtured some of America's most reactionary forces: white supremacist terror, sexist violence, intellectual backwardness, environmental destruction, and economic underdevelopment.

Too often historians of the founding and early republic— whether they are called neo-Beardian, like Gordon S. Wood, or neo-progressive, like Woody Holton and Terry Bouton—suggest, without ever proving, that local and state governments were more democratic than the national government. In the following pages I take a more contingent view. Surveying the state governments of the 1780s, one frequently sees elite, self-dealing gangs that were very local but also very undemocratic, oppressive, exploitative, and often profoundly incompetent.

In *Radical Hamilton* I have attempted to transcend the aristocracy-vs.-democracy debate that often frames discussion of the founding, the Constitution, and the early republic. Instead I argue that a third agenda also operated: *the struggle for national survival and state making*. While shaped by internal class forces, this agenda was also born of the international context, specifically the national project's relationship to other states. As the "realists" of International Relations theory note, every state seeks survival within the international system of states. At one level all states threaten one another, even as groups of states cooperate. This suggests a dialectic between the external and internal strength of a state.

If the political right and liberal center ignore the *Report* because it attacks their sacred fetish, the market, then much of the left has ignored the *Report* because they see state power and economic development as always oppressive and bad. That is to some extent strange. For most of the twentieth century, socialism and welfare-state liberalism were deeply engaged with the state and development as concepts and practices. Even much of the right took the state and development for granted. All this began to change in the 1960s. Both the right and the left increasingly championed the individual and grew hostile to large state-centric projects. If the New Right veered toward extreme libertarianism, much of the New Left embraced quasi-anarchist or "anarcho-liberal" politics.

Available for use by both political tendencies was the nostalgic call to localism of E. F. Schumacher's *Small Is Beautiful* and Helen and Scott Nearing's *Living the Good Life*.[18] During the 1980s, as many leftists migrated from movements into universities, post-structuralism and the "cultural turn" further eroded faith in big projects. Today, any metanarrative suggesting teleological processes of improvement (as the notion of economic "development" clearly does) comes under assault for carrying embedded oppressive normative judgments.[19]

To be fair, the high modernist developmentalism of the Cold War—be it of the liberal democratic or Soviet variety—very often did involve oppressive politics and horrendous unintended consequences, such as massive ecological devastation.[20] Yet the left correction went too far and soon morphed into a moralizing religiosity that, mirroring the libertarian right, developed its own fetishism: decentralization, localism, and individual empowerment. Poststructuralism, tending toward a fixation on the micro-politics of resistance, cast the state as out of date, or merely the effect of micro-practices. In the symbolic struggle to restore individual agency, institutions with their rules, specialized functions, expertise, and hierarchy became anathema, none more so than government. Problems are cast as residing in states and institutions, while freedom, agency, and thus morality reside in the individual or notional formations like the community.

Structure of the Book

In the chapters that follow I first explore the historical context from which Hamilton's ideas were born: the war and the Critical Period. Then I explain the *Report*'s core arguments and examine its impact in the U.S.

Chapter 1 looks at Hamilton's experiences fighting in the Revolutionary War and how this shaped his mature political economic thinking. In that chapter I suggest that there is something of an "epistemological rupture" in Hamilton's writing, marked by his strange two-month-long collapse in the winter of 1777–78. From this "nervous fever" Hamilton emerged with a new intellectual voice, and in a torrent of long letters disgorges his systematic program of political economic transformation. Chapters 3 and 4 explore how the rebellion against Britain was funded and supplied. Far from being a guerrilla conflict, the Revolutionary War was fought in the conventional style of the eighteenth century, and that meant it was expensive. At first, the rebels funded their cause by simply printing money. Call it confiscation by inflation. Chapter 5 introduces the Critical Period as beginning during the war in the form of widespread and increasing military mutinies toward the end of the fighting, including the Newburgh Conspiracy. Chapter 6 looks at how the end of the war, and with it the end of the hothouse economic stimulus of military procurement, led to a devastating economic depression that was the bedrock of the multilayered crisis of the Critical Period.

Chapter 7 addresses political and military events during the Critical Period, such as the intercommunal violence on the frontier; slave and Maroon resistance; and escalating combat between white settlers and Native Americans in Kentucky and the Ohio Country. Chapter 8 looks at Shays's Rebellion, the Critical Period's bloody culmination.

Chapter 9 addresses the political reaction to these interwoven crises, the U.S. Constitution, while Chapter 10 reads the Constitution as a developmentalist toolkit of state economic powers without which the *Report* would have been orphaned. Chapters 11 and 12 cover Hamilton's financial reports and creation of the First Bank of the United States. Chapter 13 unpacks the *Report*'s clotted prose to get at its clear ideas. Chapter 14 explores the War of 1812 as the logical result of the Jeffersonian agenda. Chapter 15 looks at the *Report*'s impact and afterlife, both in the United States and abroad.

Now, let us turn to a contextualizing account of the crisis-plagued years of the Revolutionary War and the Critical Period that gave rise to the *Report on the Subject of Manufactures*.

2

Cometh the Hour, Cometh the Man

How did Hamilton develop his political preference for a strong and activist state? It is tempting to see his policy ideas as rooted in his personal biography; particularly the insecurities that resulted from being an "illegitimate" child who was then orphaned at a relatively young age. No doubt these early experiences help explain Hamilton's later politics; call that theory "the state as missing guardian."[1]

More specifically, or more materially, Hamilton's mature political ideas were born of his experiences fighting in the Revolutionary War, during which he saw the Revolution's deep dysfunction and vulnerabilities, and from the economic crisis and general slide toward chaos that was the Critical Period of the mid-1780s. Hamilton saw the rebellion's vulnerabilities and weak structure up close when he joined General Washington's staff, or "family," as the Virginian called his administrative and executive team. A mysterious two-month illness during the lowest point of the military campaign seems to mark a turning point in Hamilton's thinking, almost an "epistemological rupture" between the young Hamilton and the intellectually mature Hamilton. It is only after his illness that the outline of Hamilton's future work suddenly appears, sketched in an outpouring of letters. Given modern America's obsession with the self and psychology, it is strange that Hamilton's illness, a two-month-long "nervous fever," has not received more

attention. But this breakdown and the intellectual transformation it seems to punctuate must be understood in the context of
Hamilton's overall experience of politics and economics during
the war.

From Immigrant to Officer

Born of humble origins on the Caribbean island of Nevis,
Hamilton's mother had not divorced her previous husband
when Alexander was born. He was thus the "bastard brat of a
Scotch Pedler," as John Adams would later put it.[2] By age thirteen
Hamilton was orphaned, inheriting nothing except a few books.
Taken in by family friends on St. Croix, he found work as a shipping clerk. Hamilton had prodigious intellectual talent and applied
himself with fanatical discipline. Soon the young shipping clerk
was penning essays for the island's press. His work caught the
attention of local notables, who in 1772 sent the teenager off to
preparatory school in New Jersey, and then to King's College, now
Columbia University. Revolution would soon interrupt his studies.

As Hamilton began his formal education, structural forces
were driving the colonies toward war and independence. Three
grievances stood out. The first was the Crown's stifling, monop-
olizing overregulation of trade and manufacturing. The British
actively prohibited colonial efforts to develop industry. Colonial
hat makers, for example, were prevented from hiring more than
two apprentices, nor could they export hats. Such restrictions frustrated both elites and common laborers in the Northeast and the
Mid-Atlantic region.

The second grievance was Britain's prohibition on colonial settlement west of the 1763 Proclamation Line that ran along the
ridge of the Appalachian Mountains. Agreed to after British victory
in the French and Indian War, this prohibition was designed to
keep the peace with France by preventing American settlers from
encroaching on French-allied Native American lands. This aggravated poor farmers who looked west for opportunity, as well as
wealthy land speculators like George Washington, who, even after

the 1763 Proclamation, illegally surveyed western lands. As he put it in a letter to a business partner: "I can never look upon that Proclamation in any other light (but this I say between ourselves) than as a temporary expedient to quiet the Minds of the Indians."[3]

The third grievance emanated primarily from the South. An implicit threat to slavery had emerged with the Somerset Case of 1772, in which Lord Chief Justice Mansfield found slavery to be illegal in England. While slavery remained legal in the colonies, banning it in the metropole nonetheless threatened American slave owners and slave traders and threatened most of all slavery's super-wealthy elites, men like South Carolina's Henry Laurens, who would later be president of the Continental Congress. As Gerald Horne has shown, removing the threat of royal restrictions on New World slavery was a significant motivation for Southern elites to join the rebellion.[4]

Politics Outdoors

With the Boston Tea Party in 1773, British-American colonists made manifest their resentment of mercantilist restrictions on their coastal trade. The colonists also resented the Crown's restrictions upon western settlement and land speculation.[5]

In 1775, fighting erupted. There was combat at Lexington and Concord in Massachusetts. Ethan Allen captured Fort Ticonderoga in what is now upstate New York. The Continental Army formed in June with George Washington in command; shortly thereafter it invaded Quebec. In New York City, the struggle remained limited to pamphleteering and raucous protest, but military preparations were underway. Hamilton and his fellow students formed a militia company that drilled, paraded, and waited.

In 1776, New York's Provincial Congress commissioned Hamilton to create and lead a new artillery company.[6] Captain Hamilton was strict but suffered the same hardships as his men, and, it would seem from the remaining records that show him advocating for their pay and equipment, he looked out for them.[7] The men, in turn, were said to respect him.[8]

In March 1776, after an almost yearlong siege, Washington forced the British to evacuate Boston by sea. The British sailed north to Halifax, but intelligence indicated they would next attack New York City. Washington marched his army south to meet them. In late June, up to a hundred British transport ships appeared in New York Harbor. They were carrying the forces of General Sir William Howe, rested, refurbished, and ready for round two against the rebellion. Thousands of Redcoats promptly occupied rural Staten Island without meeting any opposition.

While Howe awaited reinforcements, Washington's army took up defensive positions in Manhattan, Brooklyn, and Long Island and awaited a British attack. In late August, Howe, now having some 25,000 men, made his move, transiting his forces across the Verrazano Narrows, landing in what is now Bay Ridge, Brooklyn.[9] On August 27, the British attacked the American positions, which mostly held. Then the British swung past the American left flank and attacked again, driving rebels back to a position farther north in what is now Brooklyn Heights. The British followed and attacked again, and then again. Rebel casualties mounted.

Now Captain Hamilton was deep in the war. His men fought well, were noted for their discipline, and were given difficult and dangerous assignments. More than once during this early fighting, Hamilton's artillery covered Washington's retreats. By September 15 the British had occupied Lower Manhattan, but the rebel forces still occupied Harlem Heights. By October, the Redcoats had forced Washington's men up into White Plains, and then into New Jersey. In this string of defeats, Hamilton's artillery company usually served as the rear guard, holding the superior British forces at bay with barrages of cannonballs and grapeshot while the main body of the Continental Army retreated.

In militarized societies, war can present young men who are willing to fight the possibility of great reward at the price of great risk. Hamilton saw the opportunities in war and grasped them aggressively. Over the course of 1776 and early 1777, Hamilton's reputation as a commander and strategic thinker grew. Soon a variety of generals were offering him staff positions. First came Major General William Alexander, then Major General Nathanael

Greene. Hamilton declined both, preferring instead the glory and potential martyrdom of field command. Hamilton was very much a romantic of the morbidly gallant eighteenth-century style.

Washington's Family

Finally, in January 1777, a letter from General Washington arrived. It offered Hamilton promotion to lieutenant colonel and a place on the headquarters staff. Accepting would mean Hamilton had to relinquish command of his artillery unit. There would be no more heroic shouting of orders through clouds of cannon smoke, no group of direct subordinates to look up to him. Instead, Hamilton —only twenty-two or twenty-four years old (there is some debate about his real date of birth)—would be Washington's immediate subordinate, tasked with thinking, planning, and communicating. While others would live and die heroically, Hamilton weighed the prospect of being hunched over a desk studying maps, reading intelligence reports, managing the flow of material, and cranking out endless letters (by the volume that survive, it seems he was always writing). Hamilton, the man of action, would be made a bureaucrat if he took the appointment; but then again, the offer promised him entry to the highest levels of American power. Ultimately, the propertyless immigrant soldier accepted.

As usual, Hamilton's overflowing mind, manic work ethic, and tremendous personal discipline made him indispensable. In short order he was Washington's most important aide-de-camp, managing highly sensitive intelligence, diplomacy, and inter-command negotiations between the many clashing egos of generals, colonels, congressmen, and governors. Apparently excelling at everything all the time, Hamilton even played a key role in the military's entire retraining and restructuring![10]

By the summer of 1777, Congress had obtained a fair amount of weaponry from France. The court of Louis XVI was officially at peace with its ancient rival Britain, and thus hid its support for the American rebellion with the "plausible denial" of a privately structured, off-the-books arrangement: a tobacco-for-guns swap between Congress and a private French arms dealer.[11] This new arsenal included state-of-the-art brass cannons, and with them arrived a young aristocrat and adventurer, the Marquis de Lafayette. Most American officers at first dismissed Lafayette as just another posturing European soldier of fortune. However, Lafayette soon proved his worth and would become close friends with Hamilton. Also arriving with the guns, ammunition, and uniforms was the "Baron" von Steuben, who had been on Frederick the Great's staff, but was not actually a nobleman. Steuben would work closely with Hamilton on modernizing and retraining the Continental Army.[12] European assistance aside, the years 1777 and 1778 would be full of trials for both the rebellion and Hamilton.

As an artillery captain, Hamilton experienced the war on the intimate terms of frontline combat: tactics, discipline, calculating munitions trajectories, and bravery in the face of chaos, gore, and terror. On Washington's staff, Hamilton's view expanded to encompass all the war's moving pieces. That view was neither pretty nor glorious. Rather, it was marked by weakness, dysfunction, and crisis.

It was from his experience on the headquarters staff that Hamilton's political economic vision, culminating in the *Report on Manufactures*, would emerge. When he first joined Washington's "family," Hamilton was, despite his brilliance and his early combat experience, still fundamentally a striving kid. We see this in his early articles and letters, which stand out for their style and intelligence but not so much for their original ideas. Hamilton's essays were clever, sharp, well informed, but they also had something of the pamphleteer's boilerplate to them. Like many young authors, he was a philosophical name-dropper and his tone was often what we would today call snarky. For example, from one of his first truly famous early essays, "The Farmer Refuted" (1775): "If you will follow my advice, there still may be hopes of your reformation. Apply yourself, without delay, to the study of the law of nature. I would recommend to your perusal, Grotius, Puffendorf, Locke, Montesquieu, and Burlemaqui. I might mention other excellent writers on this subject; but if you attend, diligently, to these, you will not require any others."[13]

Politically, the young Hamilton took positions more often associated with Jefferson than with Hamilton's own later ideas. He was committed to "liberty" and "the rights of man" and liked to paraphrase John Locke, as he did in "The Farmer Refuted": "Upon this law, depend the natural rights of mankind, the supreme being gave existence to man, together with the means of preserving and beatifying that existence ... and invested him with an inviolable right to personal liberty, and personal safety. ... Hence also, the origin of all civil government, justly established, must be a voluntary compact, between the rulers and the ruled."

As late as May 1777, Hamilton, still sounding like a Jeffersonian Republican rather than the Federalist he would become, worried that even the existence of a Senate was dangerous: "In time, your senate, from the very name and from the mere circumstance of its being a separate member of the legislature, will be liable to degenerate into a body purely aristocratical."

All this would change during the winter of 1777–78. At Valley Forge, amid the hunger, disease, death, and moments of intense political despair, a different Hamilton emerged. Tasked with enormous responsibility, Hamilton witnessed terrifying levels of political dysfunction. At the nadir, Hamilton suffered a debilitating "nervous" fever and thought he was dying—a crisis that sounds very much like a nervous breakdown.[14] Hamilton would survive the illness and return to the war, but the man who came back was transformed. Gone was the clever boy democrat; in his place arose an angry visionary, possessed and driven by a sense of historical mission. As if in communication with an industrialized future that only he could see, this was the man who would design America's financial system and lay out the template for its industrialization.

The Crisis Begins

The path to Valley Forge for Washington and Hamilton was unfortunate. When Washington fell back to White Plains he left a large garrison in northern Manhattan at the eponymous Fort

Washington. In mid-November 1776 the British attacked, took the fort, and captured 3,000 rebel prisoners. Now, fearing the British would advance farther north, Washington crossed west over the Hudson at Peekskill, New York, and then moved south down into New Jersey. The British followed, and by December Washington's main force had been driven into Pennsylvania. But then Washington's army turned around, crossed the Delaware River on Christmas Day and, the following morning, attacked unsuspecting, somewhat drunken, Hessian mercenaries garrisoned at Trenton, New Jersey. It was a small but victorious battle with a pivotal impact. After months of defeat, victory at Trenton boosted morale and brought in new, badly needed recruits.[15]

That winter, Washington's army dug in at Morristown, New Jersey, and there awaited another British attack. But, for reasons internal to the British Army's own dysfunction, General Howe did not oblige. Instead, Howe tried to lure Washington's army out for a fight. The Continentals did not take the bait.

To be fair to Washington, the string of defeats, though painful, expensive, and humiliating, did not necessarily undermine his (and it should be said, Hamilton's) larger military strategy. Even as their tactics remained primarily those of eighteenth-century conventional warfare, the Patriots' overall strategy looked ahead to the cardinal maxim of the guerrilla: as long as they were not totally defeated on the battlefield, the rebel colonists "won" politically; conversely, the British "lost" politically as long as the rebellion continued. Thus, Howe's string of victories added up to less than the sum of their parts.

As was so often the case, it was Hamilton who first outlined this logic in print, as early as February 1775. Note the geographic element in his thinking, for it comes up in later works: "Let it be remembered, that there are no large plains, for the two armies to meet in, and decide the contest. ... The circumstances of our country put it in our power, to evade a pitched battle. It will be better policy, to harass and exhaust the soldiery, by frequent skirmishes and incursions, than to take the open field with them, by which means, they would have the full benefit of their superior regularity and skill. Americans are better qualified, for that kind of fighting, which is most adapted to this country, than regular troops."[16]

As the fight picked up pace again in early spring 1777, the British had a new plan, or rather two linked but poorly coordinated plans. Howe would land far up the Chesapeake, march north, and take Philadelphia. At the same time, his subordinate and rival General John Burgoyne would invade from Quebec, push down the Hudson Valley, and link up with Howe's forces occupying New York City, thus cutting the rebel colonies in two.

On September 11, 1777, Washington tried to block Howe's force of 15,000 at Brandywine, Pennsylvania. But the British drove away Washington's forces, killing about 300 rebels, wounding 600, and taking about 400 prisoners.[17] With that, Philadelphia, and the Continental Congress gathered in it, were open to British capture. Lieutenant Colonel Hamilton was charged with the midnight task of rousing Congress and evacuating Philadelphia. As Congress fled, Hamilton organized a mass requisition of horses, blankets, and other essentials. In this, Hamilton spared the poor and the laboring classes. For example, anyone who made a living from their horse was allowed to keep it. But the gentleman with his coach and six was expropriated. The politicians, with their baggage and papers (they took great care to preserve their papers), rushed to Morristown, New Jersey, then Lancaster, Pennsylvania, and finally to the small city of York, Pennsylvania, where they stayed for the next nine months. The crotchety John Adams summed up the situation as follows: "Congress was chased like a covey of partridges from Philadelphia to Trenton from Trenton to Lancaster."[18] And as he had noted on an earlier occasion, "In general, our Generals were out generalled."[19]

The British soon took the rebel capital, Philadelphia. Before long, the civilian leaders, particularly those of the Pennsylvania State Government, were urging Washington to retake Philadelphia. On October 4, 1777, Washington tried to oblige. His attack began at Germantown, on the outskirts of Philadelphia. Thick fog led to confused fighting and the Americans were again forced to withdraw. This was the nadir of Washington's prestige. As one modern author summarized: "Washington had made serious mistakes. In two years he had lost New York City and all of New Jersey, and then Philadelphia. Congress had been forced to vacate the capital twice and was well within its rights to question his abilities."[20]

The American campaign was now in real crisis. Supplies were lacking, the men hungry, exhausted, and demoralized. Too many of their comrades had died, were maimed, or were emotionally broken—and for what? Many Continental soldiers were at or near the end of their one-year enlistments. Desertion was increasing. Washington's army was melting out from under him. A winter siege of Philadelphia, as the civilian politicians were urging, was beyond the Army's capacity. All they could do was dig in and hope to survive the winter. Washington's remaining 11,000 men fell back to a piece of defensible high ground called Valley Forge. This new position was between Congress and the British, close enough to the lost capital city to harass and monitor the enemy, yet far enough away to allow some rest and retraining. The nearby Schuylkill River offered the benefit of quick transport and, at certain times, abundant fish. The men built crude log huts, gathered wood and what supplies they could, and awaited the arrival of winter.[21]

Command Fragments

Then, amid the gloom, came miraculous news: American forces had scored a major victory in upstate New York. While General Washington was shielding the flight of Congress, Major General Horatio Gates, leading a force of about 12,000 up the Hudson Valley, had intercepted and blocked British General John Burgoyne's army of 7,200, which had invaded southward from Montreal.[22]

Outnumbered and running low on food, Burgoyne stopped near Saratoga, New York, and waited for reinforcements from the British forces occupying New York City. But none arrived. Meanwhile, the two opposing armies probed each other's lines. American sharp-shooters, some using highly accurate, state-of-the-art, rifle-bored muskets, and firing from behind cover rather than in formation, systematically targeted British officers and artillery crews.[23] On September 19, the two armies clashed, almost by accident. The

British held their ground but suffered heavy casualties. The waiting, probing, and sniping continued. Then, on October 7, Burgoyne attacked the American lines. Again the British suffered heavy casualties and fell back. Now, Burgoyne's forces were basically trapped and surrounded, and still there was no sign of reinforcements from New York City. On October 17, he surrendered.

Into the hands of a jubilant Gates fell 5,804 prisoners and equipment amounting to "thirty pieces of artillery, 4,647 muskets, 190 sets of harness, and a large supply of ammunition."[24] It was a tremendous victory. The British lost nearly one-quarter of the men serving for them in America at that time.[25] News of Saratoga would eventually persuade France to formally join the American cause.

There was, however, a duplicitous twist. The victorious General Gates viewed his victory as license to act unilaterally and independently of the larger plan. In a destabilizing power play, Gates reported the Saratoga triumph not up the chain of command to General Washington, but rather directly to Congress. Gates was acting as if he was independent of and equal to Washington. And Gates started making noises about launching an assault on Fort Ticonderoga or some other target of his own design. Were Washington and Gates now equals?

Congress hardly helped matters when it quickly rewarded Gates by appointing him president of the Board of War, the congressional committee overseeing administration of the Continental Army. In other words, Gates was placed in charge of the civilian body to which Washington answered, even as Washington was his commanding officer. At the same time, a whispering campaign commenced, urging Congress to replace Washington with Gates. Each general had troops. Each had powerful civilian allies. Neither wanted to back down. A catastrophe was taking form.

Hamilton's Mission

Fearing an assault from the British forces in Philadelphia (and perhaps to check the power of General Gates), Washington now decided that Gates should send reinforcements south to Valley

Forge. As with the evacuation of Philadelphia, delivering these orders, and more importantly *getting the orders to be followed*, fell to Lieutenant Colonel Hamilton. Washington's delicately worded instructions gave Gates the flexibility to interpret the reinforcement request in light of conditions on the ground.[26] This was a shrewd move that created face-saving wiggle room if Gates were to refuse Washington's request.

Hamilton's orders read as follows:

> If upon your meeting with Genl. Gates, you should find that he intends, in Consequence of his Success, to employ the Troops under his Command upon some expedition by the prosecution of which the common cause will be more benefitted than by their being sent down to reinforce this Army, it is not my wish to give any interruption to the plan. But if he should have nothing more in contemplation than those particular objects which I have mention'd to you, and which it is unnecessary to commit to paper, in that case you are to inform him that it is my desire that the reinforcements before mentioned, or such part of them as can be safely spared, be immediately put in motion to join this Army.

Thus, Hamilton's mission was to pass through enemy-occupied New Jersey, travel upriver, find Gates's forces, link up with his command, and convince him to send Washington as many troops as could reasonably be spared.[27] On the penultimate day of October 1777, Hamilton started riding north accompanied by only an aide. At Fishkill, New York, on November 2, Hamilton encountered General Israel Putnam, a stout, brash, veteran Indian fighter, farmer, and New England innkeeper. He relayed Washington's request for support and, it seemed, he convinced "Old Put" to redirect a portion of his forces south towards headquarters.

Then Hamilton pressed northward and on November 6 found General Gates at Albany, well supplied with captured gear and basking in the glory of victory. Tense negotiations ensued. "I used every argument in my power," wrote Hamilton in a dispatch back to headquarters, "to convince him of the propriety of the measure, but he was inflexible in the opinion that two Brigades at least of Continental troops should remain in and near this place."[28]

Gates argued that British General Sir Harry Clinton might be "returning up the River which might expose the finest arsenal in America (as he calls the one here) to destruction should this place be left so bare of troops." Furthermore, Gates said, "the difficulty of the roads would make it impossible to remove the Artillery & stores." And then, implicitly invoking the power of civilian politicians and their clashing regional agendas, Gates noted that in detaching so many men "the New England States would be left open to the depredations & ravages of the enemy."

Finally and rather presumptuously, Gates made it clear that sending such a large portion of his men south would "put it out of his power to enterprise any thing against Ticonderoga, which he thinks might be done in the Winter, and which he considers it of importance to undertake." Gates was letting it be known, or confirming, that he saw himself as increasingly autonomous from, and equal to, Washington.

Four days later, Hamilton again wrote to update Washington: "Having given General Gates a little time to recollect himself I renewed my remonstrances on the necessity and propriety of sending you more than one Brigade of the three he had detained with him, and finally prevailed upon him to give orders for Glover's in addition to Patterson's brigade to march this way."

Ultimately, Hamilton pried loose two of the three brigades Washington had requested. Not trusting Gates, who at first had tried to palm off only one below-strength brigade as if it were in full fighting order, Hamilton stayed put at Albany until he saw the men moving out.

On his southbound return, Hamilton again encountered Putnam and was shocked to find that the General was ignoring orders. "I am pained beyond expression," wrote Hamilton in his next dispatch, to "inform your Excellency that on my arrival I find everything has been neglected and deranged by General Putnam, and that the two brigades Poor's and Learned's still remained here and on the other side the River at FishKill. Col. Warner's Militia [Green Mountain Boys from Vermont], I am told, have been drawn to PeeksKill to aid in an expedition against New York which it seems is at this time the Hobby horse with General

Putnam. Not the least attention has been paid to my order in your name for a detachment of 1000 men from the troops hitherto stationed at this post. Every thing is sacrificed to the whim of taking New York."

Having seen how Gates was ignoring Washington by communicating directly to Congress, Putnam was now planning his own independent assault upon occupied New York City. To gather reinforcements he was waylaying columns as they came past, including the two brigades Hamilton had extracted from General Gates.[29]

Renegade generals cultivating distinct civilian allies in Congress and planning their own autonomous military actions—the command structure was fragmenting. The onset of winter plus chaos in the supply lines only made the crisis worse. The cracking structure had to be held together. Somehow, Hamilton, a physically slight youth, with not even a bodyguard of troops at his service, had to convince the cantankerous old Putnam to submit.

Furious, Hamilton now wrote directly to Putnam. "I am astonishd. and Alarm'd beyond measure, to find that all his Excellency's Views have been hitherto flustrated, and that no single step of those I mention'd to you has been taken to afford him the aid he absolutely stands in Need of, and by Delaying which the Cause of America is put to the Utmost conceivable Hazard. ... My Expressions may perhaps have more Warmth than is altogether proper: But they proceed from the overflowing of my heart in a matter where I conceive this Continent essentially Interested."

Collecting himself, Hamilton then ordered Putnam to comply, "I now Sir, in the most explicit terms, by his Excellency's Authority, give it as a positive Order from him, that all the Continental Troops under your Command may be Immediately marched to Kings Ferry, there to Cross the River and hasten to Reinforce the Army under him."[30]

It was a gamble. By giving an order in Washington's name Hamilton was technically overstepping his bounds. A worried Hamilton immediately wrote to Washington apologetically saying as much.[31] But Hamilton's bluster worked. Putnam backed down. The reckless freelance plan for an assault on New York City was put aside. The two waylaid battalions were released to move south.

Then came trouble from the rank and file. The men heading south had not been paid for six to eight months, nor properly resupplied or decently fed. They had become openly mutinous, saying they "would not march for want of money and necessaries." As Hamilton explained, "There has been a high mutiny among the former on this account, in which a Capt. killed a man, and was shot himself by his comrade. These difficulties for want of proper management have stopped the troops from proceeding." Desperate to stop the mutiny, Hamilton turned to his connections among the New York elite to beg them for money. "Governor Clinton has been the only man, who has done any thing toward removing them; but for want of General Putnam's cooperation has not been able to effect it."

Hamilton's Collapse

Although successful, the stress of this mission had been too much. On November 12, Hamilton wrote to Washington: "I have been detained here these two days by a fever and violent rheumatic pains throughout my body. This has prevented my being active in person for promoting the purposes of my errand, but I have taken every other method in my power, in which Governor Clinton has obligingly given me all the aid he could."[32]

Hamilton's condition worsened. He was now bedridden in Peekskill at the house of Dennis Kennedy, a civilian supporter of the cause. On November 20, Hugh Hughes wrote to Washington: "I am with Col. Hamilton, who I find very ill of a nervous Fever, the Event of which the Doctors say is altogether uncertain. ... At Times he has been a little delirious, but not so now."[33] On November 23, Hamilton's assistant on the trip, Captain Caleb Gibbs, wrote to Washington: "I found Colo. Hamilton much worse than I expected, labouring under a Violent nerves fever, and raging to the greatest extremity, he continued through the day, & last night very Ill. He is this morning something better, the fever in some small degree abated. every possible measure is taking to restore him, & it is the oppinion of the Doctr two or three days will determine his fate." For his part Hamilton seems to have thought he was dying, for Gibbs concludes, "Colo. Hamilton bears his sickness with becoming fortitude but is Confident he shall not survive long."[34]

A day later, Hamilton's fever broke and he left. But almost at once the illness returned with full force. Again deathly ill, Hamilton was taken back to Kennedy's house. While lying sick and delirious, worrying about fissures at the highest level of Army command and growing regional tension within Congress, Hamilton learned of another form of rot: systematic looting by officers. "A particular instance, among others," Hamilton wrote to New York Governor Clinton from his sickbed, "a great number of cattle belonging to the inhabitants were driven off—sold at a kind of mock auction by order of a general officer—sent into Connecticut, and no kind of account rendered of the proceeds. Such enormities, if real, are evidently of the most mischievous tendency; a timely stop ought by all means to be put to them, and the perpetrators brought to an exemplary punishment."[35]

One suspects that it was during this two-month-long convalescence at the Peekskill home of Dennis Kennedy that Hamilton read and wrote his notes on Plutarch's *Lives*. Though deathly ill, this break from the war would have contained moments of relative recovery and calm in which Hamilton could fill the empty pages of his old state militia artillery pay book with quotations, summaries, and reflections. He likely continued those notations once back at Valley Forge, but his workload there was again immense. Whatever the case, these notes are full of ideas about democracy, state power, and economic development that he would return to throughout the rest of his life.[36]

The dissension among Washington's generals continued for many more months, spreading south to the Carolinas to encompass insubordination by General Charles Lee. The reckless freelancing by Gates and Putnam would be known as the Conway Cabal, for Brigadier General Thomas Conway, an Irish officer and Gates supporter who drunkenly divulged the true scale of the machinations against Washington. The crisis was only resolved after a few reputation-changing battles, a court-martial, and two duels.

In one duel, a Washington ally, General John Cadwalader, shot Conway through the mouth.[37] As the story goes, upon seeing his handiwork Cadwalader allegedly said, "I've stopped the damned rascal's tongue anyhow." Miraculously, Conway survived and died years later in Ireland.

In the other duel, Hamilton's extremely close friend (and perhaps lover), Lieutenant Colonel John Laurens, shot and lightly wounded General Lee. The character of John Laurens deserves elaboration. He was the son of the fabulously wealthy Henry Laurens, president of the Continental Congress, and one of the biggest slaveholders in South Carolina. The younger Laurens was sent off to boarding school in Geneva, Switzerland, and then legal studies at the Middle Temple in London.

Laurens was influenced by the 1772 Somerset Case, in which Lord Chief Justice Mansfield ruled that any enslaved person became free simply by setting foot on English soil. By the time "young master Jack" came home to South Carolina he was an outright abolitionist.[38] As Ron Chernow put it, "Laurens became a passionate convert to abolitionism, which was to create a strong ideological bond with Hamilton." Laurens correctly saw slavery as the Revolution's primary moral contradiction. He successfully lobbied to form two battalions of manumitted slaves, even convincing his father to free many of the Laurens family's bondsmen for military service.[39]

Laurens and Hamilton were extremely close. Later historians have described their bond as "homosocial." Their bond may or may not have involved sex, but it was certainly romantic in tone and intensity. Hamilton, in particular, wrote Laurens letters that exude sexual passion. "Cold in my professions, warm in my friendships," read one such missive, "I wish, my Dear Laurens, it might be in my power, by action rather than words, to convince you that I love you. I shall only tell you that 'till you bade us Adieu, I hardly knew the value you had taught my heart to set upon you. ... You should not have taken advantage of my sensibility to steal into my affections without my consent. But as you have done it and as we are generally indulgent to those we love, I shall not scruple to pardon the fraud you have committed."

Laurens, like Hamilton, was recklessly brave, exhibiting what one biographer called "indirect self-destructive behavior." After the Battle of Brandywine in 1777, the Marquis de Lafayette said of Laurens, "It was not his fault that he was not killed or wounded ... he did every thing that was necessary to procure one or t'other."[40] After serving on Washington's staff, Laurens was captured, paroled, freed, led troops in South Carolina, and was there killed in action on August 27, 1782 while leading an unnecessary charge against trapped but well-defended British troops.

Cantonment at Valley Forge

In late January, Hamilton's health was finally restored and he rejoined Washington's headquarters staff at Valley Forge. The army, now less than half its peak strength, lived in log huts with frozen earthen floors. Supplies of every type were lacking. The would-be nation's political disorganization and decentralization stoked hunger, malnutrition, cold, overcrowding, and illness. Dysentery, pneumonia, typhoid, typhus, smallpox, all festered. Ultimately, around 2,500 men, or a quarter of Washington's army, died. More would have perished if Washington had not ordered systematic inoculations. Inoculation, then very much in its infancy, carried the risk of death; many religious leaders condemned the practice as sinful.[41]

The men supplemented their meager half-rations, when possible, with some winter fishing in local streams. This yielded some chub, gar, and suckers. Then, in early spring, the Schuylkill River showed mercy with a robust and early run of shad.[42]

We get a hint of the crisis in Washington's letter to President of the Continental Congress Henry Laurens: "I am now convinced beyond a doubt, that unless some great and capital change suddenly takes place in that line this Army must inevitably be reduced to one or other of these three things. Starve—dissolve—or disperse, in order to obtain subsistence in the best manner they can."[43]

When states did send provisions, typically only a fraction of what had been promised arrived. Even in these situations, state politicians were known to assert their privileges; for example, when Governor Thomas Wharton, Jr. of Pennsylvania sent clothing, he instructed Washington that it "will be directed for 3rd, 6th, 9th & 12th Pennsa. Battalions."[44] As it turned out, the supplies in question had already been looted by "the disaffected in Philadelphia and Bucks Counties." These mobs, according to Washington, had "seized and carried off a number of respectable inhabitants in those Counties, and such Officers of the Army as fell in their way, among others, Major Murray of the 13th Pennsylvania Regiment, who was at Newtown with his family. What adds to the misfortune is, that they carried off near 2000 Yds of Cloth which had been collected in the County and was making up for the Regiment."[45]

While discontented civilians resisted Army foraging operations —meaning "house-to-house visitations for clothing, blankets, shoes, and every kind of food that could be spared by noncombatants"[46]—there was half-suppressed mutiny in camp. In the same letter to Henry Laurens, Washington described his inability to mobilize his men for defensive action: "Yesterday afternoon receiving information that the Enemy, in force, had left the City, and were advancing towards Derby, with apparent design to forage and draw subsistence from that part of the Country, I ordered the Troops to be in readiness, that I might give every Opposition in my power; when behold! to my great mortification, I was not only informed, but convinced, that the Men were unable to stir on account of provision, and that a dangerous mutiny, begun the night before and which with difficulty was suppressed by the spirited exertions of some Officers, was still much to be apprehended for want of this Article."[47]

By February 1778, there was near logistical collapse and a catastrophic shortage of provisions. Poor management at commissary, and a breakdown of transport due to wet weather and lack of wagons, meant resupply almost stopped. Horses died of hunger. Men's diaries contain lines like: "It snows—I'm Sick—eat nothing —No Whiskey—No Forage—Lord—Lord—Lord."[48]

In desperation Washington ordered a "grand Forage." His instructions read:

It is of the utmost Consequence that the Horses Cattle Sheep
and Provender within Fifteen or Twenty miles west of the River
Delaware between the Schuylkil and the Brandywine be immediately removed, to prevent the Enemy from receiving any benefit
therefrom, as well as to supply the present Emergencies of the
American Army. I do therefore Authorise impower & Command
you forthwith to take Carry off & secure all such Horses as are
suitable for Cavalry or for Draft and all Cattle & Sheep fit for
Slaughter together with every kind of Forage that may be found in
possession of any of the Inhabitants within the Aforesaid Limits.[49]

At moments like this, desperation crept into Hamilton's letters.
In a February order to commandeer wagons for the foraging he
concludes: "For god's sake, Dear Sir, exert yourself upon this occasion. Our distress is infinite."[50]

The Vision Emerges

It was amid this concatenation of crises—Hamilton's debilitating
fever and breakdown; around him generals going rogue, men starving, deserting, and rebelling; officers looting; politicians bickering
and plotting; illness everywhere; a powerful enemy in possession
of two major cities—that we can see Hamilton's broader vision
emerging. From his swirling fears, frustrations, and fever emerged
a new, ruthless clarity and the outline of his mature political and
economic theories. Gone from that point on was the romantic boy
democrat; in his place, the brutally pragmatic nationalist.

Beginning in early 1778, just after his return to Valley Forge,
Hamilton's letters show him sketching out the blueprint of his
future political work. The essential problem was the dependence of
the military upon the national government, and the national government's dependence upon the states. Under the as-yet-unratified
Articles of Confederation, the Continental Congress had no real
power to compel tax money from the states. It made requests, but
these were only sometimes honored.

To make matters worse, the new nation had no navy, no banks,
no financial system, not even any government departments or

standing bureaucracies. What passed for administration was conducted by ad hoc congressional committees and boards. The entire structure seemed destined to fail.

To make the new government even less coherent, ocean travel and shipping, upon which the largely roadless colonies had depended for internal communications, were now blockaded by the British Navy. Everything moved at the arduously slow rate of overland traffic. Meanwhile, lack of stable funding made it difficult for the Continental Army to obtain necessary provisions and pay its soldiers. Very often states preferred to support their own militias.[51] Compounding the predicament, the officers of the Continental Army, Hamilton's peers, looked down on the militia as undisciplined and only dubiously reliable.[52]

The Want of Power

On February 13, 1778, less than a month after returning from his illness, Hamilton sent an outline of his critique to Governor George Clinton of New York. At the heart of the problem lay Congress, or "a degeneracy of representation in the great council of America. It is a melancholy truth Sir, and the effects of which we dayly see and feel, that there is not so much wisdom in a certain body, as there ought to be, and as the success of our affairs absolutely demands." The letter accuses Congress of "a want of foresight, comprehension and dignity" and "instances of the most whimsical favouritism in their promotions." The letter concludes with a Machiavellian admission: "The sentiments I have advanced are not fit for the vulgar ear. ... But it is time that men of weight and understanding should take the alarm, and excite each other to a proper remedy. ... Indeed Sir it is necessary there should be a change. America will shake to its center, if there is not."[53]

By September 1780, Hamilton was less circumspect. In a letter to the New York politician James Duane, Hamilton expressed himself in more explicit terms: "The fundamental defect is a want of power in Congress." And that, in Hamilton's view, "originated from ... an excess of the spirit of liberty which has made the particular states show a jealousy of all power not in their own hands." In other words, the states "exercise a right of judging in the last resort of the measures recommended by Congress." And Congress hardly helped. Instead of asserting its power, Congress was "timid and indecisive in their resolutions, constantly making concessions to the states, till they have scarcely left themselves the shadow of power." In this context, Congress had ruined its "influence and credit with the army," causing the Army "to establish its dependence on each state separately rather than ... on the whole collectively."⁵⁴

In Hamilton's long letter to James Duane we also see, in embryonic form, the idea of a Constitutional Convention—the first time a Founder mentions anything of the sort in print: "The confederation itself is defective and requires to be altered; it is neither fit for war, nor peace. The idea of an uncontrolable sovereignty in each state, over its internal police, will defeat the other powers given to Congress, and make our union feeble and precarious."

The logic of Hamilton's developmentalism as expressed in the letter to Duane was fundamentally military: a constitutionally strong and activist state could build a strong and wealthy economy, which in turn could fund a strong military and thus ensure national survival and sovereignty.

"The confederation gives the states individually too much influence in the affairs of the army; they should have nothing to do with it," Hamilton wrote. "The entire formation and disposal of our military forces ought to belong to Congress. It is an essential cement of the union; and it ought to be the policy of Congress to destroy all ideas of state attachments in the army and make it look up wholly to them."

The letter to Duane is a truly portentous document. Scrawled out late at night by an overworked, ferociously motivated twenty-three-year-old immigrant officer, it is not only the first time anyone floated the idea that seven years later would become the Constitutional Convention, it also delineated what would be the central issue in American political union up to the end of the Civil War, and in many ways beyond to our current era—in the struggle between states' rights and national sovereignty.

A week and a half after his robust dispatch to Duane, Hamilton wrote to John Laurens, who was on parole as a prisoner of war in New Jersey. Provisioning the Army was still a struggle, he told his dear friend:

> You can hardly conceive in how dreadful a situation we are. The army, in the course of the present month, has received only four or five days rations of meal, and we really know not of any adequate relief in future. This distress at such a stage of the campaign sours the soldiery. 'Tis in vain you make apologies to them. The officers are out of humour, and the *worst* of evils seems to be coming upon us—*a loss of our virtue*. ... I say this to you because you know it and will not charge me with vanity. I hate Congress—I hate the army—I hate the world—I hate myself.[55]

3

The Supply Effort, from Grand Forage to Manufacturing

The military supply effort was central to America's initial steps into industrialization. Supplying the Continental Army was an epic struggle as important as any battle. It gave Hamilton, and many others, an experiential education in dirigiste economics. The constant emergency of war revealed the government's power to create economic conditions, drive technological innovation, and spur capital accumulation. From the military crisis emerged something like war communism, a system of production, exchange, and procurement that had little to do with competitive markets or the price signal, resting instead on coercive bands of armed men, their power to confiscate, and the creative destruction of inflation.

Before the war, British mercantilist policy constrained American economic development. The colonies had a thriving wool industry, but as early as 1699, Parliament barred any export of woolen products such as yarn, cloth, clothing, or drapery. The colonies had plentiful beaver pelts and a burgeoning hat industry, but in 1732 Parliament "forbade the exportation of hats from the colonies, and prohibited any hatter from taking more than two apprentices." The colonies had coal and iron deposits, and built foundries, but in 1750, Parliament forbade the colonies from processing iron beyond a rudimentary stage, or from making steel.[1] In other words, a contradiction had emerged between the forces of production and relations of production.

There was also, as has already been noted, an emerging threat to slavery. The Somerset Case of 1772 left American slave owners fearing a slippery slope toward total abolition. This was a significant motivation for Southern elites to join the rebellion.[2] And, very crucially, the Revolution freed white settlers to move west and acquire Native American lands beyond the Proclamation Line of 1763 that ran along the high point of the Appalachian Mountains.[3]

In liberating the colonies from British rule and creating the American government, the Revolutionary War created a new political economy. Lasting eight years, the war disrupted old economic arrangements and forged new ones. The material crisis of the war forced emergency experimentation in dirigiste economics. The politics of the war pushed the colonies into formal political unity, and that led to greater economic integration. The costs of the war demanded not just confiscation but also taxation. Taxation, in turn, forced autonomous farmers, the American peasantry, into the cash economy and thus drove commodification and production for sale rather than use. And through it all the organizational and productive powers of the state grew. Central to this was the state debt, which as we shall see, became the platform upon which to build an entire financial and credit system. Thomas Paine was ahead of events in 1776 when in *Common Sense* he wrote, "the necessities of an army create a new trade," and "No nation ought to be without a debt. A national debt is a national bond."[4]

The economic story of the war confirms a disturbing truth: both capitalism and the modern fiscal military state emerge from the furnace of war. War is not external to capitalist political economy; rather, war is fundamental to capitalism's historical existence. War is to capitalism as ponds are to frogs. During war the truth is revealed: violence is at the heart of the state's form, function, and purpose. When mass violence is unleashed, the state is revealed as one of the central organizing structures of modernity.[5]

In the spirit of Paine's insights about the economics of war making, Hamilton would build a powerful central state and national financial system. The primary economic challenges of the war —procuring and manufacturing supplies for the Army, and doing so *on credit*—would shape all three of Hamilton's famous reports:

the *Report on Public Credit*, *Report on a National Bank*, and *Report on Manufactures*. In these, Hamilton worked out remarkably sophisticated ideas about state power, finance, and long-term economic planning. When the *Report on Manufactures* is read through this history, we see that Hamilton's ideas about government driving economic transformation were not only the product of his intellectual powers and voracious reading, they were also the crystallization of his experiential education as a participant in the conflict.

To understand the war as political economy and its impact on Hamilton's ideas, we need to consider its geography, technology, and social forms. What forces built the economy? Where did the national debt come from? At the apex of those "necessities of an army" sat Hamilton, viewing the broad and distressing sweep of events.

War as Fetter

Real economic performance during the Revolutionary War is hard to measure because we lack the necessary data.[6] The customhouses of port towns kept records of what was in the holds of departing and arriving ships. But the household, the family farm, and the home workshop, which were the basic units of production, generally did not keep records. Probate and tax records have not been well preserved nor were they always well produced. When compared with the decades prior to the war, and with the decades after the formation of the current federal government and its first census, the fifteen years from 1775 to 1790—that is, the Revolutionary War and the so-called Critical Period—are very poorly documented.[7] We lack consistent data on rates of investment, employment, and income. In other words, much of what would be needed for a rigorously detailed economic history of the conflict and its immediate aftermath is missing.[8]

We do, however, have fragmented data, and these allow us glimpses into the political economic realities of the war and the postwar crisis. From these, it is safe to say that the Revolutionary

War created contradictory economic pressures. On the one hand, the British blockade hurt imports and exports at a time when the colonies were heavily dependent on both, and before a robust internal national market existed. Violence took a heavy toll on the colonies' working capital: when the British burnt Falmouth, in what is now Maine, the flames took workshops, mills, and storehouses. In summer 1779 British naval forces raided the Connecticut coast, plundering and burning much of New Haven, Fairfield, Norwalk, and New London. "The property damage in New London included a large part of the shipping, almost all the wharves, sixty-five dwelling houses, thirty-one stores filled with merchandise, and many other buildings."[9]

War drew away some laborers from production, though not a devastating amount. As J. Franklin Jameson explained it: "In 1776, when the army was at its largest, it numbered, including both Continentals and state militia, not quite ninety thousand men, about one-eighth [12.5 percent] of the men of fighting age. In the years 1779 and 1780 it was but half as large, not more than a sixteenth part [6.25 percent] of the male inhabitants of military age ... for most men in the thirteen American states industrial life went on during these seven years, not without disturbance, to be sure, but without cessation in its development."[10]

The war's worst economic damage hit American shipbuilding. No dockyard in the colonies was as developed as the Royal Dockyard at Portsmouth, England, which employed "considerably above 8,000 working men, of whom about 1,500 were shipwrights and caulkers, nearly 500 joiners and house carpenters, 200 smiths, 250 sawyers, nearly 700 laborers of various kinds, and about 350 employed in the rope-yard."[11] Indeed, most American shipyards lacked permanent buildings, and there were no working drydocks. According to C. Stevens Laise, the number of employees within the shipyards "varied greatly with both the season and the volume of work to be done. Under the direction of a master shipwright, the workforce in an active period might include four to six shipwrights hired either by the day or for a specific part of the vessel's construction. Each shipwright might have an apprentice or two whose wages he collected. House carpenters, sawyers, and others would be hired as needed and a few unskilled laborers were always required. Thus a busy colonial shipyard might employ between one and two dozen workmen at times of peak activity."[12]

Shipbuilding was an important, technologically and organizationally advanced form of manufacturing and accounted for a large portion of exports. By 1750, Colonial America had about 125 shipyards. In 1769, the American colonies built 389 ships.[13] Lloyd's Register recorded an astounding 1,680 vessels built in 1776. At that time, "at least a third of the British merchant fleet was American-built."[14]

Before the war, America built ships for its own use and for export. We get a glimpse of how the export of ships worked from this description, penned by a British observer in 1729: "We have a great many young men who are bred to the sea, and have friends to support them; if they cannot get employment at home, they go to New England and the Northern Colonies with a cargo of goods, which they there sell at a great profit, and with the produce build a ship and purchase a loading of lumber, and sail for Portugal or the Straits, etc., and, after disposing of their cargoes there, frequently ply from port to port in the Mediterranean till they have cleared so much money as will in a good part pay for the first cost of the cargo carried out by them, and then perhaps sell their ships, come home, take up another cargo from their employers, and so go back and build another ship."[15]

The war largely stopped such trade. British blockade, coastal raiding, and the partial suppression of American fishing and trading all hurt American shipbuilding. By the latter part of the war there was another problem: a shortage of capital. As Richard Buel put it, "The Continental Navy benefited from embarking on a large building program in 1776, when prices were still reasonably low and Congress's credit intact. As the currency progressively lost value, however, building new vessels became more expensive. This is one reason why Congress turned in 1778 to purchasing frigates abroad. In 1779, after Congress had exhausted its credit at home and overseas, the Continental Navy's principal resource was its captures."[16]

During the war, the various regional markets all had widely different price structures. Prices in the Mid-Atlantic markets, for example, remained substantially higher than those in Massachusetts Bay for the duration of the war.

War as Stimulus

In other parts of the economy, the war increased domestic production and investment. The British Naval blockade acted as a de facto tariff, a wall that protected domestic industry from cheaper, often better foreign imports. The war created new and ravenous consumers, in the form of the British, French, and Continental armies, each of which needed vast amounts of food, fodder, clothing, paper, metal, and munitions. Consumption is half the equation for economic growth. Booming production without commensurate consumption produces glutted markets, slower rates of accumulation, and inevitable slowdowns. War pushed the economic throttle forward about as far as it could go; it drove up farm prices, yielding farmers more income, which in turn allowed more investment, which meant more employment and yet more consumption. As Ferguson put it in his classic *The Power of the Purse*: "The expense of the war far exceeded anything in colonial experience. As the conflict broadened, it stimulated a business boom and caused a real price inflation, which was in turn spurred by government and private buying. A seller's market prevailed throughout the war; domestic products and services rose in price, and scarce foreign articles were extravagantly dear."[17]

Of course, some classes fared better than others. In general, class inequality was higher after the Revolution than before.[18] The merchants, smugglers, and speculators made out best. Such was their prosperity that we have evidence of "growing demand for consumer goods and the increasing means to satisfy a taste for luxuries among those profiting from the war." In particular, men connected to Congress's so-called "Secret Committee," which authorized importation of supplies for the Continental Army, did very well. The patriot financier Robert Morris, who was at the center of this wheeling and dealing, wrote to an associate: "The prices of all imported articles have been enormously high. I could have sold any quantity of European manufactures for 500 to 700 percent and bought tobacco for 25s. to 30s. per ct. It is not too late, but goods are becoming rather more plenty and tobacco is rising, but there is plenty of room to make as much money as you please."[19] Meanwhile, on at least "thirty occasions between 1776 and 1779," crowds of hungry civilians violently confronted hoarding and price-gouging merchants, often looting the offenders' storehouses.

In 1791, Tench Coxe, assistant secretary of the Treasury under Hamilton, studied the question of the economy's transformation during the war and concluded: "Any man, who makes a comparison of a variety of branches [of industry] as they were in 1774, and as they stood in 1782, will perceive a great advance to have taken place." Coxe noted the war's impediments to growth but then concluded that on the whole the conflict forced an expansion of manufacturing:

> Though manufactures were little encouraged, through the intermediate eight years, by reason of the total occupation of government in the prosecution of the war: their importance moreover was not duly estimated. The British manufacturers, who can now emigrate with the greatest convenience, then viewed the people of this country as enemies. Neither they, nor the people of other nations cared to risque themselves in an invaded country, nor would they hazard a capture in their passages hither. Notwithstanding these impediments, the manufacturers of the United States have been found to be the most successful competitors with those of Great Britain in the American market. They have not made fine linens, fine cloths, silks, stuffs, and other articles requiring a great degree of skill, labour, or capital; but they have made common cloths of linen, woollen, and cotton, steel, nails, sheet iron, paper, gunpowder, cabinet work, carriages, shoes, and fabrics of the simple but most important kinds.[20]

As Gordon S. Wood put it, "the inexhaustible needs of three armies—the British and French as well as the American—for everything from blankets and wagons to meat and rum brought into being hosts of new manufacturing and entrepreneurial interests and made market farmers out of husbandmen who before had scarcely ever traded out of their neighborhoods."[21] In other words, the war not only created expansion, as in quantitative growth, it also brought qualitative transformations; with the spread of market relations came the increasing commodification of previously subsistence economies. The war, and the interventionist state policies it forced into being, brought together new producers and consumers, created new connections between previously isolated regions, and thus vastly stimulated "inland trade" while also laying the legal and physical foundations of the market economy's later rapid development. All of which helped establish the necessary preconditions for the country's economic takeoff.[22]

Ravenous Armies

The patriot military effort was no low-tech, low-cost guerrilla undertaking. Certainly such tactics were used at key times. At Lexington and Concord, the Minutemen fought from behind stone walls, attacking, retreating, then attacking again in classic guerrilla fashion, and irregular tactics and terror were used by militias in smaller skirmishes and by sharpshooters within larger set-piece battles. But most of the fighting in the Revolutionary War was in the European style: uniformed troops confronting each other in massed formations, or attacking and defending heavy fortifications, both sides using artillery bombardments and dependent on long supply lines. It was, in other words, capital-intensive and very expensive. All of this helped shape Hamilton's political economic ideas.

The Continental Army's peak strength reached about 22,000.[23] Between 100,000 to 200,000 Americans, "perhaps one in ten of the available population served" at some point during the war. Provisioning this force pushed the development of both manufacturing and finance.[24] Working on Washington's staff, Hamilton was at the center of this effort, the war-driven economic planning that was also a form of ad hoc state building.

During the first year of the war, supplying the American troops was left to each commanding officer. Thus, Hamilton had to both recruit and fundraise for his New York State militia company. As such smaller units were incorporated into larger units, supplying fell to the generals. In charge of "brigades" of 1,000 to 3,000 men, generals fundraised, foraged, and purchased as and where they could. This disorganized supply system gave the Continental Army a locust-like quality. In 1777, Washington would admonish his officers on this point: "That fences are ever burnt must be imputed to inattention, and want of care in officers; but at this time will be deemed to arise from the most inexcusable negligence—How disgraceful to the army is it, that the peaceable inhabitants, our countrymen and fellow citizens, dread our halting among them, even for a night and are happy when they get rid of us? This can proceed only from their distress at the plundering and wanton destruction of their property—To prevent these evils is the manifest duty of the officers."[25]

So time-consuming was the economic side of things that during the early fighting in New England "the vast majority of American and British forces spent their time," David Hsiung writes, "finding and acquiring supplies for themselves, and denying their enemy those same items. For months the Royal Navy had cruised the Atlantic coast, seizing livestock, hay, and timber for the main British forces in Boston."[26] That winter, the "most serious threat facing the Continental Army ... came not from British forces but from its own diminishing woodpiles." Meanwhile, the British troops, trapped in occupied Boston and having no forests to cut down, dismantled buildings and burned the timbers. Hsiung shows that the problem of limited supplies helped drive General Howe away to Nova Scotia and then to a more amply supplied New York.[27]

James A. Henretta estimates that each day the 35,000-strong British Army "consumed thirty-seven tons of food, thirty-eight tons of hay and oats, and (during winter) huge supplies of wood." Most of this would have been purchased from local farmers and merchants using scarce and valuable hard currency, specie money. Much of this hard currency eventually found its way into the hands of patriot agents who used it to pay their European arms suppliers. The French Army was another major source of stimulus. "Military contractors estimated the French demand for flour for the five months beginning in May 1779 at thirty-five thousand barrels. This total was more than triple the amount of bread and flour shipped annually from New England to the West Indies between 1768 and 1772."[28]

Supplying Sullivan

To understand how expensive the war was, consider the scale of one of the Army's more pharaonic efforts: General Sullivan's campaign against the British-allied Iroquois Confederacy.[29] The Iroquois had been raiding western settlements, so Washington ordered "the total destruction and devastation of their settlements and the capture of as many prisoners of every age and sex as possible," adding that "it will be essential to ruin their crops now in the ground and prevent their planting more."[30]

Logistics for the campaign started in the spring of 1779, when General Clinton's brigade of about 1,600 men, plus camp follow-ers, rendezvoused at Canajoharie, New York, on the Mohawk River and there gathered supplies.[31] Meanwhile, seventy miles to the east along the river, carpenters built boats at Schenectady, which, when ready, were taken upstream to Canajoharie. In June, the boats and supplies were portaged about 25 miles to Otsego Lake, headwaters of the Susquehanna. There, Clinton's men dammed the south end of the six-square-mile lake, impounding as much water as they could. In August, with the flotilla of supply boats loaded, they broke the dam and made their way down the artificially swollen Susquehanna River.

Farther south, General Sullivan assembled his forces at Easton, Pennsylvania, cut a road some sixty miles northwest through woods and swamps to meet the Susquehanna at Wyoming, Pennsylvania, and there received the supply boats as they came in over the next month.[32] From there, Sullivan marched off to kill Indians and burn their villages, destroying some forty in all and forcing most surviv-ing British-allied Iroquois to retreat to Fort Niagara and beyond, into present-day Ontario.

Though not directly involved in the campaign, Hamilton had to follow its logistics. "By a letter we have received from General Sullivan it appears that Poor's Brigade have left their tents behind," jotted Hamilton to the relevant parties. "The General requests you will have them supplied from your nearest deposit, and, in general, that you will make up every deficiency in this article for the expedition as speedily as possible. General Sullivan appears to be very anxious to have his supplies of every kind forwarded to him, that he may begin his career. He is in his usual pother; but dispatch is certainly very desireable."[33]

Commissary

The decentralized catch-as-catch-can system of each general equipping his own force was quickly recognized as a recipe for disaster. Accordingly, Congress created the Board of War and a Commissary Department, which, after June 1776, ran much of the supply effort—or tried to.[34]

Usually made up of five congressmen, a secretary, and a few clerks, the Board of War was essentially the Defense Department of its time. The board was charged with keeping an accurate register of all officers and the dates of their commissions and accounts of the number and condition of all soldiers, and with keeping track of arms, ammunition, artillery, and other military equipment. It was to receive regular reports from commanders in the field and communicate to them all dispatches from Congress. It managed all monies appropriated for the war and supervised the recruiting, training, supplying, and transporting of all land forces. And finally, the board was in charge of all enemy prisoners. All of this required supplies.

By 1779, the Commissary Department, divided into a Purchasing Commissary and Issuing Commissary, had five departments managing five geographic districts in the North, East, Middle, South, and a district covering western Connecticut and eastern New York. In the Continental Army, almost all orders other than battlefield commands were issued in writing and disseminated throughout the ranks on slips of paper or as posted broadsheets. Washington and his officers' orders were always rather detailed and often veered away from straightforward instructions into political pedagogy and outright sermonizing. Though physical punishment was a regular and brutal feature of Continental Army life, Washington noted that "a people unused to restraint must be led, they will not be drove—even those who are ingaged for the War must be disciplined by degrees."[35] Viewed through its archives, Washington's army can appear as a gigantic letter-writing machine.

All of this meant more paper, ink, candles, food, fodder, buildings, and horses were needed—yet more stimulus for the myriad layers and networks of craftspeople, artisans, apprentices, loggers, farmers, teamsters, laundresses, seamstresses, and merchants. Guns were only one piece of gear. Textiles, paper, shoes, hats—every line of production ramped up during the war. Soldiers needed "bayonets, bayonet scabbards, bayonet belts, espontoons, extra flints, spare musket locks, cartridge boxes, swords ... blankets, knapsacks, extra flints (about 6 flints to a man), balls (about forty or fifty to a man). ... tents, camp kettles, linen covers for kettles, canteens and haversacks."[36] Cannon of brass or iron were essential. "A heavy brass 12 pounder weighed 3,200 pounds; a brass 6-pounder, 500 pounds; Iron pieces weighed more." To move this artillery required horses, lots of them. "A 12-pounder required 12 horses." Ammunition wagons needed four horses. In 1776, a British military writer estimated that an army of 30,000 men and sixty pieces of heavy artillery would need 9,000 horses. That meant "6000 tons of bread would be necessary every six months, allowing for deterioration, also the same amount of hay and oats" for the horses.[37]

Domestic Production

Manufacturing of all articles, from cloth, paper, salt, and glass, to weapons, bricks, and beer, was by no means moribund in the colonies. But neither was it robust. Even before fighting erupted, the rebellion took on developmentalist, proto-nationalist—that is, proto-Hamiltonian—aspects. Before their grievances were "referred to the terrible arbitrament of the sword," the colonial rebels used not only petition and protest, but also boycott and economic counter-blockade.[38]

As early as 1774, while the whole struggle was still a matter of generalized agitation, the First Continental Congress passed resolutions urging the colonies to curtail unnecessary consumption of imports and to encourage sheep breeding and a domestic wool industry. Many states paid bounties for the best domestically produced linens, wools, and cotton textiles.[39] When, in April 1775, fighting began and the Continental Army was formed, the country was in no way economically self-sufficient. Manufacturing in the form of petty commodity production was in its infancy and nowhere near ready to meet the requirements of fielding a conventional army. Production of textiles, shoes, hats, tents, wagons, metals, weapons, ammunition, shovels, medicine were all lacking, and imports were hampered by the British blockade.

In support of the patriot cause came a great outpouring of decentralized, domestic manufacturing. During the first two years, government at every level exhorted society to *produce, produce, produce!* Domestic production became something of a fetish among patriots. "I will tell you what I have done," wrote a lady of Philadelphia to a British officer at the outset of the war. "My only brother I have sent to the camp with my prayers and blessings. I hope he will not disgrace me; I am confident he will behave with honor, and emulate the great examples he has before him; and had I twenty sons and brothers, they should go. I have retrenched every superfluous expense in my table and family; tea I have not drank since last Christmas, nor bought a new cap or gown since your defeat at Lexington; and, what I never did before, have learnt to knit, and am now making stockings of American wool for my servants; and this way do I throw in my mite to the public good. I ... assure you that these are the sentiments of all my sister Americans. They have sacrificed assemblies, parties of pleasure, tea-drinking, and finery to that great spirit of patriotism that actuates all ranks and degrees of people throughout this extensive continent."[40]

Patriot promotion of domestic production led to creation of what was likely the first joint-stock company for manufacturing ever formed in North America. The United Company of Philadelphia for Promoting American Manufactures was formed in 1775 to produce wool and linen cloth. Tench Coxe, later a collaborator with Hamilton, was an early investor. The United Company mostly used a "putting-out" system: giving raw wool and flax to artisans to spin and weave in home workshops; but it also seems to have gotten hold of an imported spinning jenny, one of the very earliest, for the mechanical creation of yarn and thread in a workshop, or proto-factory, of its own.[41]

At the same time, Virginia's state constitutional convention passed an ordinance "to encourage the manufacture of salt petre, gunpowder, lead, the refining of sulphur, and providing fire-arms for the use of the Colony." The ensuing zeal and industry of Virginians for producing homemade manufactures were "described as almost surpassing belief." By the end of the war, one of the best cannon foundries in the country operated outside Richmond.[42]

These were successful efforts, but they took place in a context of relative underdevelopment. Gun ownership in Revolutionary America, for example, was fairly limited; many people were simply too poor to own weapons. A study of 221 estates in Surrey County, Virginia, from 1690 to 1715 found that among the poorest 30 percent of decedents only about one-third owned guns, while among the wealthiest 10 percent about two-thirds left guns. A similar study covering six Maryland counties between 1657 and 1719 found a similar pattern, in which only 50 to 58 percent of poorer households owned guns. Thus many early colonial militias were not even fully armed. In Virginia during the years 1777 to 1784, "only 46 percent of the militia" arrived with their own weapons.[43]

Contrary to the image of the self-armed yeoman farmer, a large portion of American soldiers came from the proletariat. As the prominent American historian John Ferling put it: "After 1777, the average Continental soldier was young, single, propertyless, poor and in many cases an outright pauper. In some states, such as Pennsylvania, up to one in four soldiers was an impoverished recent immigrant."[44] Thus, Congress and the state governments had to purchase enormous amounts of weaponry, ammunition, and gunpowder just to field lightly armed militias, not to mention the effort necessary to maintain an army capable of beating what was then perhaps the best equipped, best trained, and most seasoned military in the world.

Public spending expanded massively. Between 1776 and 1779, the government of Maryland spent money at twelve times the rate it had prior to hostilities. "The drain on Maryland's treasury doubled during the following three years. Supplying military needs became a major enterprise. Before 1779 clothing, munitions, and other military supplies consumed 60 percent of the state's budget."[45] The effects of state procurement can be seen in the swelling number of gunsmiths. In the years leading up to the war, 1751 to 1774, there were an estimated 803 gunsmiths in all thirteen colonies. During the war years, 1775 to 1783, that number almost doubled, rising to 1,573.[46] As we shall see in a later chapter, the number would drop off precipitously with the arrival of peace.

The colonies had only a few foundries, and these were not sufficient to meet the demands of war. Only at Westham, Virginia; Bridgewater, Massachusetts; and Reading and Warwick, Pennsylvania, were there metalworks that "turned out cannon and cannon ball."[47] And so government at every level took action. The Connecticut Council of Safety seized a royalist-owned furnace at Lakeville "and spent £1,450 preparing it to cast cannon and ammunition." North Carolina appropriated £5,000 to lease or purchase existing works in Guilford County. Foundries in Pennsylvania and New Jersey did a robust trade on large contracts for the rebel forces on land and sea. Small, sometimes-illegal foundries popped up throughout the rebellious colonies. Maryland had eighteen or twenty small foundries that mostly supplied local farmers.[48]

Prior to the war, many foundries used slaves and indentured servants. During the war finding labor of any sort became difficult. To assist, Congress and many individual States passed laws "exempting workmen employed at furnaces and forges from enlistment, and by various encouragements given for the establishment of new works or the operation of those already in existence." Some Pennsylvania operations used Hessian prisoners leased from the Continental Congress.

Despite robust effort, American-made weaponry remained inferior to European imports; American cannons were "cast with a cylindrical cavity of a diameter somewhat smaller than the intended calibre, which was afterward bored to a proper size" but such "guns were extremely liable to be spongy in that part where strength and smoothness are required." In Europe "the gun was cast solid" and the caliber afterward laboriously bored out.[49]

A nineteenth-century political economist, offering more evidence of government-led manufacturing, reported that "the first trials of anthracite for manufacturing purposes were made by Congress at its armory at Carlisle, Penn., in 1775, established in consequence of the Revolutionary war. The combined resources of Congress and people were only barely sufficient at first to supply the country with the iron it needed. It took some time to train workmen, and the Tories frequently interfered with proceedings by burning the iron-works."[50]

Production of gunpowder was particularly important. Congress and the colonial assemblies encouraged "the repair of old powder mills that had fallen into ruin since the French and Indian War and the erection of new mills." The Committee of Philadelphia built a "saltpetre Manufactory" in July 1775, while the Rhode Island Assembly "offered a bounty of 3 shillings a pound on every pound of saltpeter made in the colony during the next year." By the fall of 1777, at least 115,000 pounds of gunpowder had been produced from domestically made saltpeter, yet an estimated 90 percent of all gunpowder was imported or captured by American privateers.[51]

One old economic history noted the durability of the powder industry: "As soon as hostilities with the mother country were seen to be inevitable, powder-mills were established at Andover, Stoughton, Bradford, Morristown and other points. Five years after the surrender of Cornwallis, Pennsylvania had 21 such mills, with a reported annual capacity of 625 tons. This industry continued to flourish in America, not only on account of the demands of the frontier, but because of the rapid extension of mining, canal-building, and other development work, where the use of explosives, like that of machinery, was stimulated by the high price of labor."[52]

Domestic production, though expanding during the war, was also constantly hampered by such military depredations as tightening British patrols. Most frustrating for Washington and his closest aide and frequent ghostwriter, Hamilton, was the serious lack of interstate coordination. For example, in the summer of 1780, production in Connecticut halted, for though the mills there had plenty of saltpeter, they lacked sulfur. But when Washington suggested that the well-supplied powder mill at Springfield, Massachusetts, send down some of its sulfur, nothing happened.[53]

The number of paper mills increased prodigiously during the Revolutionary period. Newspapers were major consumers of paper. While staying in Marlborough, Massachusetts, the Duke of La Rochefoucauld noted that the inhabitants "busy themselves much with politics, and from the landlord down to the housemaid they all read two newspapers a day."[54]

In salt manufacturing a similar pattern obtained. Prior to hostilities, salt, essential for preserving food and for the health of livestock, was cheap to import as it was often used as ballast in the holds of ships arriving from Europe. The salt itself was produced in England and the Caribbean, and in a rare exception to British Mercantilist restrictions, also arrived from the Portuguese and Spanish islands of Madeira, the Azores, and the Canaries, and was traded directly for American fish.[55] As one much later account put it: "Salt was as essential to the armies of 1776 as gasoline is to the armies of 1945. When it was not obtainable the horses of the quartermaster's corps and of the cavalry became weak, meats spoiled, and soldiers mutinied."[56] The process of canning food in glass jars or tins was not invented until 1809, so during the Revolutionary period salting, smoking, and drying were the only methods of food preservation. Washington's wartime letters are full of reference to salt: "I have allready Spoke to the Commissary General to Send off as much Salt provisions as he Coud, but you must urge him on this head, as they are in very great want, & have no other place to depend on, but what goes from New york, he must Lay in all he Can get, to Supply the quantity which he Sends up, for he must take Care to Keep up his Stock."[57]

During the war, demand for salt increased while imported

supplies largely disappeared. Salt prices skyrocketed. In Virginia, as early as 1775, there was "a series of disturbances by people who, destitute of salt, used force to provision themselves. One of these disorders occurred when a band of armed men from the frontier, where it was virtually impossible to obtain salt, descended upon Henrico County, and coerced residents of the county into delivering small quantities of salt to them."[58]

By May 1776, the price of a bushel of salt in Philadelphia had risen from £2 to £7.[59] This caused a small boom in salt produced by artificial heat from wood or coal fires rather than by passive evaporation. Boiling saltwater to get salt was, in the economy of the eighteenth century, energy- and therefore also labor-intensive. Seawater is typically about 3.5 percent salt. A report from Kentucky estimated that it "took 840 gallons of the weak brine [from a saline spring] to yield one bushel."[60] In early 1776, "at least four colonies—New Jersey, Maryland, North Carolina, and Connecticut —all passed acts to encourage domestic salt-making," while Congress established a bounty for domestic salt production.[61] In Maryland, despite state-imposed price controls, "salt appreciated in value 3,900 percent between 1777 and 1780."[62] There, too, a domestic salt boom commenced.

Smuggling and Privateering

The Continental Army's dependence on debt-funded French imports of uniforms and weaponry proved that without looms and foundries of its own, the new nation was not only economically underdeveloped but also militarily vulnerable. To remedy this weakness would require aggressive public-sector action.

Most of these European-produced supplies were smuggled through the Caribbean and were paid for with tobacco and every other commodity, except livestock. Congress always kept livestock so as to build up woolen and leather industries at home. French financing also helped. As Richard Buel put it, "Without access to French money and goods the Continental Army would not have been able to clothe and rearm itself."[63] Thus, even as shipbuilding was hurt, American shipping in the form of smuggling and privateering boomed. A report in April 1776 found that profits of 120 percent could be had selling European gunpowder on the Dutch-controlled island of St. Eustatius. So great was the gain there that even some British smugglers were enticed to supply their nominal enemies by diverting cargos listed as bound for Africa to the sub rosa market at St. Eustatius.[64]

New England shipping interests did the best from all of this. In May 1779, eighteen captured ships were brought home to New London, Connecticut. During 1780, the Admiralty Court of the Essex district of Massachusetts registered 818 ships taken by privateers. In 1781, Salem, Massachusetts, was homeport to "fifty-nine vessels, carrying four thousand men." Over the course of the war, various American states commissioned at least 500 privateers. J. Franklin Jameson estimated that as many as 90,000 Americans served on privateers, "a number of men almost as great as served in the army, and greater than that of the army in any single year save one. Two-thirds of these men were from Massachusetts, the rest from the other New England states and from the Delaware river."[65]

A quick look at the number suggests that the loss of American shipbuilding due to the blockade and assaults upon shipyards was made up for in the number of ships stolen from the enemy by America's audacious and swashbuckling privateers.[66] The importance of the privateers is reflected in the letters of the Quartermaster and Commissary officers. For example, in a letter to Washington, Major General Thomas Mifflin wrote: "An armd Sloop is arrivd at Sinepuxent with military Stores—She has 500 Tents on board— The Capt. says that there are now at Martinique 6000 Tents imported there for Congress which are to be sent to the Continent in different Bottoms to prevent a total Loss. The french Ship La Seine is taken by the pincus Frigate are carried into Dominigue. She had on board a great Number of Tents. The Governor of Martinique has sent a Frigate to demand her on Pain of Reprisals. A Brigantine belonging to this Port is arrivd at Baltimore with 24000 Yds of Tent Cloth—but as they run great Risque in the Importation the Owners demand a most exorbitant Price which in the Opinion of many Gentlemen of Congress ought not to be paid—The Owners are willing to take their Chance at public Sale here, but as Housekeepers are generally in Want of Sheeting &ca for which the Cloth mentiond above is well calculated I think it cannot be purchasd for Congress at any reasonable Rate."[67]

Alongside the growth in privateering came an expansion of American, rather than British, marine insurance underwriting.[68] "Marine insurance in eighteenth-century America was still an individual rather than a corporate enterprise," Buel explains. "Ports with substantial commerce usually had one or more insurance offices that wrote policies, posted them, and settled balances between the insurers and the insured for a fee. The actual capital was put up by individuals or partnerships, who signed their names at the bottom of the policies—hence the term underwriter—for the posted rate."[69] Both risks and rewards were high. During peacetime, insurance rates in England for American ports had been as low as 2 per cent. By the late war, 35 percent was considered moderate in Massachusetts and Rhode Island.[70] One mercantile firm that smuggled in and out of Virginia during the war paid insurance premiums worth "50 percent of a cargo's value" by the late 1770s.[71] Merchants and shippers also adapted to the high-risk trade by switching to smaller, faster ships.[72]

And yet, despite the transformative growth in domestic production, the Continental Army remained heavily dependent on imports. My point is not that domestic manufacturing displaced imports, but rather that the supply effort was central to America's initial steps into industrialization. The struggle to produce, procure, and finance gave Hamilton an experiential education in the power of government to create economic activity, drive technological innovation, and spur capital accumulation. During the war, Adam Smith's "invisible hand" was very invisible indeed, while the visible hand of nascent state power held everything together.

4

"The Badness of the Money": Inflation and War

To supply the Army and militias, Congress and the states at first simply printed money. Ultimately, this resulted in hyperinflation. Just as the supply effort had taught Hamilton about the utility of government economic action, the inflation helped him develop his plan for a national financial system pivoting on a mixed public-private central bank.

In Colonial America, money was a chaotic thing. As one historian described it: "In 1774 each of the provinces in North America had its own paper currency, which not only varied in value from province to province, but varied in relation to the coins of England, Spain, Portugal, France, and the Netherlands, all of which circulated throughout America. In addition, some provinces had two sets of currency, one differing in value from the other. Newspapers and almanacs published lists of [the] comparative value of the several monies from time to time for the use of merchants and farmers."[1]

From 1775 through 1779, Congress would emit almost $200 million in Continental dollars. This accounted for fully "77 percent of congressional spending."[2] The states operated similarly, printing state money to buy the necessities to field their militias. "By the spring of 1778, emissions were five and ten millions at a time, and were about a million a week."[3] In the three years leading up to "1778 nearly 90 per cent of the revenue generated came from currency issues."[4] One modern study estimated that fully 67 percent of the direct costs of the war were paid for with a combination of congressional and state-issued paper money.[5]

This money printing actually worked in theory and practice, up to a point. As economist Bennett Baack has explained: "As long as the Continental dollar held its real value, then Congress could simply match the quantity of issues with the resource demands of the war." But managing a national money supply was undermined by a decentralized political structure. "Congress was not the only entity issuing money. During the period from 1775 to 1777 each state relied primarily on its own currency issues for revenue." Rather shockingly, fewer than half the states had given themselves the power of taxation![6]

Thus, as the money supply chaotically and haphazardly expanded, the value of Continental dollars began to drop. Between 1775 and 1777, the Continental's "average specie value fell by over 70 percent."[7] In 1778, Congress took the first step away from its own rapidly depreciating national currency when it declared about 41 million dollars of it to be British counterfeit. Much of it likely *was* fake, part of the empire's economic warfare.[8] To ease the blow, Congress allowed holders of counterfeit series notes to purchase other congressional "loan certificates" with them.[9] Between 1777 and 1779, the depreciation continued, but at a slower rate until late in 1779 the Continental dollar, "like an aged man, expiring by the decays of nature, without a sigh or groan, fell asleep in the hands of its last possessor."[10]

Extreme inflation had dangerous strategic effects; among other things, it badly damaged military morale. Soldiers were predominantly from the landless proto-proletarian classes, and while historians generally rate them as patriotic and politically sophisticated, the value of their signing bonuses and other pay were also important motivations. Aggressive inflation meant that even initially substantial sums of money depreciated so thoroughly that soldiers received nothing of real value. The Connecticut surgeon Albigence Waldo put it thus: "Much talk among Officers about discharges. Money has become of too little consequence. The Congress have not made their Commissions valuable Enough. Heaven avert the bad consequences of these things!!"[11]

This "confiscation by inflation" served as a form of taxation. Benjamin Franklin even argued that it was progressive in nature: "The general Effect of the Depreciation ... has proved a Tax on Money, a kind of Property very difficult to be taxed in any other Mode; and it has fallen more equally than many other Taxes, as those People paid most who being richest had most Money passing thro' their Hands."[12] In a desperate bid to combat inflation, Congress recommended price controls, then recommended their removal, and then in 1779 again supported price controls.[13]

Confiscation and Certificates

As faith in money collapsed, the Continental Army began requisitioning supplies. This was unpopular with the population and offended many state-level authorities. Congress thus urged, "every possible attention should be paid to the Laws of States and the Rights of Individuals." In December 1777, Congress asked the states to pass laws authorizing the Continental Army's ongoing impressments of goods and services. The confiscations were so unpopular that Congress avoided formally endorsing the practice. But at the same time the confiscations were necessary, so neither did Congress prohibit the practice.[14]

On the ground, among the hungry soldiers, survival often depended on requisitions of civilian property. Usually this took the form not of outright confiscation but of forced sales at a set price, theft papered over with nearly worthless scrip and IOUs. Only loyalists and those refusing the set price had their property expropriated without at least token compensation.[15] Letters from the Commissary and Quartermaster are full of reference to the practice. In October 1776, the quartermaster general, Thomas Mifflin, explained the situation to his colleague, the military supplier and later commissary general, Jeremiah Wadsworth: "Now my sweet scolding Jeremiah ... be pleas'd to impress for the public Service all such Teams [of horses and oxen] as you want ... If the Inhabitants will hire their Teams at reasonable Rates you will not I dare say proceed to impress—If they refuse to aid you you are to impress without Loss of Time."[16]

Here is a typical note from Colonel Ephraim Blaine, commissary general for the Middle District of the Continental Army, to George Washington. Written in 1778, it captures some of the struggle between suppliers and the Army: "I made Contracts for a Considerable Quantity of pork, I received orders from the Board of War to seize every Kind of provisions and spiritous liquors necessary for the Army, have been in this County and Berks this ten days & hope to procure six hundred head of Fatt cattle and a Considerable Quantity of Whisky, but Forestallers [speculators] are giving great prices and Stealing it off daily, I sincerely wish one or two examples cou'd be made of them."[17] There are indications that on occasion resistance to the forage was suppressed with violence. Bloodshed is said to have "attended the collection of forage in New Jersey."[18]

In late 1779, yet another de facto currency emerged in the form of "loan-office certificates."[19] Originally these were meant to function like war bonds. Many wealthy Americans actually paid money to get the certificates in the hope of making more money when the loans were paid back. The certificates were not supposed to circulate as currency. Yet the Army, Ephraim Blaine in particular, started military suppliers with certificates. Under requisition, if payment were refused, property would be confiscated without compensation. So the suppliers—farmers, manufactures, teamsters, coopers, and gunsmiths—took the paper and in turn used it to meet their own obligations. Soon the certificates were operating as currency. The certificates were at first handwritten, later printed, forms on which the commissary official listed the products or services purchased, the date of the transaction, and the amount of money to be paid later. Artisans, farmers, and merchants soon preferred the certificates to worthless Continental dollars.[20]

At the war's end yet another military currency was born when many soldiers and officers receiving discharge bonuses were paid with a new form of IOU called "final settlement certificates" and known colloquially as "Pierce's notes" because the paymaster general of the Continental Army was John Pierce.[21]

Inflation was not merely the result of too much money chasing too few goods. It was also driven by war profiteers and speculators. As the currencies grew more worthless, states took increasingly drastic action against speculative hoarding. "Virginia declared in 1778 that any one who bought country produce for resale was an engrosser and his goods liable to seizure. The governor was authorized to seize all grain and flour purchased by any forestaller, engrosser, or monopolizer."[22] As fighting shifted south, the government of Virginia became even more aggressive in its confiscations. "In May 1780 commissioners were appointed in each county to seize or purchase provisions at adjudicated prices, payable in certificates; all goods above family need were declared forfeit on these terms. The next year, on the eve of the Yorktown campaign, the governor was given unlimited power to produce the resources of the state."[23] Washington shared this hostility toward war profiteers, whom he called a "tribe of black hearted gentry" and "murderers of our cause," who should "be hunted down as the pests of society" and "hung in Gibbets upon a gallows."[24] Finally, starting in 1781 seven states, despite everything, again issued paper money. It lost value very quickly and left widespread resentment.[25]

Hamilton Sketches an Attack on Inflation

Amid this crisis of war-driven inflation, Hamilton for the first time laid out the full scope of his ideas about money and banking. Sometime in the winter of 1779–80, while still on Washington's staff, Hamilton wrote a long letter most likely to Robert Morris, who was the Revolution's chief funder and later the superintendent of finance. Hamilton's letter explained that the author's "principal concern" was "the state of our currency." In typical form, Hamilton begins the letter with a disabusing critique of the intellectual status quo: "Most people think that the depreciation might have been avoided by provident arrangements in the beginning without any aid from abroad, and a great many of our sanguine politicians 'till very lately imagined the money might still be restored by expedients within ourselves."[26]

Aware of how important French, Dutch, and Spanish loans were to the war effort, Hamilton dismissed this overconfidence in American self-sufficiency. "The war," he wrote, "particularly in the first periods, required exertions beyond our strength; to which neither our population nor riches were equal." The proof of this was "the decrease of our staple commodities and the difficulty of every species of supply."

As for inflation, or, "the badness of the money," while it had become a real problem, it was "originally an effect not a cause" of the economic trouble. The deeper problem was, to use modern language, the new nation's economic underdevelopment combined with the war's colossal expense.

As Hamilton explained: "The public expenditures from the dearness of everything necessarily became immense, greater in proportion than in other countries and much beyond any revenues which the best concerted scheme of finance could have extracted from the natural funds of the state. No taxes which the people were capable of bearing ... would have been sufficient for the current exigencies of government." He went on: "it was not in the power of Congress when their emissions had arrived at the 30,000,000 of dollars to put a stop to them. They were obliged, in order to keep up the supplies to go on creating artificial revenues by new emissions; and as these multiplied their value declined. The progress of the depreciation might have been retarded but it could not have been prevented. It was in a great degree necessary."

In other words, confiscation by way of inflation had been inevitable. But it also had to change.

Devaluation and a Foreign Loan

By early 1780, the near total depreciation of the national currency was hampering production and procurement. On March 18, 1780, Congress revalued the nearly worthless Continentals "at the rate of one Spanish milled dollar in lieu of 40 dollars of the bills now in circulation."[27] This instantly wiped out a huge portion of the national debt: obligations of $200 million now became a mere $5 million.[28] But the plan, which was to be operationalized through the state governments, largely failed. In theory the states would recall the old currency by imposing taxes that could only be paid in the old currency. Then each state would, as Buel explains, "issue one dollar of the 'new emission' for every twenty dollars of the old that they retired. ... The new currency also entitled the bearer to 5 percent annual interest. The states were asked to pay the interest on their assigned quotas of the new emission annually. Congress authorized each state issuing the new currency to retain six dollars of every ten in its own treasury to fill vacancies in its line regiments and to collect specifics; the remaining four dollars would be at the disposal of Congress." Unfortunately, Congress was slow in promulgating the plan to the states, and many states did not fully comply. "Inevitably, the value of the new state and continental currencies fell. ... They also had to contend with the general atmosphere of mistrust engendered by Congress's aban-donment of its repeated pledges to honor the nominal value of the old continentals. Surprisingly, the new money remained in less demand than the old, though there was more of the old in circu-lation than the new."[29]

As Hamilton saw it, there was "but one remedy, a foreign loan." Because the "hope of appreciating the money by taxes and domes-tic loans is at an end." And indeed, American representatives were in Europe raising money. As early as 1777, the government of France had given a secret grant of two million *livres* and assured that it would be annually renewed if American products were sent to pay for supplies purchased in France. Before 1780, the total value of foreign loans had been small when compared with the total cost of the war. Most of those foreign loans were immediately spent in Europe on weapons, so despite their military importance they had little economic impact in America.[30]

A more difficult question was how to handle new loans. Two plans were floated. The first would use the loan to buy back bad debt in the hope of restoring confidence in the Continental dollar and congressional loan certificates. In Hamilton's view, this plan was bad because it failed to transform the dynamics driving the crisis. It involved too little state intervention in the economy; the government would simply attempt to bribe the speculative class into having confidence. It would be all carrot and no stick. The other plan, "to convert the loan into merchandize and import it on public account," suffered from the opposite problem—it relied too heavily on state power. The state would take full control of the supply effort, even cutting out many private suppliers. Hamilton found this idea of essentially nationalizing the war profiteering sector "incomparably better than the former." However, its flaw was that it did nothing to structurally contain the profiteering interests that had developed with the supply effort. If the state took all responsibility it also took all the risk, and was thus open to being attacked by the speculative class.

Thus, in his letter to Robert Morris, Hamilton proposed a plan that sought to harness and use speculative interests. "The only plan that can preserve the currency is one that will make it the *immediate* interest of the moneyed men to cooperate with government in its support."[31] To do that, Hamilton argued, Congress had to use new hard-currency foreign loans to create a central bank that combined public and private ownership. This would bind the moneyed men to the state and its currency and thus hopefully prevent their speculative scheming from sabotaging national finances. It was the logic of "keep your enemies close." The means to do this would be "an American bank, instituted by authority of Congress for ten years under the denomination of The Bank of The United States."

As John C. Miller put it in his classic 1959 biography: "the inventiveness and boldness that characterized Hamilton's later financial schemes clearly emerged for the first time. Nothing remotely resembling the Bank of the United States had ever existed in America—in fact, the country did not even boast a bank—nor did any other American propose at this time to combat the inflation and establish the authority of the government by such heroic measures."[32]

Scaffolding a Bank and the Fiscal Military State

About ten months after his letter on finances to Morris, Hamilton wrote a similarly epic and prescient letter to James Duane, the New York politician with whom he had been corresponding for about one year. In this letter of September 3, 1780, Hamilton addressed the question of a national financial system pivoting on a public-private central bank. He also detailed the need for a new constitution.

"How far it may be practicable to erect a bank on the joint credit of the public and of individuals can only be certainly determined by the experiment," Hamilton wrote, "but it is of so much importance that the experiment ought to be fully tried. ... Paper credit never was long supported in any country, on a national scale, where it was not founded on the joint basis of public and private credit."[33]

Why did Hamilton wish to enlist the rich? Was it merely to serve them? No, it was to bind them more closely to the national project. In effect, Hamilton sought to do the latter by means of the former. Hamilton considered a purely public bank, but feared it would remain open to private attack. As Hamilton explained to Duane, "the monied men have not an immediate interest to uphold its credit. They may even in many ways find it their interest to undermine it. The only certain manner to obtain a permanent paper credit is to engage the monied interest immediately in it by making them contribute the whole or part of the stock and giving them the whole or part of the profits." His goal was to neither smash nor coddle the "monied men" but rather to harness that class to the political project of state building. Hamilton's model was the Bank of England, which combined public authority and private credit so as to raise "a vast fabric of paper credit" upon this "visionary basis." Hamilton saw the bank as a means to economic growth, which was in turn a means to his ultimate geostrategic objective: unconquerable sovereignty.

"And why can we not have an American bank?" asked Hamilton in the letter to Duane. "Are our monied men less enlightened to their own interest or less enterprising in the persuit? I believe the fault is in our government which does not exert itself to engage them in such a scheme. ... Let the Government endeavour to inspire that confidence, by adopting the measures I have recommended or others equivalent to them. Let it exert itself to procure a solid confederation, to establish a good plan of executive administration, to form a permanent military force, to obtain at all events a foreign loan. If these things were in a train of vigorous execution, it would give a new spring to our affairs; government would recover its respectability and individuals would renounce their diffidence."

As in the financial realm, so, too, in the political: decentralization was the enemy. "Congress should have complete sovereignty in all that relates to war, peace, trade, finance, and to the management of foreign affairs," Hamilton wrote. Along with "the right of declaring war of raising armies, officering, paying them, directing their motions in every respect, of equipping fleets and doing the same with them, of building fortifications arsenals magazines &c. &c., of making peace on such conditions as they think proper."

Here were all the themes that Hamilton would later develop in *The Federalist Papers*. And here, too, is an early encapsulation of Hamilton's developmentalist economic nationalism. Hamilton wanted Congress to centralize the nation's chaotic and fragmented financial system and also shoulder economic planning through regulations, subsidies, direct investment, setting industrial standards, and other types of rule making. These are the economic policy tools he would later call "the Means proper." As he saw it, the new government needed the power

> of regulating trade, determining with what countries it shall be carried on, granting indulgencies laying prohibitions on all the articles of export or import, imposing duties granting bounties & premiums for raising exporting importing and applying to their own use the product of these duties, only giving credit to the states on whom they are raised in the general account of revenues and expences, instituting Admiralty courts &c., of coining money, establishing banks on such terms, and with such privileges as they think proper, appropriating funds and doing whatever else relates to the operations of finance, transacting every thing with foreign nations, making alliances offensive and defensive, treaties of commerce, &c. &c.

Translation: the new state must have the power to build a national credit system "coining money, establishing banks." It must have the power to shape the nation's economic intercourse with the rest of the world "by regulating all international trade." It must have the power to create internal markets and industries by "granting indulgencies laying prohibitions on all the articles of export or import" and by "granting bounties & premiums." This would be the tariff by which infant industries would be shielded, and it would generate the taxes needed for public investments.

Ultimately, almost all of this would come to be. In the short term, Congress would take new foreign loans and charter a new private bank under the leadership of Roger Morris. Later, as Treasury secretary, Hamilton would calculate the nation's total outstanding debt to foreign creditors, including arrears, as equal to $11.7 million.[34] The total price tag for liberty Hamilton estimated at $79 million.[35]

Final Assault

Eventually Hamilton's vision for a bank would be realized. But in the meantime, the whole Revolution seemed to be rotting. Hungry and unpaid soldiers mutinied in both Pennsylvania and New Jersey. Increasingly frustrated, Hamilton pestered Washington for a commission commanding troops. Eventually, Washington relented.

Hamilton returned to the front lines in search of glory at the head of a New York light infantry battalion in 1781. During the final assault on Yorktown's redoubts No. 9 and No. 10, Hamilton led a combined force of three Continental battalions, John Laurens led one battalion, and the Marquis de Lafayette another; alongside the Americans, French troops fought under Lieutenant General de Rochambeau. The siege culminated in a nighttime bayonet charge that breached the two positions and ultimately forced the surrender of General Cornwallis and the 7,000 hungry and disease-ravaged men he commanded.[36]

The victory at Yorktown brought an end to major military operations, though in the South fighting went on another two years and New York remained occupied until November 1783. The war officially concluded with the 1783 Treaty of Paris. And with that, new troubles began while old problems festered.

5

Military Mutiny and
the Critical Period

As the end of the Revolutionary War approached, discipline in the Continental Army began to crumble. The spreading mutinies were part of Hamilton's experiential education. They also mark the beginning of the Critical Period, the new nation's near collapse into anarchy during the 1780s.

The Beardian tradition in American historiography reads the conflicts of the Critical Period as fundamentally a set of class struggles: debtors against creditors, poor against rich. And it reads the Constitution as an elite bulwark against populist rebellion. Indeed, class struggle was an important part of the mounting crisis. Shays's Rebellion in Massachusetts should be read as a class conflict. The fight against Maroons in the South was a racial struggle, but one that pivoted on the class interests of Southern elites whose system of economic exploitation was threatened by the existence of militarily self-emancipated, autonomous communities of armed Black people. (More on that in Chapter 7.)

However, other Critical Period conflicts were not rooted in class antagonism. One intra-elite conflict pitted New York City merchants and New York State government-connected money-men against a similar alliance of elite commercial interests from Connecticut. There were also conflicts that involved mutually opposing, regionally rooted, cross-class alliances. For example, the Connecticut-based alliance of speculators, political operatives, and

yeoman settlers who clashed with a very similar intraclass formation from eastern Pennsylvania, over who would settle and own
Pennsylvania's Wyoming Valley. And of course, up and down the
frontier, there were clashes pitting American settlers and speculators against Native Americans.

The increasingly contentious politics of slavery also involved
cross-class formations. Southern pro-slavery defensiveness, though
always having an air of paranoia to it, was becoming increasingly
rational and grounded in facts. Vermont, for thirteen years a de
facto independent republic and locked in a bitter struggle with
New York, had abolished bondage for adults in its 1777 state
constitution. (Despite that, a few Vermonters were still listed as
"slaves" as late as the census of 1810.)[1] In 1780, Pennsylvania
passed a law ending slavery, though it also expanded indentured
servitude. In 1783, Massachusetts interpreted the state's 1780 constitution as outlawing slavery. This resulted from a set of legal cases
known collectively as "the Quock Walker case."

Then, Connecticut passed a law making anyone born a slave
after March 1, 1784, free at age twenty-five. The state also, unfortunately, legally codified a racial hierarchy that kept African
Americans at the bottom. A year later, New York passed a similar
law that set off gradual emancipation even as it legalized disen-
franchisement and segregation. Inadequate as these laws are in
retrospect, they were at the time and in the eyes of wealthy Southern slave owners profoundly threatening. First it was cold, distant,
rocky little Vermont. Then it was mighty New York. Who would
be next and where would it stop?

Madison summarized the larger set of conflicts as follows:
"What has been the source of those unjust laws complained of
among ourselves? Has it not been the real or supposed interest
of the major number? Debtors have defrauded their creditors.
The landed interest has borne hard on the mercantile interest. The
Holders of one species of property have thrown a disproportion
of taxes on the holders of another species."[2] The first signs of the
crisis emanated from within the Army itself. Thus, we turn to the
question of mutiny.

Mutiny

Even before the Critical Period proper, signs of violent discontent were growing. Throughout the American Revolution, soldiers and sailors mutinied with increasing regularity. The reasons they mutinied were usually a combination of hunger, lack of clothing, lack of pay, and abuse at the hands of "ill-trained and arrogant officers."[3] Soldiers were whipped for even minor infractions, and the material disparities between officers and men were outrageously unfair.

John A. Nagy's *Rebellion in the Ranks: Mutinies of the American Revolution* is the most thorough recent book on all this. Nagy found fifty-six mutinies in the American Army from 1775 to 1783. The first small rebellion happened only four days after the war began. The last mutiny occurred two months before the 1783 Treaty of Paris. Even among the "winter soldiers" at Valley Forge, Washington wrote of "a dangerous mutiny, begun the night before and which with difficulty was suppressed by the spirited exertions of some Officers."[4]

Nagy estimates that about 6 percent of courts-martial involved allegations of mutiny, with the largest mutinies happening in the later years of the war. Not only did the mutinies grow in number and size, they also became more political, with violence increasingly directed at politicians rather than at military leaders.[5]

A clear example of this happened on December 30, 1778, when General Jedidiah Huntington's hungry and ill-clothed Connecticut Brigade, encamped at Redding Ridge, in Redding, Connecticut, assembled with their weapons and prepared to march on the state government in Hartford and demand support. Their commanding general, our friend "Old Put," talked them down very delicately, then arrested the ringleaders.[6]

A similarly "political" mutiny happened on October 4, 1779, when militiamen in Philadelphia, angry about their poverty, marched on the home of a wealthy attorney named James Wilson, where a meeting of the local elites was underway. The mutineers supported price controls; rich men like Wilson did not. As the crowd passed Wilson's house, a shot rang out, then more shots; soon the firing "became smart on both sides." The firefight raged for about ten minutes until members of the aristocratic "silk-stocking" City Troop of Cavalry, along with some Continental cavalry, charged the militia. "Six or seven people were killed; between seventeen and nineteen were 'dangerously wounded.'"[7] Twenty-seven were arrested.[8] "We are at this moment on a precipice," wrote Henry Laurens after this so-called Fort Wilson Riot, "and what I have long dreaded and often intimated to my friends, seems to be breaking forth—a convulsion among the people."[9]

The slow-building problem of mutiny reached crisis point in January 1781 and took the form of three connected mutinies that together lasted the entire month. The first of these mutinies began on New Year's Day and lasted a full ten days. Trouble began in Morristown, New Jersey, among soldiers of the Pennsylvania Line under the command of General Anthony Wayne. It started as a raucous New Year's celebration. The men were drinking, but not very heartily, as their ration per man was a mere four-ounce "gill" of rum. The men had served three-year enlistments filled with hunger, filth, fear, killing, and dying, yet they had not been paid since their initial, badly depreciated signing bounties. Now, by a certain reading of their enlistment terms—"three years or the end of the war"—the men considered their contracts completed.[10]

The mutineers formed a leadership structure, which they called a Board of Sergeants. Their plan was to march toward Philadelphia and demand their back pay from Congress and the Pennsylvania Council. The next day, about 1,500 men, more than half of Wayne's entire command, shouldered arms and prepared to march away.[11] "The names of only two leaders are known for sure: William Bowzar, secretary of the twelve-man Board of Sergeants that represented the mutineers, and Daniel Connell, who signed the board's final communication. A man named Williams—probably John Williams—was president of the Board of Sergeants, but does not appear to have been the real leader or organizer of the revolt."[12]

The departing mutineers took supplies, horses, and some artillery pieces. Other cannon that could be used against them were "spiked"; that is, made inoperable. During these preparations, scuffles and confrontations broke out. One officer who tried to stop the mass exodus was killed, as were several enlisted men.

General Anthony Wayne did his best to dissuade the departing column, riding out vulnerable and alone to reason and plead with soldiers. But he had no resources to offer them and they knew it. To his credit, Wayne had been warning Washington and civilian authorities that his men were in desperate need. Hungry, ill clothed, penniless, and angry, the mutineers marched on toward Philadelphia where they hoped justice awaited. As they went, Wayne dashed off a description of the situation to Washington: "Capt. Billing is killed Capt. Tolbert Mortally wound, some Others are also Hurt." The great fear was that the British might take advantage of the violence. But Wayne assured Washington, "nor have any of the Soldiers gone towards the Enemy their General cry is to be Discharged—& that they will again enlist & fight for America a few excepted."[13]

Wayne's reassurances aside, the situation was quickly spinning out of control. A nearby New Jersey militia contingent thought the mutiny was an enemy attack and lit a string of hilltop signal fires and discharged cannon to summon reinforcements. General Wayne, seeing the fires and hearing the guns, thought the British had invaded from New York and ordered Continental troops at Pompton to move toward the coast and repel the British. In occupied New York City, the British commanders heard about the mutiny and sent two civilian smugglers to entice the rebels into switching sides. The mutineers refused, and the captured emissaries were hanged.[14]

Meanwhile, the mutineers marched south toward Philadelphia, where sat Congress and the Pennsylvania Council. Along the way to Philadelphia lay Princeton, even then a toney college town. Fearing that the impoverished, battle-hardened mutineers might ransack Princeton, the town fathers gathered supplies of food and firewood with which to placate the expected guests. On January 3, word of the approaching column reached Philadelphia. Realizing the gravity of the situation, both the Pennsylvania Council and Congress dispatched representatives to open negotiations.

General Washington, at his headquarters in New Windsor, New York, high on the west bank of the Hudson River, forty-five miles north of the action, feared the mutiny might spread. He prepared to move south, but then changed plans when it became clear that his soldiers were also on the verge of rebellion. So Colonel Israel Shreve, who was closer to the problem, was ordered to muster a force and confront the insurgents. But Shreve's troops were also unready. As Shreve explained to Washington: "I could not have marched more than a Captain's command ... I am Sorry to inform Your Excellency that the soldiers present appear to be exceedingly mortified and disgusted on account of the unspeakably bad quality and scanty supply of clothes."[15]

Unable to confront the mutiny, Army brass and politicians had to negotiate. The mutineers won. It was agreed that the men were, in fact, at the end of their contracts and would thus be discharged.[16]

Setting an Example

Word of the successful mutiny spread, stirring up trouble as it went. On January 17, a committee of sergeants from the Massachusetts Line stationed on the west bank of the Hudson submitted a list of grievances. They wanted the unpaid enlistment bounties, back wages, their clothing allowance, and adequate provisions. Washington wrote to politicians in Connecticut, Massachusetts, New Hampshire, New York, and Rhode Island describing the deprivation. Three days later, another mutiny broke out, this time among men of the New Jersey Line at Pompton, commanded by Shreve—the same troops who two weeks earlier had failed to deploy against other mutineers for lack of clothing. This time there was no shooting, no confrontation with officers, no killing. Instead, a few hours after darkness fell, about two hundred hungry, cold, angry, and armed men just marched out of camp, headed for Trenton, seat of New Jersey's government. Handbills decrying Congress and the common soldier's misery had been circulating for two weeks; some were posted on the doors of officers' huts. One read: "To the officers and soldiers of the Continental Army, shake off the Congress and despise them of their France and Spain allies. Their paper money trust no more. We have all been cheated enough."[17]

"It is with pain I inform Your Excellency," Colonel Shreve wrote to Washington, "that the troops at this place, revolted this evening, and have marched towards Trenton—their behavior and demands are similar to those of the Pennsylvania Line; though no blood has been spilt."[18]

Now, Washington and his chief aide and primary ghostwriter of orders, Hamilton, were very worried. Washington ordered Shreve to crush the uprising. "This affair, if possible, must be brought to an issue favourable to subordination, or the army is ruined. ... If the revolt has not become general, and if you have force enough to do it, I wish you to compel the mutineers to unconditional submission. The more decisively you are able to act the better."[19]

To assist Shreve, Washington sent Major General Robert Howe with 600 soldiers to suppress the mutiny. On January 27, Howe's force took the mutineers by surprise. Outnumbered, the mutineers surrendered. A firing squad of twelve particularly active mutineers was ordered to execute two of their fellow rebels; they wept as they did so. Four months later, another small mutiny was put down with similar punishments. But still the mutinies continued.

Newburgh

Hamilton left the army shortly after the 1781 victory at Yorktown. In July 1782, he was appointed to the Congress of the Confederation and began his term that November as part of the New York delegation. Peace talks with Britain were already underway, having begun that spring. Huge issues had to be sorted. How far west would the new nation's territory extend? Would American fishermen have fishing rights on the Grand Banks off Newfoundland? Who would have access to the Mississippi River? Negotiations proceeded slowly.

British forces still occupied New York City while the bulk of the Continental Army camped on the high bluffs at Newburgh, New York, some sixty-five miles to the north. Still poorly supplied and unpaid, officers were forced to use their own resources to feed themselves and their men. Politically decentralized and heavily indebted, the country was essentially insolvent. The national government, such as it was under the Articles of Confederation, still lacked the power to tax. It could merely request money from the sovereign state governments. In 1781, Congress almost amended the Articles of Confederation to allow itself to levy an import tariff, but then Virginia overturned its earlier ratification of the bill. Congress remained broke.[20] Officers desperately lobbied their state governments for help. Little to nothing arrived.

Now it would be the officers' turn to mutiny. Historians have often cast what followed in late 1782 as an attempted coup d'état by power-hungry elites. The record, however, reveals something more complicated. Although many of the officers came from landed and moneyed families, they were not economic parasites for whom war had been a great boon. While their cousins may have been "forestalling" (hoarding and speculating), the officers—let us give them their due—were risking their lives, often while going unpaid.

Yes, the Continental Army was a class-ridden thing. Officers often drank wine with meals while their men drank water and maybe a dram of rum or whisky. Officers had attendants to assist them, and got the best clothing and boots, while the rank and file cut their own firewood, hauled their own water, and made do with meager rations. Yet officers also suffered and died. And not all officers were wealthy; some were merely middle class. Daniel Shays, the indebted Massachusetts farmer turned class rebel (more on him later), had been a captain in the Continental Army.

Proof of the officers' relative penury is reflected in the fact that, being paid like regular soldiers in the IOUs called Pierce's notes, "most of the officers sold their securities soon after receiving them."[21] While the wealthy were buying discounted public debt, the officers were selling. In short, the officers at Newburgh had legitimate grievances. "During those long, boring months of 1782, a growing feeling of martyrdom, an uncertainty, and a realization that long years of service might go unrewarded—perhaps even hamper their future careers—made the situation increasingly explosive."[22]

The crisis began in December 1782 when officers at Newburgh sent a petition to "The United States in Congress assembled" from

"Cantonments, Hudson River." It was signed by leading men of the Massachusetts Line, the New York Line, the New Hampshire Line, the New Jersey Line, and the General Hospital. The petition described "hardships" of "hunger" and "nakedness" and explained that many of their comrades had been forced to sell state-issued promissory notes "to prevent their families from actually starving." They complained "that shadows have been offered to us while the substance has been gleaned by others." The petition linked their plight to wider economic problems: "The citizens murmur at the greatness of their taxes, and are astonished that no part reaches the army." They had, in short, "borne all that men can bear—our property is expended—our private resources are at an end, and our friends are wearied out and disgusted with our incessant applications. We, therefore, most seriously and earnestly beg, that a supply of money may be forwarded to the army as soon as possible. The uneasiness of the soldiers, for want of pay, is great and dangerous; any further experiments on their patience may have fatal effects."[23]

Two months after a committee of three colonels had delivered the petition to Congress, there was still no response. On March 10, 1783, the situation took a turn for the worse. A short anonymous letter circulated calling for a meeting of all the officers the following day for the purpose of answering Congress's lack of action. At the same time, a second, longer, rather heated letter also made the rounds. We now know it was written by Major John Armstrong, an aide to General Horatio Gates. (Recall that Gates was the general who had gone rogue and challenged Washington's leadership as part of the so-called Conway Cabal back in the winter of 1777–8, when Hamilton had his feverous collapse.)

The military historian Richard Kohn, relying on admittedly circumstantial evidence, suggests that the other officers behind the letter were from a mostly young "small extremist wing of the corps, which was angrier, more dogmatic and hot-headed," and had gravitated to Gates, "whose bad blood with Washington was long standing." In Kohn's view, this group included John Armstrong, Jr., Christopher Richmond, William Barber, and very likely William Eustis and Timothy Pickering.[24]

The second letter had none of the supplication of the December petition. The author, described as "A FELLOW-SOLDIER, whose interest and affections bind him strongly to you," explained how he had left a much-beloved civilian life and fought to force "the enemies of his country, the slaves of power, and the hirelings of injustice" to "acknowledge America as terrible in arms as she had been humble in remonstrance." He had "long shared in your toils, and mingled in your dangers ... felt the cold hand of poverty without a murmur, and has seen the insolence of wealth without a sigh."

Then came his challenge: "To be tame and unprovoked when injuries press hard upon you, is more than weakness." It would, he suggested, "show the world how richly you deserve those chains you broke." Who was to benefit from the peace and independence they had won? "A country ... that tramples upon your rights, disdains your cries, and insults your distresses?"

His recommendation: Congress needed to be scared straight. "Tell them that ... the army has its alternative ... nothing shall separate you from your arms but death; if war ... you will retire to some unsettled country, smile in your turn, and 'mock when their fear cometh on.'"[25]

The threat was not a coup d'état, but rather a type of military secession or defection. The threat was to abandon Congress and march west "to some unsettled country" such as the Northwest Territory. That would have created a vacuum and invited a British return. Regardless of the details, this was not good.

As soon as Washington understood what was happening, he announced his "disapprobation of such disorderly proceedings" and called his own meeting for "12 o'clock on Saturday next," March 15, at which time would be relayed "the report of the Committee of the Army to Congress."[26]

At that next meeting, Washington read the men a stern and direct rebuke. He began by chiding the impropriety of an unauthorized meeting as "unmilitary!" and "subversive of all order and discipline." He described Armstrong's anonymous letter as "addressed more to the feelings of passions, than to the reason & judgment" but sarcastically granted that the author was "entitled to much credit for the goodness of his pen." Washington condemned Armstrong's letter as "insidious" and "calculated to impress the mind, with an idea of [the] premeditated injustice ... of the United States, and rouse all those resentments which must unavoidably flow from such a belief."[27]

Washington reminded the men of his own place among them: "I have never left your side one moment ... I have been the constant companion & witness of your distresses." And then he most aggressively condemned the letter's suggestion of "deserting our country in the extremest hour of her distress, or turning our arms against it ... My God! What can this writer have in view, by recommending such measures?" The mere suggestion of this threatened to "tarnish the reputation of an army which is celebrated thro' all Europe, for its fortitude and patriotism."

To put an end to it all, Washington called on his officers to "express your utmost horror & detestation of the man who wishes ... to overturn the liberties of our country, & who wickedly attempts to open the flood gates of civil discord, & deluge our rising empire in blood."

A common and perhaps apocryphal story holds that after finishing his rebuking speech, Washington tried to read a communication from Congress and, stumbling over unfamiliar handwriting, put on a pair of spectacles saying: "Gentlemen, you must pardon me. I have grown gray in your service and now find myself growing blind."[28] Allegedly moved by this vulnerability, the officers soon complied with the general's request, and passed a unanimous resolution renouncing mutiny and reaffirming their loyalty. While the sentimental vignette of the spectacles is often repeated, Washington's sobering speech invoking the specter of national collapse and reconquest likely brought most officers back to their senses.

Laying Siege to Congress

June 1783 saw another large mutiny. This time several hundred soldiers marched from Lancaster into Philadelphia. The rumblings began on June 17, when troops stationed in Philadelphia, perhaps emboldened by a furloughed regiment passing through on their way home to Maryland, sent Congress "a very mutinous remonstrance," as James Madison put it, that told of "the hardships which they had suffered in defense of their country" and of the "duty of their country to reward them."[29]

Two days later, Congress received word that eighty soldiers from the Third Pennsylvania Regiment stationed at Lancaster had mutinied and, under command of their sergeants, were marching toward Philadelphia to settle accounts with Congress. As usual, the troops wanted to be paid. Hamilton, acting in his capacity as a politician, sent instructions to a Major Jackson to intercept and placate the mutineers. "You will represent to them with coolness but energy the impropriety of such irregular proceedings. ... You will assure them of the best intentions in Congress ... In short you will urge every consideration in your power to induce them to return; at the same time avoiding whatever may tend to irritate."[30]

A day later, the mutinous detachment from Lancaster, which had grown as it marched, linked up with men from Philadelphia barracks and surrounded the State House in which operated both Congress and the Supreme Executive Council of Pennsylvania. In one of numerous reports on the matter, dated June 24, Hamilton and Oliver Ellsworth informed Congress: "That the Militia of the city in general were not only ill provided for service [against the mutiny], but disinclined to act upon the present occasion."[31] In other words, Congress needed to find some money.

Eventually, Congress did scrape up some cash and promissory notes to pay the men.[32] But this method was fundamentally played out. Even worse, when the war finally ended, the economy slid into brutal recession. For many veterans, political struggle continued. As James D. Drake put it, "The cacophonous calls and seemingly anarchic actions of veterans and others who struggled in the postwar world became the most proximate cause for the Constitutional Convention."[33]

6

Postwar Depression

As peace becalmed the Army, Hamilton resigned his commission and went to live in Albany with his new wife, Elizabeth Schuyler, daughter of Philip Schuyler, one of the New York elites with whom Hamilton had begun a correspondence while still on Washington's staff. Both Schuyler and his wife, Catherine Van Rensselaer, were from long-established and wealthy New York Dutch landowning families. Hamilton married up, quite far up.

In Albany, as Hamilton explained to his old friend the Marquis de Lafayette, he spent "ten months in rocking the cradle" and "studying the art of fleecing my neighbours," meaning the legal profession. He passed the bar, became "a Grave Counsellor at law," and in July 1782, the New York Legislature appointed him representative to the Congress of the Confederation, so called by historians because the Articles of Confederation had finally been ratified.[1]

From inside Congress, Hamilton got yet another troubling and overarching view of the new nation's real condition. When the war officially concluded with the 1783 Treaty of Paris, the American economy fell into a deep economic slump. The stimulus of wartime procurement had ended. And just as the war had created significant areas of economic expansion, so did its conclusion bring economic contraction. Now the nation's accumulated debts had to be paid. Incomes and economic activity stagnated even as heavy taxes hit the populace. Worse yet, while the state now took much, it spent little. The revenue it collected was largely used to pay debts and was thus sent overseas or given to financial speculators at home. There being no real credit system, many of these speculators literally sat on their wealth without plowing it back into real economic activity. Meanwhile, many parts of the real economy were starved for investment and, not receiving it, shrank.

Like the experience at Valley Forge, the Critical Period of the 1780s—roughly the years stretching from the end of major hostilities, through the Constitutional Convention, ratification, and election of Washington's first government—helped shape Hamilton's thinking in ways that led directly to his dirigiste *Report on Manufactures*.[2] This chapter sketches that story.

Postwar Depression

The severe economic depression brought by peace and independence was, we now know, the worst in American history. Looking back from the twentieth century, Joseph Schumpeter described the dynamics of the postwar slump: "The war of independence ... affected industry much as prohibitive tariffs would have done and encouraged investment that was bound to become unremunerative as soon as those conditions were removed."[3] Only in recent years, as archival research has deepened and innovated, have scholars grasped the full extent of this economic suffering. A 2012 working paper for the National Bureau of Economic Research by Peter Lindert and Jeffrey Williamson went through most previous economic research on this era and found a 20 percent per-capita decline in income, making the 1780s as bad "as the 1929–1933 drop into the Great Depression."[4]

Lack of systematic data on rates of investment, employment, and income hamper our ability to describe the post-Revolutionary slump. Yet we can catch glimpses, illuminated by scraps of surviving data. For example, recall the count of gunsmiths from a previous chapter—the colonies had an estimated 803 between 1751 and 1774, and during the war that figure rose to 1,573. But after the war, the number of gunsmiths slumped by almost a third, to a mere 1,011.[5]

War brought, as we saw in Chapter 3, a boom in domestic salt production. But with the war's end, most American salt works went out of business. Bishop et al. relay that a group of businessmen "at Broad Point, in Brewster," Massachusetts, "erected works of that kind with three vats" and joined one previously existing saltworks; "and in 1779, the first on the new plan were built in Barnstable." Salt's high price and this region's proximity to the fisheries led many others into salt production, "but on the revival of foreign trade, after the peace, a large number of the works were abandoned."[6] Several decades later, a local newspaper recalled that "after the peace of 1783, foreign salt was again introduced, the price fell, and for several years the business was almost, if not wholly abandoned."[7]

Similarly, we read of the rise and fall of metal production. In Trenton, New Jersey, steel was manufactured during the Revolution, "but the business afterward declined."[8] An old book on American economic history put it this way: "The iron-manufacture began in New Hampshire about 1750, where several bloomaries were built to make use of the bog-ores. A good deal of iron was made during the Revolution; but, after that, the business died out."[9]

Recall the role of Congress in supporting anthracite mining to fuel the armory at Carlisle, Pennsylvania, in 1775, to supply the country with the iron it needed.[10] After the war, that operation also went into decline. "Towards the close of the Revolution the industry gained a good start." But, like other war industries, the end of hostilities meant collapsing demand and inevitable contraction. Had "the treaty of peace in 1783 been followed up by a policy favorable to native manufactures, its rise would have been thence forward rapid," wrote a nineteenth-century political economist. "But the Continental Congress had no power to initiate a policy of the proper sort; and a period of six years followed, during which the country was flooded with cheap manufactures from England; and a large number of the native American furnaces and factories, finding no demand for their iron, ceased to exist."

Shipbuilding was also hit hard. In New Hampshire's shipbuilding region along the Piscataqua River "some thirty to forty vessels of two to three hundred tons" were built every year. But from 1783 to 1789, this region built only six vessels of this size. In other words, during the Critical Period, New Hampshire's "shipbuilding output was equal to just 10 to 15 per cent of the annual prewar rate."[11] Similarly, commercial fishing suffered. Before the war, dried fish was New Hampshire's largest single export. "But during the Confederation period, fishing as a source of employment had all but disappeared. And those seamen who attempted to eke out a living by fishing were reported by the *New Hampshire Gazette* as 'starving.'"[12]

Historian Cathy Matson notes that business startups largely stopped for lack of investment: "Large-scale enterprises that required more capital outlay than commercial ventures, such as sugar refining and candy making, distilling, papermaking, tobacco refining, or glass and pottery working, were hit hard with bankruptcies by 1785, as were most peltry and lumber exporters. Plans to initiate new manufactures were discussed only rarely between 1785 and 1787."[13]

In the countryside, the situation was also very bad. Lorena S. Walsh summarizes the situation in the Chesapeake as follows: "Most planters found themselves in reduced if not desperate straits by 1781 as a result of planter absenteeism in government or military service, loss of income from market crops, destructive British raids, slave desertion, loss of rents from tenants who could not or would not pay, depletion of livestock herds and timber reserves, high taxes, scarce specie, and deterioration of farm buildings and fences. Only those who had contrived successful speculations in alcohol or produce or those who had had access to overland markets survived the war without major losses. Few planters were able to resume full crop production before 1785. ... Market disruptions, falling land prices due to westward migration, scarce money and credit, planters' unpaid prewar debts, and continued high taxes all contributed to economic malaise."[14]

The general slump and its enforced austerity are also visible as rapid postwar deflation. In 1779, wholesale prices were "about three times higher" than in 1775. Six years later, wholesale prices had dropped back to "only 23 percent over the 1775 index."[15] Another scholar finds that "between 1787 and 1789 prices fell between 4 and 7 percent across the country."[16]

More dramatic is the case of Philadelphia, where "inflation reached its peak in 1781 with prices at a level 400 times (40,000 percent) those in 1775." By 1785, two years into the peace, prices were back down to prewar levels.[17] Another study found that from 1784 to 1790 Philadelphia experienced "a 20 percent deflation rate overall."[18] Anecdotal evidence gleaned from surviving letters confirms the picture of a painful deflationary torpor. In a news-filled 1785 letter to Jefferson, Madison bemoaned the low price of tobacco: "The price of our Staple since the peace is another cause of inattention in the planters to the dark side of our commercial affairs."[19] Declining prices meant declining tax revenues. Thus, Madison wrote Jefferson in December 1786 that "Our Treasury is empty, no supplies have gone to the federal treasury, and our internal embarrassments torment us exceedingly."[20] Amid this, George Washington wrote to the incoming Virginia governor, Edmund Randolph, and lamented, "Our affairs seem to be drawing to an awful crisis: it is necessary therefore that the abilities of every man should be drawn into action in a line, to rescue them if possible from impending ruin."[21] The picture is not perfect, but we can see enough to confirm that the 1780s brought a very severe economic slump.[22]

The causes of the slump include the loss of imperial subsidies, the sudden end of wartime government purchasing, the exclusion of American ships from British ports, depredations upon American vessels by the British Navy and Algerian pirates, Spain's decision in 1784 to close the Mississippi to U.S. trade, loss of population due to disease, war casualties, the departure of loyalists, the liberation of slaves by the British Army, and the rapid decline in public-sector wartime procurement.

Here is how a nineteenth-century book described the crisis: "The Revolutionary war caused the greatest destruction of value which this country has ever known. It cost, in money and money's worth, not less than three hundred millions of dollars, every dollar of

which somebody had to pay. The years of stagnation and pros-
tration which began with 1780, and continued till 1789, were the
years in which the country, (without knowing it), was paying for
the war. Congress had issued one hundred and sixty millions of
paper money, which after falling lower and lower in value, became
in 1780 absolutely worthless, and ceased to circulate. The people,
impoverished by the war, without a currency of any kind, except
a few millions of specie, without union, without a practicable government, without credit either at home or abroad, would have
utterly despaired had not the bounty of the soil and their own
industrious hands always secured a sufficiency of the bare necessaries of life."[23]

Flood of Imports

The end of hostilities brought with it a wave of imported products. "Eager to replenish depleted inventories and make quick
profits," Matson writes, "American merchants placed orders with
former correspondents in British ports. As before, British imports
were cheaper, of higher quality, and of greater variety than those
of any other foreign country. Despite increased domestic productivity during the war, Americans could not supply enough
of the woolens, Irish linens, and hardwares and housewares to
satisfy demand. ... Commercial correspondence with British firms
resumed; prices and terms of sales were communicated easily in
familiar channels."[24]

Much of this trade was done on credit. "The country was hungry
for the European luxuries which had been dear so long and in
limited supply. The merchants imported freely, and, as usually
occurs when the demand is unnatural, the market was soon over-
stocked. Sellers were even more imprudent than buyers, and English
exporters forced their shipments on 'unlimited credit' to America,
this credit being a large factor in pressing out the oversupply of
goods from England."[25]

In the years just after the war, British imports to America flowed
in at roughly triple the prewar volume. The average annual export

to New England for five years before the war was £409,000. In the two years between 1783 and 1785, some £3 million's worth of manufactured goods had been shipped from Great Britain to America. That put serious pressure on American manufacturing. But at least American ships would be free to carry goods like salted cod to the Caribbean. Shipbuilding and export would resume.

But on July 3, 1783, Britain closed the West Indies to American ships, cutting off one of America's most important foreign markets. Within a year, the British also "cut off the Newfoundland and Nova Scotia whale and fishing traffic to American vessels and prohibited American fish, whale oil, and salted meats from entering England." American port cities fell into an economic slump, with the damage from loss of markets soon rippling out to hinterland producers. "The total result, after the carnival of trade that immediately followed peace, was a violent business crisis, terminating in a prolonged depression. ... town artisans and small manufacturers experienced enough distress to create the sentiment behind the New England and Pennsylvania tariff laws of 1785 and 1786."[26]

As one author summarized it: "The country was flooded with foreign goods, largely from England. The industrial isolation during the war, as well as the demand for material for sustaining the army and navy, gave a decided stimulus to the struggling manufacturers of the colonies. Many iron works and other manufacturers were called into existence, and in some cases were given encouragement by a system of bonuses. Upon the resumption of imports these industries suffered immediate and disastrous setbacks. Many were not firmly established and were forced out of existence."[27] As the economic crisis intensified, wartime experience with planning, subsidies, and de facto protection was reinforced. "An economic theory of public welfare was developing that included protected manufactures as fundamental to a well-balanced commonwealth."[28]

There was little Congress could do to stop the inflow. As John Fiske put it: "British manufactured goods were needed in America, and Congress, which could levy no duties, had no power to keep them out."[29]

Revolutionary Debt and Postwar Austerity

All these factors were aggravated by yet another: the massive postwar debt was now due, and paying it sucked investment capital out of the economy. Recent research into the crisis by Woody Holton, as well as Terry Bouton and Jeffrey S. Selinger, has shown that debts and the heavy taxes needed to pay them were central to the crisis.[30] Just as the emergency dirigiste economic patterns of the war shaped Hamilton's developmental nationalism, so, too, did the postwar debt crisis, with its profoundly destabilizing sociopolitical consequences.

As we have seen in previous chapters, during the initial stages of the war, Congress and the thirteen state governments funded the effort by printing currency. From 1775 through 1779, Congress emitted almost $200 million in Continental dollars, accounting for three-quarters of all congressional spending.[31] The states operated similarly, printing state money to buy what they needed to field their militias. Then, starting in late 1779, the government paid its suppliers and even its soldiers in loan-office certificates.[32] The other major source of funding was international. Congress took loans from France, Holland, and Spain; most of that hard currency was immediately spent abroad, to pay for imported weaponry and uniforms.

When Hamilton became the first Treasury secretary in 1789, he did the first full calculation of America's total foreign debt; the sum, owed in various currencies, was equal to $11.7 million.[33] Hamilton also estimated the total debt, which came out to $79 million. Servicing these postwar debts required extremely high state and national taxes. The burden of these taxes, falling on the depressed economy of the 1780s, fueled increasingly tumultuous politics.

Woody Holton's superb book *Unruly Americans and the Origins of the Constitution* describes well the suffocating waves of taxation. "Between the Yorktown victory of 1781 and the federal assumption of state debts in 1790, Americans were hit with taxes that averaged three or four times those of the colonial era. The principal purpose of the levies was to pay interest on state and federal government securities, many of them bought up by speculators. In the mid-1780s, most states earmarked at least two-thirds of their tax revenue to pay foreign and domestic holders of the war-related debt bonds. The tax burden was magnified by a shortage of circulating coin."[34] In Massachusetts, taxation on farmers was estimated at four to five times higher in 1786 than it had been under most of British rule.[35]

By Holton's estimate, during the 1780s the national government needed "nearly a million dollars a year to service its foreign and domestic debts."[36] That was about a third of its revenue. The national government was being starved in the cradle. State finances were even more threadbare, in "nearly every state two-thirds of direct tax revenue was earmarked for public creditors."[37]

Sheldon D. Pollack, an economic historian of American finance, put it this way: "Between 1781 and 1786, the Congress assessed the states a total of $15.7 million, but only $2.4 million was paid."[38] By the late 1780s, "most of the states dedicated between 75 and 80 percent of their budgets to retire state debts and to pay congressional requisitions to service the federal debt."[39] As a result, the public sector, such as it was, invested very little. Roads, ports, schools, experimentation, and exploration—all these languished.

Tax Levy of 1785

The harshest tax levy of all came in 1785, when Congress sent a $3 million bill to the states. More than half the amount had to be paid in scarce hard currency, meaning gold, silver, or special government paper called "indents" which could only be purchased if at least one-third of their face value was paid in gold or silver. Holton has shown that the 1785 requisition was the Critical Period's proverbial last straw. The pressures of that levy, which unfolded throughout 1786, led directly to the armed uprising of indebted farmers in Massachusetts known as Shays's Rebellion.[40] (We take a closer look at those events in Chapter 8.)

By the peak of the crisis—during Shays's Rebellion—the national government received almost nothing from the states. According to Pollack, "Between October 1, 1786, and March 31, 1787, the treasury took in only $633, leaving the national government unable to pay its debts."[41] As John Fiske noted, by this time in many parts of the country "the payment of taxes had come to be regarded as an amiable eccentricity."[42] By one modern academic reckoning, the "states at best provided one dollar for every eight dollars requested by the Congress, and compliance dropped considerably from nearly 12 percent in mid-1784 to less than 2 percent from mid-1786 to mid-1787."[43] Because the states failed to pay their assessments, the national government, which had no direct powers of taxation, starved.

In 1785, Congress had to suspend payment of interest on the debt to France and "defaulted on installments of the principal which fell due in 1787."[44] Although state contributions picked up in 1787, the financial position of the national government remained critical and its debts enormous. Hamilton estimated that to service "the foreign debt, and to pay four per cent [interest] on the whole of the domestic debt, principal and interest," would require the federal government have "a yearly income of 2,239,163 dollars, 9 cents."[45]

These suffocating tax obligations created austerity, and that hurt investment, employment, and consumption, which led to economic contraction and price deflation. Deflation led to less investing and more hoarding. During the war, government had been a major consumer; with peace and demobilization public procurement shrank, states cut spending, and they invested little in infrastructure. Meanwhile, the tax-burdened populace saw its income shrink even as its spending on taxes increased. To cope, people reduced consumption, and thus reduced demand, which in turn led to further decline in private investment, and so on, fueling a downward spiral. Economic recovery and the development of internal markets stalled.

The tax burden also created new private debts. Taxes had to be paid in specie, gold and silver, or Continental Certificates. Taxes could not be paid in grain, cattle, goods, or labor services. Thus even people who had usable wealth but who were not much engaged with the cash economy often had to borrow hard currency just to pay their taxes. This was true for, among others, the small, diversified, trading-oriented yet essentially barter-dependent farmers of Western Massachusetts described by Christopher Clark.[46] This could be the case even when they had significant amounts of wealth in the form of land, tools, grain, and animals.[47] In the cash-poor, deflationary, crisis economy of the Critical Period such use value could not be realized, or transformed into the necessary exchange value—i.e., money—demanded by the state.

As the economy failed to grow, these new tax-driven debts became impossible to service. Foreclosures began to escalate. More farmers and artisans now lost their working capital to the bailiff and auctioneer. Without their tools, lands, animals, and materials, production and consumption necessarily contracted further and, as it did, prices declined. As prices declined, the real economic pain of each dollar paid to the government increased. If high prices meant the sale of five sheep would cover the tax bill of X amount of hard currency, then falling prices meant one had to sell eight or ten sheep to get X amount of hard currency. Thus was established a vicious cycle of debt-fueled austerity and recession, leading to deflation that deepened the recession.

A solution for the internal debts might have been found in some sort of controlled inflation, by which debtors could pay off their debts with new and ever depreciating currency. But creditors opposed this. Most states continued to print paper money, but they did so sparingly and had little, if any, inflation. Only three states —Georgia, North Carolina, and most of all, Rhode Island—had continually high inflation.[48]

In Rhode Island, a proto-populist pushback against merchant creditors had gained some political power and made inflating away debts an explicit state policy. There, the rural people used elections and town meetings to take over a government otherwise dominated by the coastal merchants. A party of debtors won state elections and in spring 1786 issued a huge emission of paper currency. As usual, the new money quickly lost value and creditors shunned it, demanding that their debts be paid in hard currency like silver, gold, or foreign bills of exchange, redeemable in specie. The debtors' government then passed a law mandating that creditors accept Rhode Island's new, essentially homemade paper money at face value. Many creditors literally hid from debtors; some boarded up their shops and left the state rather than accept payment. So the new government passed another law in the summer of 1786 that "permitted debtors to file their payments with the local courts, and it was then up to the creditors to appear at the court and receive their pay (such as it was)."[49] Rhode Island's inflation was so bad many creditors fled the state so as to avoid debtors eager to pay off the face value of debts with nearly worthless paper scrip.

Not all advocates of a tight money policy were conservative, wealthy elites, nor were all advocates of easy-paper emissions radicals from the laboring classes. Struggling backcountry farmers tended to want paper money. But many artisans, who waited long periods between purchasing materials and being paid and were thus hurt by inflation, opposed paper emissions. Thomas Paine, from concern for the artisan and mechanic class, switched from paper money advocacy to opposition.[50] As Paine explained in 1786, "They say Paper Money has improved the country—Paper Money carried on the war, and Paper Money did a great many other fine things." Disagreeing, Paine drew a key distinction: "It was CREDIT which did these things, and that credit has failed, by non-performance. ... We have so far mistaken the matter that we have even mistaken the name. The name is not Paper Money, but Bills of Credit."[51] If *credit* was the real issue, then *creditworthiness* was essential for a functioning economy.

Similarly, there were landed elites, like Thomas Jefferson, who carried major debts, died in debt, and would have benefited overall from controlled inflation. But Jefferson, as a man who was rich in land and human beings but money poor, had a classically agrarian suspicion of all things financial. Also, in his role as an investor in land schemes he had lost wealth due to paper money inflation, and memorably disparaged it as "oak leaves."[52]

Contrary to what is suggested by most liberal historians of this period, Hamilton's preference for a strong currency was not rooted in an elitist class allegiance to wealthy creditors, as such. Rather it flowed from a *realpolitik* understanding of crisis-plagued, post-colonial statecraft.

Hamilton was *Homo publicus*: a man materially and psychologically linked to the military, the law, and government. His glory-fixated ego, his sense of self, did not pivot upon owning land and slaves, or upon business interests like shipping or manu-facturing, or upon accumulating money via speculation. Nor did he want power merely for its own sake. Rather his personal tra-jectory, for better or worse, was bound up with the success of the national project, the success of the state. For the state to survive, the American economy had to develop and transform, because if the nation was to defend itself militarily in a future war, the government—no matter how well balanced its books were—would need to borrow. Survival would depend on an international line of credit, because war meant debt spending. Adam Smith captured this truth at the heart of "the fiscal military state" when he wrote: "the moment in which war begins ... the army must be augmented, the fleet must be fitted out, the garrisoned towns must be put into a posture of defence. ... An immediate and great expense must be incurred in that moment of immediate danger, which will not wait for the gradual and slow returns of the new taxes. In this exigency government can have no other resource but in borrowing."[53]

National survival depended on the state's ability to go into debt and to pay off its debts. And that required the confidence of European financiers. In addition, economic recovery required investment, including foreign investment. Lack of faith in American creditworthiness created capital flight and an investment drought; foreigners kept their capital away while wealthy Americans who could, hid their hard currency overseas. Hamilton realized that if the economy failed to improve, and capital stayed away, political turmoil would increase, fueling more disinvestment, more social strife, and soon, civil war.

Parasitic Speculation

Throughout the Critical Period manic speculation took hold among those wealthy few with money to invest. Much of the debt held as certificates—especially certificates of smaller amounts that had been paid to rank-and-file soldiers—circulated like money as a form of payment. Typically these certificates traded at a fraction of their face value. Investors bought them cheap and waited for their value to rise. This speculation in debased and fragile but likely to appreciate public debt drew capital that might otherwise have been invested in the productive sectors of the economy.

Often state governments made matters worse. To instill confidence in the creditworthiness of the various types of bonds and certificates, many created new consolidated certificates, which paid annual interest on the face value of paper that was treading at knocked-down rates on the secondary markets. Intended or otherwise, this had the effect of increasing both state debts and the speculative frenzy.[54]

Thanks once again to Woody Holton, we have a detailed view into the mind of a major speculator and thus also an account of the paper mania. The financier in question was none other than the future first lady Abigail Adams. No mere quiet New England farm woman, the wife of John Adams gambled aggressively in what was then the cutting edge of finance. When John suggested from his post in Europe that she buy more land, Abigail countered, "There is a method of laying out money to more advantage than by the purchase of land's, which a Friend of mine advised me to," and that, she wrote, was to invest "in State Notes."[55]

She went on: "Provision is now made for the anual payment of Interest, and the Notes have all been consolidated. Foreigners and monied Men have, and are purchaseing them at 7 shillings upon the pound, 6 and 8 pence they have been sold at. I have mentiond to you that I have a hundred pounds sterling in the hands of a Friend, I was thinking of adding the 50 you sent me, and purchaseing 600 pounds LM ['lawful money' meaning official Massachusetts currency] in state Notes provided I can get them at 7 shillings or 6 and 8 pence. This would yeald me an anual interest of 36 pounds subject to no taxes."[56]

If speculators bought the Massachusetts Consolidated Note at about one-third of face value and received the standard 6 percent annual interest on the note's face value, they would earn 18 percent on their investment every year.[57]

Later, when Abigail joined John in Europe, she wrote to her financial manager Tufts (for whom the university is named) with instructions to buy yet more public debt: "I should think it might not be a miss to invest one hundred pounds in the Army certificates which though not so valuable at present, will become so in time."[58] To pay the interest on Abigail Adams's government securities, the taxes kept coming. This was an early example of government-facilitated "accumulation by dispossession," to use David Harvey's phrase.[59] Elites were using state power to take from the many and give to the wealthy few. Like so many other dynamics of the Critical Period, it was part of the recipe for disintegration and state failure.

Small Trade Wars

The struggle over who would receive the lion's share of state taxes pitted wealthy creditors (investors like Abigail Adams) against the indebted, tax-paying majority. But there were also struggles among state governments. With peace, state governments increasingly asserted their powers and exercised their prerogatives, and not in concert with but against one another.

Among the worst offenders was Hamilton's own New York State, where Governor George Clinton had devolved into a tax-hoarding bully. Once an ally to Hamilton, Clinton had become a hardcore states'-rights man. To pay the speculators on state securities and run a government, New York began a vigorous tariff regime of 5 percent on British imports, but then extended this to produce entering from New Jersey and Connecticut. Furthermore, as the entrepôt through which many imported manufactured goods destined for New Jersey and Connecticut first arrived, New York State captured a steady stream of tax revenue that rightly should have benefited neighboring states. All of this proved highly lucrative for New York government and speculators in New York–issued securities, but it was obviously detrimental to the larger project of national economic development and political stability.[60]

As John Fiske put it: "The city of New York, with its population of 30,000 souls, had long been supplied with firewood from Connecticut, and with butter and cheese, chickens and garden vegetables, from the thrifty farms of New Jersey. This trade, it was observed, carried thousands of dollars out of the city and into the pockets of detested Yankees and despised Jerseymen. It was ruinous to domestic industry, said the men of New York. It must be stopped by those effective remedies of the Sangrado school of economic doctors, a navigation act and a protective tariff. Acts were accordingly passed, obliging every Yankee sloop which came down through Hell Gate, and every Jersey market boat which was rowed across from Paulus Hook to Cortlandt Street, to pay entrance fees and obtain clearances at the custom-house, just as was done by ships from London or Hamburg; and not a cart-load of Connecticut fire-wood could be delivered at the back-door of a country-house in Beekman Street until it should have paid a heavy duty."[61]

This mini trade war became so intense that in 1786, "New Jersey declared that it would not comply with the requisitions laid by Congress [in the massive levy of 1785] until New York had reduced its tariff."[62] In Connecticut, businessmen convened a meeting at New London and "unanimously agreed to suspend all commercial intercourse with New York. Every merchant signed an agreement, under penalty of $250 for the first offence, not to send any goods whatever into the hated state for a period of twelve months. By such retaliatory measures, it was hoped that New York might be compelled to rescind her odious enactment."[63]

Obvious and worrying to observers like Hamilton was that these tactics of economic leverage were the very same methods the rebel colonies and Britain had used against each other in the run-up to war. Increasingly, the crisis was apparent to powerful outside powers. A French minister summarized the mess: "There is now no general government in America, no head, no Congress, no administrative department."[64] This lack of government, at the heart of the economic slump, also produced increasingly violent instability.

7

Challenging the Weak State: Frontier Secessionists, Maroons, and Native Americans

Along with the struggle between speculators and the taxpaying majority, and the struggles between state governments, the Critical Period saw a smattering of other increasingly violent conflicts. Some of these conflicts were class struggles. For example, in Shays's Rebellion in Massachusetts, indebted middle-class farmers in the western mountains fought debt-owning coastal elites and the state government they controlled. And the fight against Maroons appears as a racial struggle, but it was fundamentally a class conflict pitting those who sought to own and work people as slaves against those who refused to be enslaved.

Other clashes erupted between class factions or involved mutually opposed cross-class alliances, such as the small intra-settler war in the Wyoming Valley of Pennsylvania, the conflict in what is now eastern Tennessee, and the conflict in Vermont. The violence between settlers and Native Americans in the Ohio Country was about racial hostility, civilizational conflict pitting a state against a tribal federation. But it was also very much about class, in that acquisitive American land speculators were a driving force in the violence. This chapter and the following explore this panorama of Critical Period conflicts.

Small Wars and Little Secessions

In the Wyoming Valley of northeastern Pennsylvania, "Wild Yankees," settlers from Connecticut, had since the 1760s clashed sporadically with Pennsylvanians, known as "Pennamites." Like the ongoing struggle of Vermont to break away from New York, the Wyoming Valley conflict was rooted in overlapping and conflicting colonial land grants. The Yankees were backed by the Connecticut-based Susquehannah Company and relied on long-dormant land claims detailed in Connecticut's 1662 charter extending out to the Pacific Ocean, and upon a deed (of questionable legality) bought from the Iroquois. Trouble started because Pennsylvania claimed the same lands under its 1681 charter and also had deeds bought from Native Americans.[1]

In the first stage of the conflict, the Yankees allied with the notorious, Indian-murdering, Scots-Irish thugs known as the Paxton Boys. As Paul Moyer, the expert on this conflict, put it, "Dozens of people were killed and wounded and hundreds more violently dispossessed in the years preceding the outbreak of the Revolutionary War."[2] Connecticut officially annexed the contested region and in December 1775 got the Continental Congress to recognize its claims. Around the same time, a Yankee force of 400 under Colonel Zebulon Butler defeated a larger Pennsylvanian force at Nanticoke Falls, in what is known as the Battle of Rampart Rocks.[3]

Then the fighting with Britain began and, like the Vermont conflict, the local, low-grade Pennamite-Yankee war was largely eclipsed by the much bigger war for independence. When the Revolutionary War ended, Congress returned to the Wyoming question. This time, Congress gave Pennsylvania jurisdiction over the disputed territory in the Trenton Decree of 1782. But that did not end the conflict.[4]

Eager to rekindle its case, the Susquehannah Company issued land rights to John Franklin and a few other political leaders in Connecticut. For good measure the company also "awarded twelve shares to the architect of agrarian insurgency in Vermont, Ethan Allen, in order to win his pledge of support."[5]

Then, in March 1784, nature exacerbated political tension. Heavy winter snows plus a sudden thaw caused the Susquehanna to overflow the valley; "great blocks of ice drifted here and there, carrying death and destruction with them. Houses, barns, and fences were swept away, the cattle were drowned, the fruit trees broken down, the stores of food destroyed, and over the whole valley there lay a stratum of gravel and pebbles."⁶ The flood's victims were mostly Yankees, and, instead of aiding their country-men, Pennsylvania militias evicted and mistreated them. Yankee farmers armed and fought back; there were a few killed and a number of wounded. Civil war seemed imminent. The Yankees' leader, John Franklin, claimed that Yankee prisoners had been starved and mistreated and that several women had been raped: "We are now in a State of War," Franklin wrote.⁷

Violence continued to rise through the rest of 1784, producing "a level of bloodshed surpassing that of Pennamite-Yankee con-flict in the 1760s and 1770s." In May 1784, Pennamite militiamen drove "more than 150 Yankee families from their farms ... and burned their homes." Yankees struck back, forcing "more than six hundred Pennamite men, women, and children from the land."⁸

In July, patrols of Pennamites and Yankees stumbled into each other, and the ensuing shootout left two Pennsylvanians wounded and two Yankees killed. "Four days later, Yankee settler Benjamin Blanchard received a gunshot wound in the thigh and, the follow-ing day, a rifle shot killed another Connecticut man. Later that week, Pennamites shot John Franklin through the wrist and killed New Englander Nathan Stevens."⁹ That same month, Yankees laid siege to a Pennamite fort for nine days. In August, Yankees killed a Pennamite militiaman and wounded three others in a shootout. Several weeks later, they killed two Pennsylvania Militia lieutenants during a raid on Wilkes-Barre. On October 19, Pennamite fighters ambushed and wounded another Yankee. Around the same time, Yankees killed and wounded "half-a-dozen Pennamites and Penn-sylvania militiamen" during heavy fighting near Abraham's Creek. On October 28, Pennamites attacked Yankee settlers, who fought back with musket fire. On November 4, Pennamites attacked a dif-ferent group of Yankee homesteads and another gunfight followed.¹⁰

Just as important though less dramatic was the steady sabotage in the form of barn burning, animal stealing, and killing, theft, and destruction of crops. "In January 1785, Enos Randel recounted how a Yankee mob tore down his house, plundered his crops, and 'destroyed' his cattle. Afterward, Randal went to the New Englanders and begged for 'a little of his corn for the subsistence of a numerous family thro' the winter.' But the Yankees denied him any support, saying that 'they would want it all the next summer for the supply of the Troops.' In her deposition, Catherine Bower-lane testified that after fleeing their home in the face of Yankee violence, her husband returned 'to gather Corn when they [the Yankees] killed him' and 'took all his grain of every Sort.'"[11]

In 1785, Pennsylvania's government called on several county militias to evict the Connecticut settlers. But in violation of the law, men in Berks, Bucks, and Northampton counties flat-out refused to mobilize. As Terry Bouton explains, the mutinous militiamen protested "that they had been called to serve private, self-interested purposes rather than the public good." The Bucks County militia described their "abhorrence of the Idea of Staining their hands with the blood of their Countrymen & Fellow subjects."[12]

The Vermont rebel Ethan Allen, being of the larger Connecticut diaspora and prone to aggressive hyperbole, was not so nationally minded. In April 1786, he traveled to the Wyoming Valley saying he would create a new state, a "New Vermont Plan." Allen threatened to bring down a hundred Green Mountain Boys to help finish off the Pennamites. But soon he went back home.[13]

In 1787, Pennsylvania authorities arrested the Yankee leader John Franklin. The Yankees, with the apparent support of the Connecticut land speculators backing them, soon struck back by kidnapping Timothy Pickering, the former quartermaster general who had moved from his native Massachusetts to the Wyoming Valley and tried to calm the festering conflict there. Pickering was rescued after twenty days as a captive of the Yankees. Two men were badly wounded in the fray. Growing sick of the mayhem, a Connecticut newspaper disparaged the Wild Yankees of Pennsylvania as "a dangerous combination of villains, composed of runaway debtors, criminals, [and] adherents of Shays."[14] The conflict, like so many of the Critical Period, was not fully resolved until the 1790s.

In Vermont, although most violence had stopped, conflicting sovereignty claims remained alive. Vermont had declared independence in 1777 and drawn up a constitution. The state's military force, the Green Mountain Boys, fought in Canada and assisted Gates in trapping the British at Saratoga. But New York sent troops to the restive frontier after the Green Mountain Boys occupied not only what is now Vermont, but also parts of New York State and, to the east across the Connecticut River, parts of New Hampshire.[15] During the 1780s, this conflict remained largely dormant but set to reignite.

Vermont in the 1780s had no taxes, other than town levies. The state was run by what critics called "outlaws." Though loyal to the colonies during the revolution, Vermonters had been in open and sometimes violent rebellion against the government of the state of New York since the mid-1760s. Vermont became a haven for debtors and rebels who mixed the legal politics of protest and non-cooperation with sporadic night-riding–style property destruction and (usually) nonlethal violence. Some New Hampshire counties on the east bank of the Connecticut River sought to join Vermont and set up a formal alliance with the Green Mountain Boys.[16]

Farther south, a similar conflict was building. In what is now northeastern Tennessee, frontier settlers prepared to form an independent state. As Kevin Barksdale explains in *The Lost State of Franklin*, these regional separatists were "a powerful coalition of landed elite, yeoman farmers, and backcountry merchants" operating in "a diverse, dynamic, and interconnected regional economy" that mixed "commercial agriculture, mercantilism, and land sales."[17]

Isolated from North Carolina's Eastern power structure by the Smoky Mountains, in conflict with Native Americans, and menaced by various banditti, the region's economic, military, political, and religious leaders began probing the question of independent statehood as early as 1782. As Barksdale explains, the Franklin separatists believed independence "would allow them to expand and enhance the region's economy" by freeing them to make war

on the Cherokee and utilize regional taxes for internal improvements like roads and bridges, generally allowing "the backcountry
ruling class to wield greater political influence" than as an isolated
subset of North Carolina.[18]

Meetings throughout the summer and fall of 1784 culminated
with a declaration of independence at Washington County's log
courthouse on December 14. A Revolutionary War veteran, John
Sevier, was made governor, and several new counties were created.
The state of North Carolina pushed back with a mostly peaceful
strategy of divide and rule. This struggle between white people was
mostly nonviolent, taking the form of competing elections, courts,
protests, arrests, and fistfights.

But in 1788, the political tensions erupted into the Battle of
Franklin. In late February, a force under John Tippton seized property from John Sevier's farm in lieu of Sevier's mounting North
Carolina tax arrears. Sevier was away training the Franklin Militia
in preparation for a spring offensive against the Cherokee. Hearing
about the raid, Sevier and a column of about a hundred militiamen
tracked down and attacked Tippton and his men. Over three days
of fighting, several combatants were killed and wounded, as was
a female civilian. Another clash would occur in March. By then
it was too late for the new microstate, and rapprochement with
North Carolina began.[19]

Maroons

In the South, the military problems of the Critical Period pivoted
on the specter of slave revolts. The Revolutionary War had given
slaveholders reason to fear this. The British had freed and armed
hundreds of African Americans during the Revolution; in 1775
Lord Dunmore notably decreed, "all indentured Servants, Negroes,
or others ... [are] free that are able and willing to bear Arms."[20]

In Virginia, several hundred slaves and many white indentured
servants escaped to Dunmore and became the core of his Ethiopian Regiment. Other British units composed partly or wholly of
escaped and militarily liberated slaves included the Black Pioneers,

the Negro Horse, and the East Florida Rangers.[21] When the war ended, not all of them made it out of the United States. Recent scholarship estimates that the number of African Americans liberated and evacuated from America by the British between 1775 and 1783 "would be no less than eight thousand and no more than ten thousand."[22] In other words, many African Americans who broke out of bondage stayed behind, and there is evidence that some of these people helped fuel an uptick in Maroonage during the 1780s, particularly in the once vast Dismal Swamp on the Virginia–North Carolina border, and farther south along the Savannah River.

Survival as a Maroon required special skill; people born in Africa, so-called "saltwater slaves," seem to have been better prepared for this. "Even in the 1780s, about a third of the one hundred thousand slaves living in South Carolina had been born in Africa."[23] Given the interconnection between slavery and warfare in Africa, many of those Carolina Maroons had first fallen into slavery as prisoners of war in Africa and had military skills. The fight against Maroons grew particularly intense in the 1780s. "Maroons were often organized into small companies, each with guns, which acted as independent raiding parties or were able to launch pincer movements against enemies."[24]

At the same time as Shays's Rebellion was unfolding in Massachusetts, a small Maroon war began on the Georgia–South Carolina border. Like most Maroons throughout history, the inhabitants of the Savannah River settlements were not insurrectionists. Rather, they fought defensively, as survivalist-style social bandits. They needed supplies, which they often stole, and they needed autonomy, which they often defended with violence.[25]

The Savannah River Maroon settlements "had existed since at least 1782 and could well have developed from older Maroon communities that resided in the same location as far back as 1765."[26] Although constrained in everything from agriculture and trade to cooking by their overriding need for security, the Maroons nonetheless planted crops, built canoes, and established settlements on both sides of the Savannah River. To supplement their farming, the Maroons surreptitiously traded with a few renegade white people, but to survive they had to raid local plantations for supplies, ranging from weapons and clothing to food. One of their leaders, originally named Sharper, operated under the *nom de guerre* Captain Cudjoe and had been a slave of Alexander Wright, and during the Revolution "fought on behalf of the Loyalists."[27]

By 1786, Maroon depredations were terrorizing slave owners and men of property in both Georgia and South Carolina. Elites began demanding military action. A worried planter explained: "If something cannot be shortly done, I dread the consequences—they are as daring as any & from their independent state, from the ease they enjoy in S. Carolina, forbode what I dread to express, a capital insurrection. Their leaders are the very fellows that fought, & maintained their ground against the brave lancers at the siege of Savannah, & they still call themselves the King of England's soldiers."[28]

By the autumn of 1786, specially mobilized militia forces from Georgia and South Carolina, plus some Catawba Indian auxiliaries, were hunting for the Maroons. Eventually, two major settlements were found. The first, at Belleisle Island, was attacked in October. There was fighting and casualties, but most of the Maroons slipped away. The militia then burned "a number" of huts and 15 canoes, which in total could hold about 100 people. The invaders also destroyed an estimated 3,500 pounds of harvested rice. But the Maroon trouble continued.

In April, there was another firefight with Maroons. The South Carolina governor, Thomas Pinckney, ordered out more of his militia "to extirpate a number of fugitive slaves, who have armed & embodied themselves in the swamp bordering on the lower parts of the Savannah River, & committed depredations on the Inhabitants of the Vicinity." In a letter to the governor of Georgia, he requested assistance "in the reduction of these people" as part of a "joint exertion."[29]

Finally, in early May 1787, militiamen on the Savannah River found at Bear Creek another Maroon settlement—heavily fortified with a blockade of fallen trees across the approaching creek and a breastwork around the village in which stood twenty-one buildings—and overran it.[30] Nevertheless, Maroon raiding picked up about eighty miles east, along the Stono River. Indeed, sporadic

Maroon activity would continue in remote parts of the South until the end of the Civil War.

Many of these "King of England's soldiers" on the Savannah River were abandoned British military veterans. Training and combat during the Revolution had hardened and sharpened their sense of collective power. These Maroons were ultimately vanquished, but not before having a terrifying effect on local political elites who otherwise tended to prefer a weak central government.

Native Resistance

During the late 1780s, long-running tensions between white settlers and the Creek Nation were heating up. In 1784, Spain closed the Mississippi River to American traffic. The Creek people, feeling increasing pressure from land-hungry whites, saw the Spanish move as a sign of American weakness. The main Creek leader, Alexander McGillivary (who was of mostly English extraction and had fought for the British during the Revolution), now struck up an alliance with the Spanish. In exchange for a steady flow of trade goods from Spain, McGillivary promised to be "a powerfull barrier in these parts against the ambitious and encroaching Americans."[31]

By spring 1786, the majority of Creek leaders had agreed to take up arms against the Georgia settlers who were pressing in from the east. War parties started low-level raids against Georgians who had settled on land belonging to the Oconee people, and against settlers in the western mountains of North Carolina in what is now part of Tennessee. That spring, Creek war parties burnt homes, destroyed crops, stole animals, murdered an enslaved couple who were clearing land, and killed and scalped six white surveyors. Many of the recently arrived white settlers fled east. Because the raids worked, more raids followed.[32]

In 1787, the Georgia governor described the impact: "Our frontiers have been the scene of blood and ravages; they have killed thirty-one of our citizens, wounded twenty, and taken four prisoners; they have burnt the court house and town of Greensburgh in the county of Greene, and a number of other houses in different parts of the country."[33] North Carolina's governor gave a similarly grim tally of the raids that had plagued the western edge of his state during 1787: "forty-one of our inhabitants have been massacred within twelve Months."

The experience, as James Ostler shows, left Native peoples in the region fearing outright annihilation at the hands of settlers. The memory of a particularly egregious massacre of Conestoga Indians perpetrated in 1763 by the Paxton Boys in Lancaster, Pennsylvania, still lingered; even Indians who were not in league with the British feared coming under American control. A Moravian missionary, David Zeisberger, wrote that the Indians he worked with "prefer to stay here in Indian country despite all the wars, because we can see in advance that some harm will be done if we go to the settlements of the White people."[34]

American military operations during the Revolution had not improved relations. As discussed in a previous chapter, General Sullivan's 1779 scorched-earth campaign against the Iroquois Confederacy in New York State destroyed forty Iroquois settlements, effectively broke their military resistance, and sent about 5,000 hungry and freezing refugees fleeing as far as Canada. Speaking in anticipation of that assault, the Seneca war chief Sayengeraghta had urged other tribes to support "the King, our Father," or be "left exposed to the Resentment of the Rebels, who, notwithstanding their fair Speeches, wish for nothing more, than to extirpate us from the Earth, that they may possess our Lands." In reaction to Sullivan's assault, the Mohawk leader Joseph Brant wrote that the American "intention is to exterminate the People of the Long House."[35]

During the Revolution, Virginians from what is now Kentucky entered the Ohio country and made war, and British-backed Natives returned the favor. In 1780, Shawnee, Wyandot, and Ottawa warriors massacred 20 settlers at Ruddle's Station, Kentucky, and carried away others as captives. In April 1781, Colonel Daniel Broadhead marched into the Ohio country and destroyed the Delaware town of Coshocton.[36] Then in March 1782, not far from what is now Gnadenhutten, Ohio, Pennsylvania militiamen led by Colonel David Williamson methodically massacred ninety-six

Indians, two-thirds of whom were women and children. "By most accounts, Williamson and his men held a vote on whether to murder the Indians and, in a particularly chilling illustration of 'the dark side of democracy,' decided in the affirmative." As the militia set to slaughtering, the Indians, all Moravians, sang Christian hymns.[37]

Invading the Old Northwest

After the 1783 Treaty of Paris, thousands of American settlers and speculators poured into the Old Northwest Territory, the lands comprising current-day Ohio, Michigan, Indiana, Illinois, Wisconsin, and part of Minnesota. Indians there faced unprecedented invasion. The new nation, a collection of bickering sub-states, may have seemed like the weaker potential alliance, yet the Americans were a constant, motley, and dangerous presence— a cancer of squatters, encroaching county militias, commercial hunters, bandits, and speculators, tempered only occasionally by more rational representatives from the Army or Congress.

For their part, leading politicians in both the national government and some states were genuinely worried about the lawless incursions into Indian lands by American settlers and speculators. Their concern grew not from humanitarian zeal for Native American welfare; after all, the Declaration of Independence mentions "the merciless Indian Savages, whose known rule of warfare, is an undistinguished destruction of all ages, sexes and conditions." Rather, the concern was strategic: the new nation was too poor and disorganized to sustain another major war. And already in 1784, Spain had signed treaties with numerous tribes up and down the western frontier.[38]

Hamilton urged caution. To George Clinton, the bellicose New York governor who was antagonizing the remaining Iroquois, he wrote: "I say nothing of the Indian nations because though it will be always prudent to be upon our guard against them; yet I am of opinion we may diminish the necessity of it by making them our friends; and I take it for granted there cannot be a serious doubt any where as to the obvious policy of endeavouring to do it. Their friendship alone can keep our frontiers in peace. It is essential to the improvement of the furr trade an object of immense importance to the state. The attempt at the total expulsion of so desultory a people is as chimerical as it would be pernicious. War with them is as expensive as it is destructive. It has not a single object, for the acquisitions of their lands is not to be wished 'till those now vacant are settled—and the surest as well as the most just and humane way of removing them is by extending our settlements to their neighbourhood. Indeed it is not impossible they may be already willing to exchange their former possessions for others more remote."[39]

As historian Colin Calloway put it, on the western frontier the Treaty of Paris was the "peace that brought no peace."[40] Endemic, low-level violence up and down the frontier was a serious concern. According to Sarah E. Miller, "In the years following the American Revolution, violence between native Americans and frontier settlers spiraled into reciprocal and uncontained depredations."[41]

The Treaty of Paris to some extent facilitated the unrest, in that the British did not insist on any provisions for their Indian allies. Both the Americans and British had reason to leave Native Americans out of the settlement. The Americans wanted the Native lands and the British wanted to continue using Native Americans as military proxies to project power into otherwise lost British territory. As Hamilton observed, "when Nations now make war upon each other the object seldom is total conquest—partial acquisitions, the jealousy of power, the rivalship of dominion or of commerce, sometimes national emulation and antipathy are the motives." Still at stake were "the fisheries, the furr trade, the navigation of the lakes and of the Mississippi—the Western territory."[42]

As the historian Lisa Brooks explains, with American victory, rumors spread quickly through Native communities along the Ohio tributaries that "backcountry settlers had resumed their ferocious drive to acquire land in the valley and that the United States claimed to own, by conquest, the full span of the continent to the Mississippi River."[43]

To make matters yet more chaotic, while Britain had ceded to the United States all land east of the Mississippi River, except for

British possessions in Canada and the Spanish territory in Florida which was not Britain's to relinquish, American control of that territory was marked by numerous overlapping and conflicting state claims to the same. The national government had to gain control of these and other disputed trans-Appalachian lands. James Madison described it as imperative for "States claiming un-appropriated back lands, to cede a liberal portion of them for the general benefit," it was a matter of "the necessity of closing the union," and to his mind, land controlled by the national government was "the only expedient that can accomplish it."[44]

For Hamilton, this problem, like so many others, required a strong, well-organized army. To pay for such a force, a wealthy economy was needed. All of that required a developmentalist state, meaning a strong central government with the power to incubate and direct a transition to manufacturing. Violence between settlers and Native Americans during the 1780s set the groundwork for the new nation's first official war against Indians in the 1790s—a war that revealed the United States' profound weakness even as it eventually pushed Native Americans out of the Ohio country.

As settlers flowed into the area that is now Kentucky, Ohio, and Michigan, conflict increased with Iroquois, Delawares, Wyandots, and Shawnees. Shortly after the war's official end, as American commissioners were negotiating treaties with tribes that had fought alongside the British, news arrived of Delaware and Wyandot warriors attacking American travelers en route to Detroit. American negotiators working on the second Treaty of Fort Stanwix (the first was signed in 1768) demanded an explanation from their Iroquois interlocutors. "We have enquired into it," responded the Iroquois chiefs, "and suppose it to have been only the act of a few bad people, and not authorized by the voices of any particular tribe," adding that these "foolish young men" were not under the direct control of any tribal leaders.[45]

In many ways, neither were the encroaching American settlers under the control of their own political leaders. Squatters settled where they wanted, and, for lack of prosecution, killed Indians when they wanted, even when both the settlement and the violence were nominally illegal. Toward the end of the decade, in a report to

George Washington, Secretary of War Henry Knox would describe the Kentucky violence thus: "Since the conclusion of the War with Great Britain hostilities have almost constantly existed between the people of Kentuckey and the said Indians—The injuries and murders have been so reciprocal, that it would be a point of critical investigation to know on which side they have been the greatest."[46] The generalized conflict pitted individual settlers against individual Indians and at other times involved county militias attacking Native settlements or Indian raiding parties attacking farms. In all regards, it was destabilizing.

We see the widespread fear of an Indian war in a September 1783 letter from the Virginian congressional delegation to their state governor, Benjamin Harris: "Genl. Irvine, commanding at Fort Pitt informs that a body of abt 400 Men, from the Western Frontier of Virginia, had passed the Ohio, in order to establish a settlement on the Muskingum. The General apprehends, that an immediate Indian War, will be among the first of the many evil consequences that must result from such lawless measures. ... [T]he Virginians had passed the Ohio, & had committed many wanton & unprovoked acts of cruelty that had in some measure produced retaliation."[47]

Among other concerns was the question of which states were supposed to restrain these intruders. Harrison, who insisted these banditti were land speculators headquartered in Philadelphia, wrote back in frustration: "I have nothing to communicate to you but that my advices from our north western frontiers tell me that if the Pennsylvanians continue their settlements on the other side of Ohio a general indian war is to be apprehended which I am sure we are unable to engage in at present, and yet we must take part in it or suffer the depopulation of our Country. how this imprudent step is to be corrected I know not. is there no where a power lodged to prevent any State's acting as they please notwithstanding they may injure their neighbors in ever so great a degree."[48]

Washington was also worried about settlers antagonizing Indians. "Such is the rage for speculating in, and forestalling of Lands on the No. West side of the Ohio, that scarce a valuable spot within any tolerable distance of it, is left without a claimant. Men in these times, talk with as much facility of fifty, a hundred, and even 500,000 Acres as a Gentleman formerly would do of 1000 acres. In defiance of the proclamation of Congress, they roam over the Country on the Indian side of the Ohio—mark out Lands—Survey—and even settle them. This gives great discontent to the Indians, and will unless measures are taken in time to prevent it, inevitably produce a war with the western Tribes."[49]

In a letter to Henry Knox, Washington lamented "Land jobbers and a lawless Banditti who would bid defiance to the Authority of [Congress and the states] & more than probably involve this Country in an Indian War."[50] Again, the concern here was not humanitarian but rather strategic; the new nation was broke and exhausted, and a full-scale war with Indians genuinely scared much of its leadership.

Dark and Bloody Ground

No sooner had Congress dissolved the Continental Army in June 1784 than it created a new force of 700 men for one year of national military service. This new force was made up of militia units from Pennsylvania, New Jersey, New York, and Connecticut. They would be known as the First American Regiment. Pennsylvania, the place from which most Ohio-bound settlers came, was the only state to meet its quota of men. Thus a Pennsylvanian was chosen to lead the new force. He was, unfortunately for the men who served under him, the urbane and incompetent Philadelphian Josiah Harmar. In 1790, Harmar would lead a disastrous expedition against the Native peoples of the Ohio country,[51] but that lay six years in the future. In 1784, the crisis-plagued, economically depressed, politically fragmented United States was in no position to attack anyone.

The first order of business for the new nation was to buy time and forestall a war. That meant separating Indian people from the encroaching settlers by means of diplomacy, or by bluster, intimidation, and bribery. Emissaries were sent first to treat with the Haudenosaunee, or Six Nations of the Iroquois Confederacy, whom Sullivan had devastated during his brutal campaign in 1779. This was finalized on October 22, 1784, in the Treaty of Fort Stanwix. Then, in January 1785, Congress sent a commission into the Ohio Valley to inform the Indians that the national government intended to "establish a boundary line between them and us" that would run, roughly, just east of what is today Ohio's border with Indiana. The implication for Native peoples east of that line was that they would have to move west. Leaders of the Wyandots, Delawares, Ottawas, and Ojibwes all objected. But the American commissioners were blunt: "We claim the country by conquest."[52]

Explicitly threatened with annihilation, elements of several tribes were badgered into signing the Treaty of Fort McIntosh, agreed to on January 21, 1785, and the Treaty of Fort Finney, agreed to on January 31, 1786. Each of these traded Indian land for peace. In spring of 1785, American soldiers also removed some white settlers, destroying cabins in eastern Ohio and threatening immediate lethal force against any who resisted.[53] Yet the white settlers kept encroaching on Native lands.

Many Native leaders never accepted the treaties, and soon a terrible truth became clear: Indians would have to fight the invaders. The groups ready to resist began organizing a multinational alliance. Known to history as the Western Confederation, this political-military configuration would ultimately unite Wyandots, Delawares, Shawnees, Ottawas, Ojibwes, Potawatomis, Chickamauga Cherokees, Miamis, Weas, and Piankashaws.

In 1786, the Western Confederation sent a message to Congress: "We hold it indispensably necessary that any cession of our lands should be made in the most public manner, and by the united voice of the confederacy; holding all partial treaties as void and of no effect."[54] In the meantime, small bands of warriors launched raids against the interloping settlers, surveyors, and speculators in what is now Ohio and farther south in Kentucky. Their modus operandi was hit and run: kidnapping, murdering, stealing livestock, then engaging the responding militia in small skirmishes.

By the spring of 1786, Indian attacks in Kentucky were increasing and the county militias began responding more aggressively. In one of these fights, Shawnee warriors killed Colonel William

Christian, a former member of the Virginia Council and a brother-in-law of the new governor of Virginia, Patrick Henry. Learning of his brother-in-law's death, Henry wrote to the president of Congress, warning that "The necessity of the case will ... force the people, for the purpose of self-preservation, to go against the offending [Native American] towns."⁵⁵ And, indeed, the militia, or "Long Knives" as the Indians called them, went on the offensive.

In October 1786, the Kentucky Militia under Commander Benjamin Logan launched an invasion north across the Ohio River into the Shawnee heartland. It was a scorched-earth campaign, described somewhat more charitably by contemporaries as "a wild scampering foray."⁵⁶ On the upper Miami River, in what is now southwestern Ohio, the raiders found largely undefended Shawnee Villages. Many of the warriors had gone to the Wabash River to intercept a second column of Long Knives, so Logan's attack met little resistance. In one day, the white men burned seven towns, killed ten warriors, and took thirty-two prisoners, mostly women and children. At one Shawnee town, the old chief, Moluntha, of the Mackachack Shawnees, greeted Logan's militiamen. Perhaps thinking there was a mistake (a year earlier Moluntha had signed the Treaty of Fort Finney), the chief approached and tried to remind the militia of his neutrality. It was no use.

Moluntha "was talking with his captors when Hugh McGary, a lieutenant colonel in the Mercer County militia, approached. McGary had been in the [Revolutionary War] battle of Blue Licks where many of the leading men of Kentucky had been killed by the British and their Indian allies. He asked Moluntha if he had been at Blue Licks. It was thought by some in the group that the chief answered that he had."⁵⁷

With that, McGary smashed a hatchet into Moluntha's skull and then, by some accounts, scalped the dead chief. Many militia officers were outraged by this vicious murder and wanted McGary court-martialed on the spot for killing a prisoner and allied Indian. McGary, who by most accounts was an ill-tempered, violent, and widely disliked man, raged that he would kill anyone who tried to stop him from killing Indians. Logan refused to order a field court-martial. However, after the expedition, a case was brought against McGary. He was found guilty and sentenced to one year's suspension from the militia.

During the rest of Logan's campaign, the Kentuckians burned more than 200 Shawnee cabins and some 15,000 bushels of corn. They stole all the horses and cattle they could catch and slaughtered all the hogs, deeming them too slow and difficult to manage on the trip home. Casualties among the white raiders were minimal: three killed, two wounded.[58]

The violence would continue all through the Critical Period. With a population of only 30,000 settlers at the end of 1784 but growing fast, "the total number of Anglo-American dead in Kentucky between 1783 and 1790 approached 1,500."[59] Native casualties were also high but went unrecorded.

The settlers in Kentucky, perhaps inspired by the short-lived State of Franklin but also surely motivated by their own desire for safety, a functioning civil government, and a more orderly and equitable distribution of land (too much of which was held by rich, distant Virginians), held three conventions and endorsed independent statehood. The Virginia gentry who owned much of the land at first resisted these efforts for fear of losing other western land claims. However, as it became clear that most states would surrender their western land claims to Congress—and seeing the benefits in the possibility of a new slaveholding state—the Virginian political class eventually acquiesced. On January 6, 1786, the Virginia legislature set in motion the creation of the state of Kentucky. Unlike Vermont, Kentucky was not born of war. It was, however, born in preparation for war.

Happening at the exact same time as Shays's Rebellion, growing conflict with Native Americans in the Kentucky and Ohio country was a serious threat to stability, economic recovery, and national security. It, too, would be figured into the panoply of crises that would produce the new Constitution. During the 1780s, a U.S. victory over the Native Americans was in no way certain. Fear of Indians was based in a rational assessment of Native power, and the settler states' ability to confront them was limited. As George Washington would put it in 1789 when explaining the existence of a standing army: "These troops were raised by virtue of the resolves of Congress... in order to protect the frontiers from the depredations of the hostile Indians; to prevent all intrusions on the public lands; and to facilitate the surveying and selling of the same, for the purpose of reducing the public debt."[60]

The warfare against the Native peoples of the Ohio country would come to an end only in the early 1790s, when the United States launched three consecutive major military operations, the first two of which ended in total defeat and near annihilation for the invaders.[61]

All these conflicts of the mid- to late 1780s, even those that are often overlooked, such as the fighting against Maroons on the Savannah River, were part of a single, contemporaneous panorama of crisis. And the most destabilizing episode in this saga was still unfolding in the mountains and river valleys of western Massachusetts.

8

Shays's Rebellion:
Culmination of Crisis

If the Critical Period was marked by a low-simmering political economic sepsis, then Massachusetts was the spot where the infection erupted most intensely. Tax-hammered farmers, many of whom were indebted Continental Army veterans, had been petitioning for relief, directly to the state government and by resolutions from town meetings. The Massachusetts legislature—operating under the most undemocratic and creditor-dominated constitution of any state—rejected all these petitions.[1]

Making things even worse was the massive tax requisition of late September 1785, in which Congress demanded $3 million from the states. This had a profoundly destabilizing impact on the entire political order. Crucially, about a third of the tax had to be paid in gold or silver. Payment in kind or with rapidly depreciating state-issued paper money would not suffice. Worst of all, two-thirds of the total sum would be committed to debt servicing. This meant the expansionary stimulus effect of congressional spending would be minimal, while the recessionary economic pain of paying the tax would be significant. As Woody Holton put it, "No piece of legislation—at either the state or federal level—did more to advance the movement for the Constitution than the virtually unknown requisition of 1785."[2]

By 1786, the requisition was filtering down through the state governments to people on the ground. Economic distress

intensified. During wartime requisitions, "pay masters and purchasing agents working for the British and French armies had
scattered gold and silver through the countryside, making taxes
much easier to pay."[3] With peace, all that changed. The deflationary
postwar credit crunch meant very little hard currency circulated.
Even farmers with ample crops found it hard to pay their taxes.
For Hamilton the message was clear: the new nation was on the
brink of disintegration.

Critical-Period Climate Anomalies

A series of harsh winters and cold summers did not help. The
strange weather, noted in eastern North America and Europe,
appears to be linked to major volcanic eruptions in Japan in 1783
and Iceland during 1783 and 1784.[4] Benjamin Franklin described
the strange weather in a scientific journal: "During several of the
summer months of the year 1783, when the effect of the sun's
rays to heat the earth in these northern regions should have been
greater, there existed a constant fog over all Europe, and great
part of North America. This fog was of a permanent nature; it was
dry, and the rays of the sun seemed to have little effect towards
dissipating it." Franklin speculated that the fog might be the result
of "the vast quantity of smoke" that continued "to issue during
the summer from Hecla in Iceland, and that other volcano [Laki]
which arose out of the sea near that island." He thought this volcanic "smoke might be spread by various winds, over the northern
part of the world."[5]

Laki, a chain of craters along a volcanic seam, emitted huge
amounts of volcanic ash and sulfur dioxide, which converts to
sulfate aerosols and in large quantities can cause a general cooling
effect. The eruption released 15 cubic kilometers of lava and an
estimated 122 million tons of sulfur dioxide. This forced cooling
over the next several years and by some analyses triggered famines
in Japan, parts of highland Mexico, and continental Europe; it
likely helped usher in the French Revolution in 1789.[6] According
to one scientific paper on the climatic effects of Laki, "the years

1784–1786 appear to be the coldest years in the latter half of the eighteenth century."[7] With the cold came precipitation. In 1786, Madison wrote of Virginia that "Our summer and fall have been wet, beyond all imagination in some places, and much so every where."[8]

In Massachusetts, New Hampshire, and what is now Maine, the cooling caused heavy rain and record flooding during the economically crucial harvest months of September and October 1785. Across the region, rivers overflowed and washed away gristmills, sawmills, bridges, roads, and ironworks. The bad weather quickly translated into greater economic hardship. The devastation reduced the farmers' ability to pay taxes while simultaneously increasing the local demand for tax money to fund repairs. Still worse, this local crisis unfolded just as pressure to pay the congressional requisition of 1785 was beginning.

In southern Maine, some tax relief was granted, "ninety pounds being deducted from the tax of Wells, Kennebunk, and four adjoining towns."[9] But in North Conway, New Hampshire, where "Two barns were carried away with all the grain and hay in them, and seven dwelling houses and four barns were so much damaged that they had to be rebuilt," and the "greater portion" of that season's hay, flax, and corn were lost, and a "large number of domestic animals were drowned," there was no tax relief.[10]

Along with tax pressure, farmers often carried onerous private debts to merchants. Because the postwar credit crisis made money scarce, many Massachusetts farmers paid their debts to merchants in the form of crops or labor. But the 1785 Congressional tax levy demanded that taxes be paid in hard currency. And so wholesalers pressured retailers, who pressured their customers. By 1786, many merchants were rejecting payment in farm goods or labor and demanding specie instead. Worse yet, in Massachusetts, the tax burden fell heavily on land; one-third was paid as poll taxes, two-thirds as property taxes on land. This effectively shifted the tax burden from coastal merchants, manufactures, and speculators onto the yeoman farmers of the interior, who, though money-poor, owned land, sometimes large tracts of land. Leonard Richards has shown that the rebellion pitted common rural taxpayers against the urban owners of government debt. "Nearly 80 percent of the state debt made its way into the hands of speculators who lived in or near Boston, and nearly 40 percent into the hands of just thirty-five men."[11]

With the farmers at the bottom of the economic food chain unable to pay up in hard currency, small and struggling merchants had little recourse—but wealthier ones had lawyers and the courts. In the counties of the Pioneer Valley along the Connecticut River, where the leading families were known as "river gods," elites launched an offensive of lawsuits. "The constables are daily venduing our property both real and personal, our land after it is appraised by the best judges under oath is sold for about one-third of the value of it, our cattle about one-half the value," explained a petition from Greenwich, Massachusetts, in January 1786.[12] In Hampshire County, Massachusetts, at least eighty-eight men were imprisoned as debtors in 1785 and 1786.[13] Many others had been stripped of their property and social standing, and were thus profoundly humiliated. About 30 percent of all communities sent petitions for relief to the General Court in Boston. Nothing happened.

In Rhode Island, proto-populist forces had taken control of the statehouse in the spring elections of 1786. They emitted paper money and used the courts to force creditors and merchants to accept it or to write off debts if the money was rejected. While inflating away debt by this means provided short-term relief and was more equitable than bleeding the majority so the parasitic few could profit on speculation, it did not constitute a long-term solution, nor was it the basis of a sound and functional credit system. But Rhode Island, dubbed "Rogue Island" by critics, scared elites in every state and inspired debtors in neighboring states.[14]

Unable to control their government, indebted farmers in central and western Massachusetts started recalling representatives from the legislature and preventing courts from hearing cases. In late August, their rage finally boiled over. Likening their predicament to that of the colonies facing an unresponsive English King, some towns in western Massachusetts set up Committees of Correspondence and held convention-style meetings and petitioned the state government. Representatives from fifty towns in Hampshire County held a convention that demanded radical transformation of the state government and agreed to march upon and "break up" the local court.[15]

On August 29, 1,500 armed farmers—who in the long American tradition of agrarian rebellion and vigilantism called themselves "Regulators"—surrounded Northampton's Court of Common Pleas and shut it down.[16] As one of their documents put it: "We do Each one of us acknowledge our Selves to be Inlisted into a Company Commanded by Capt.—& Lieut. Bullard & in Colo Hazeltons Regiment of Regulators in Order for the Suppressing of tyrannical government in the Massachusetts State."[17] On September 5, a force of 500 men closed the court in Worcester. A week later, three more courts were shuttered in Taunton, Concord, and Great Barrington by groups of Regulators ranging from 300 to 800 in number.[18]

The men who marched from Pelham elected the Revolutionary War veteran Daniel Shays to lead them. In reality, he was only one of many leaders, yet the officials in Boston cast him as the "generalissimo."[19] Shays was typical of the rebellion that would bear his name. He had served in the Continental Army, fighting valiantly at Bunker Hill, Ticonderoga, Saratoga, and Stony Point. The Marquis de Lafayette even awarded Shays a ceremonial sword—but in peacetime, the indebted yeoman farmer was forced to sell the sword.[20]

The court closing made Boston merchants and moneymen apoplectic with rage. To restore order, officials called out local militia units. But to their horror, very few men arrived. During one militia muster, the men who had assembled promptly voted to switch sides and join the Regulators. Other militia musters fizzled out when the men discovered the nature of their intended mission.

Meanwhile, groups of Regulators also started appearing next door in New Hampshire. On September 20, about 500 Regulators laid nonviolent siege to the State House in Exeter, then the New Hampshire capital. Trapping many judges and politicians inside, the rebels demanded relief from debts and taxes, and the emission of paper currency. They were dispersed only when 2,000 militiamen sent from coastal Portsmouth arrived with cannons. The two forces exchanged shots, but the Regulators, outnumbered and outgunned, melted away. Some were arrested; five were tried for treason in military courts-martial.[21]

Concentrating Elite Minds

Unable to mobilize the state militia, the political gang that ran Massachusetts—that is, Governor James Bowdoin and the speculators, Boston merchants, and old families in the coastal towns who were his allies—sought to raise a mercenary army. The Revolutionary War veteran General Benjamin Lincoln went to "a club of the first characters in Boston" and "suggested to them the importance of their becoming loaners of part of their property if they wished to secure the remainder." Subscriptions were gathered, a private force was assembled, and training began.[22]

The Massachusetts rebellion sent shock waves through the new nation's upper classes. To Hamilton, Shays's Rebellion was a harbinger of total disintegration, an object lesson in what we would today call state failure. Hamilton saw the root cause of the Critical Period's turmoil as fundamentally economic. As he wrote in *Federalist* 6: "If Shays had not been a DESPORTATE DEBTOR, it is much to be doubted whether Massachusetts would have been plunged into a civil war." (Emphasis in original.)[23] The rebellion would be a recurring reference in Hamilton's *Federalist* essays.

Writing to George Washington, Henry Lee, Jr., who would later become governor of Virginia, expressed strategic concern mixed with some respect: "What renders the conduct of the insurgents more alarming is that they behave with decency & manage with system, they are encamped and regularly supplied with provisions by their friends & have lately given orders to the delegates in Assembly from their particular towns, not to attend the meeting of the Legislature." As for their leader, "the Insurgents it is said are conducted by a Captain of the late army, who continued but a small period in service & possessed a very reputable Character." Lee then wondered why this is happening: "This event produces much suggestion as to its causes—Some attribute it to the weight of taxes and the decay of commerce, which has produced universal idleness. Others, to British councils[,] the vicinity of Vermont... The next accounts will I hope produce favorable intelligence, but present appearances do not justify this hope."[24]

Abigail Adams best embodies class fury, contempt, and fear of the slippery slope: "Ignorant, wrestless desperadoes, without conscience or principals, have led a deluded multitude to follow their standard, under pretence of grievences which have no existance but in their immaginations. Some of them were crying out for a paper currency, some for an equal distribution of property, some were for annihilating all debts, others complaning that the Senate was a useless Branch of Government, that the Court of common Pleas was unnecessary, and that the Sitting of the General Court in Boston was a grieveince." For Mrs. Adams, the speculator in government debt, these demands were ipso facto evidence of evil. "By this list you will see, the materials which compose this Rebellion, and the necessity there is of the wisest and most vigorous measures to quell and suppress it."[25]

Adams then explained away the real suffering of the indebted western farmers as the result of profligacy and bad character. "Luxery and extravagance both in furniture and dress had pervaded all orders of our Countrymen and women, and was hastning fast to Sap their independance by involving every class of citizens in distress, and accumulating debts upon them which they were unable to discharge. Vanity was becoming a more powerfull principal than Patriotism."[26]

In Cambridge, John Adams worried to his diary: "As the supreme judicial Court is to sit there this week, there will be two or three companies of militia, in order to prevent riots; for the insurrections of this kind, are not yet quelled, and indeed I know not when they will be. There is not sufficient energy in the government, and the strength of the party opposed to it is increasing. Unless some vigorous measures are taken the constitution of the commonwealth must infallibly fall."[27]

Away in France, Jefferson was generally sympathetic. "The most interesting intelligence from America is that respecting the late insurrection in Massachusetts. The cause of this has not been developed to me to my perfect satisfaction. The most probable is that those individuals were of the imprudent number of those who have involved themselves in debt beyond their abilities to pay, and that a vigorous effort in that government to compel the paiment of private debts and raise money for public ones, produced the resistance. I believe you may be assured that an idea or desire of returning to any thing like their antient government never entered into their heads. I am not discouraged by this."[28]

The Virginia planter William Grayson, on a visit to New York, reported the mood in a letter to James Madison: "It is the belief of people here well informed that this insurrection threatens the most serious consequences; and that the objects are more extensive than the mere stopping the Courts of justice. It is supposed that Vermont is leagued with them, and that they are secretly supported by emissaries of a certain nation; though as to this latter conjecture, I have heard no satisfactory proof."[29]

Showdown

In January, the fighting commenced. During that month and the next, Lincoln's militia, 4,400 strong and well supplied, fought three large battles against the Regulators.[30] The crisis peaked in February 1787 when a Regulator detachment of about 1,200 tried to seize the arsenal at Springfield. Lincoln's mercenary army intercepted the Shaysites and, under cover of a harsh snowstorm, attacked with cannon. This broke the Regulators' momentum, but smaller conflicts would continue all spring. As the *New York Daily Advertiser* reported on March 8, "Gen. Lincoln is not at present so secure as we wish him to be." Part of the problem was that "Many, too many, of the rebels have fled to Vermont, where their security is much too evident."[31]

The government suspended habeas corpus in much of western Massachusetts, and its cavalry detachments continued mopping-up operations through the spring of 1787, almost overlapping with the Constitutional Convention. Throughout the spring, the Shaysites shifted to hit-and-run raids and low-level terrorism against their enemies. "For five months, hunted by better organized and equipped government soldiers, the rebels under took raids against prominent military leaders, inland shopkeepers, and lawyers."[32] Night letters, barn burning, and house looting kept known progovernment families on their toes. At one point in April, 120 rebels crossed into New York and almost caught General Lincoln as he bathed in the hot spring at New Lebanon.[33]

Eventually, many of the most ardent Regulators migrated away. Shays would finish his days on a farm in New York's Finger Lakes region. Others stayed and, giving up on "politics outdoors," took their struggle indoors, running for local offices.

The Massachusetts rebellion created special problems for elites in New York, and for Hamilton, as a member of the New York State Assembly. In defeat, many of the Regulators retreated into autonomous Vermont. That was not good for New York, which was still trying to assert control in the Green Mountains. Publicly, Vermont's military and political leaders, Ethan Allen and Governor Thomas Chittenden, disavowed the rebellion. Privately, however, Governor Chittenden invited the fugitives to camp adjacent to his farm![34] In all, some 4,000 Shaysites would sell their belongings and flee to Vermont. Allen called the Massachusetts elite "a pack of Damned Rascals."[35] And two insurgent leaders, Luke Day and Eli Parson, acting with the blessing of Shays, offered Ethan Allen command of a "revolutionary army."[36]

More armed men in Vermont scared New York politicians; would the thuggish Green Mountain Boys now try to annex yet more of New York? Would the rebellion spread? Hamilton had long been sympathetic to the Vermont cause; perhaps that resulted from his role in negotiating the release of Ethan Allen in 1778 after almost two years of brutal captivity as a British POW. As early as 1782, Hamilton had concluded that Vermont should be recognized as independent. Now, in the spring of 1787, as he prepared for the Constitutional Convention, Hamilton led a personal crusade in the New York Assembly to end the 21-year-long confrontation with Vermonters. He convinced his father-in-law, Philip Schuyler, who owned lands in Vermont, to accept defeat.[37] And on March 15,

1787, Hamilton introduced a bill directing New York's congressional delegation to support independence for Vermont. Like much of what Hamilton did, this was strictly a pragmatic action: give these Yankees what they wanted now to shut down the violence before it spread.[38]

In defense of the bill, Hamilton splashed rhetorical cold water on his fellow New Yorkers. He confined himself "to an examination of what is practicable on the part of this state alone" and reminded the assembly that under the weak Articles of Confederation, no assistance could be expected if New York tried to retake Vermont by force. Such a "scheme of coertion would ill suit even the disposition of our own citizens" who, Hamilton argued, "are not adapted to the idea of a contest for dominion over a people disinclined to live under our government." To force the Vermonters back under New York rule would be "one of the greatest evils" and "a source of continual embarrassment and disquietude."[39]

Hamilton's pragmatism prevailed. Vermont would be independent. But that was a mere subset of the larger panorama of crisis. As was so often the case, Hamilton was in the forefront of those looking for permanent solutions, which ultimately had to be *national* solutions.

9

The Constitution as Reaction to Crisis

In this chapter and the next I explore the Constitution in terms of *what* the government was empowered to do, rather than *how* the government was designed to function. This is a nonstandard approach. Typically scholars analyze the Constitution's three branches of government and its system of checks and balances. Rarely examined is the larger task that government set for itself. Reading the Constitution with an eye toward the larger mission of government soon reveals why: the document contains a hidden-in-plain-sight dirigiste political economy.

Most constitutional history addresses the document's allegedly "democratic" or, conversely, "aristocratic" features. Did it expand democracy? Or was it a countermeasure designed to contain democracy? Being a brokered text, it did both.

Below, I explore a simultaneous third element, the realist concern with sovereignty. This position considered contending internal factions, but also the new state's relationship to the anarchic international state system. In the late eighteenth century, that system was dominated by the British, French, and Spanish empires. Thus, the realist reading takes on certain anti-imperialist tones that highlight the economic mission of planning and transformation.

Toward the Constitution

The path to the Constitutional Convention began in September 1786 at Annapolis, Maryland, when several leading politicians, including the now thirty-year-old Alexander Hamilton, convened a "Meeting of Commissioners to Remedy Defects of the Federal Government." In short, they wanted to amend the Articles of Confederation. Specifically they wished to grant Congress the power to override economically destructive and now proliferating interstate trade barriers. They hoped also, if all went well, to give Congress the power to levy taxes.

Only five of the thirteen states sent delegations to Annapolis. That was not enough to rewrite the Articles. So the attendees set a date for a second meeting to be held the following spring in Philadelphia. In the meantime, Shays's Rebellion erupted, and in Massachusetts, actual class war was now a reality. This, against the backdrop of those many other troubles the elites were having with Native Americans, Maroons, and backcountry secessionists (all potentially egged on by the probing foreign powers of Spain, Britain, and France), finally shocked them into political reorganization. When the May 1787 meeting in Philadelphia convened, twelve states sent delegations. Only Rhode Island, its government in the hands of paper-money–emitting proto-populists, refused to participate. Vermont, not yet a recognized state, was not invited.

The Philadelphia meeting ran from May 27 to September 17. Decisions were made by each state delegation first arriving at a common position then casting one collective vote. When a delegation could not agree internally, it did not vote.[1] No formal minutes were taken; however, many participants took notes.[2] Of the fifty-five individual delegates who participated in the convention, only thirty-nine signed the final document.

The Constitution of 1787 was radically different from the loose Articles of Confederation, that security pact adopted by the thirteen *sovereign* states on November 15, 1777. The new document did not, despite impressions to the contrary, weaken and limit the central government vis-à-vis the individual, the subordinate states, or foreign powers. Rather, as one scholar put it, the Constitution was "designed to give power to the central government, not to take it away."[3] Yet at the same time, this new state would be divided against itself; its various branches cantilevered one against the other. As James Madison described it: "Ambition must be made to counter act ambition."[4] Or, as a critic of the Constitution, Daniel Lazare, put it, "No single element would be predominant; rather each one would check the power of the rest and see to it that no one overstepped its bounds."[5]

Article I, Section 7, for example, gives the executive branch a limited veto over legislation and allows the president considerable power within the affairs of Congress. Conversely, Article II, Section 2 allows the Senate to veto presidential appointments; this effectively subordinates a key executive power to the legislative branch. The Supreme Court has "the power of review" over potentially any and all laws, thus significantly limiting the power of the two elected branches of government. (This power was not solidified until the Marshall Court's 1803 decision in *Marbury v. Madison*.)[6] The states also retain powers. Article I, Section 4 stipulates that state legislatures control the "times, places and manner of holding elections." This means states control who can vote and how votes are apportioned through redistricting. These prerogatives give the states significant latitude in shaping both the national-level legislative and executive branches. Then there is the outrageously undemocratic nature of the Senate, in which each state has two senators, regardless of its geographic size or population. Originally, senators were chosen by the state legislatures rather than elected by voters.

Lazare summarizes: "By splitting government up into so many pieces, the document created in Philadelphia ensured that no one component would be able to get its way without cooperation of the others. Rather than sharpening disputes, the new constitutional machinery did the opposite—it fairly forced politicians to smooth them over, to seek common ground, to wheel and deal so the differences might be bridged. The new system of government would muddy the waters in order to preserve the peace."[7]

This preservation of "peace" was an elite-class project to thwart the leveling impulses of the common people. A conservative scholar of Madison correctly summed up the Constitution's class nature by noting that the "whole scheme essentially comes down to this. The struggle of classes is to be replaced by a struggle of interests. The class struggle is domestic convulsion; the struggle of interests is a safe, even energizing, struggle, which is compatible with, or even promotes, the safety and stability of society. ... In a large commercial society the interest of the many can be fragmented into many narrower, more limited interests. The mass will not unite as a mass to make extreme demands upon the few, the struggle over which will destroy society; the mass will fragment into relatively small groups, seeking small immediate advantages for their narrow and particular interests."[8]

This is the Constitution's genius, and its pathology.

But the Constitution is not merely an instrument of class control. It also includes significant democratic concessions and puts real limits on the power of the moneyed classes. Explicitly progressive elements of the Constitution include guaranteeing a republican form of government and explicitly prohibiting "titles of Nobility." (These may seem unimportant today but were significant in the late eighteenth century.) The Constitution also prohibits property qualifications and religious testing for federal officeholders. It sets limits on terms of office before re-election is necessary. The Constitution also did away with various forms of judicial caprice, specifically "bills of attainder"—legislative acts in which a person or group could be declared guilty of an offense and punishment imposed, often without a trial.[9] The first ten amendments, the Bill of Rights, explicitly guarantee a set of legal protections for the individual against the state and, by extension, for social movements seeking to shape the state.

The democracy-vs.-aristocracy framework can confuse scale for political content and thus obscure a more complex politics of intra-elite struggle. The framework implies that the Constitution's centralization of power was inherently undemocratic because the states, it is suggested, being more "local," were thus more democratic and more progressive. In reality, state constitutions contained both democratic and undemocratic features.[10] David Waldstreicher is correct in noting that many elite antifederalists "sought in state governments the same beneficent oversight by a natural aristocracy ... that the Federalists dreamed of in a new national government."[11] This applies in varying measures to men like Luther Martin of Maryland, Elbridge Gerry of Massachusetts, and the Virginians George Mason and Richard Henry Lee, as well as to Jefferson and his protégé Madison.

Hamilton and the Constitution

One of Hamilton's central concerns at the convention was the role of the states. During the war he had seen how political fragmentation caused military and economic dysfunction. For *homo publicus* Hamilton, the choice was clear: unite and grow, or divide and die. A strong state would guide economic transformation, which would underwrite the costs of building the military and administrative power necessary for insuring sovereignty. The states, with their competing petty sovereignties, threatened that larger schema. As Hamilton explained in *Federalist* 6, "A man must be far gone in Utopian speculations who can seriously doubt that, if these States should either be wholly disunited, or only united in partial confederacies, the subdivisions into which they might be thrown would have frequent and violent contests with each other. To presume a want of motives for such contests as an argument against their existence, would be to forget that men are ambitious, vindictive, and rapacious. To look for a continuation of harmony between a number of independent, unconnected sovereignties in the same neighborhood, would be to disregard the uniform course of human events, and to set at defiance the accumulated experience of ages."[12]

Hamilton had a particularly low opinion of state governments and the type of men attracted to them. He worried about "the influence of many *inconsiderable* men in possession of considerable offices under the state governments who will fear a diminution of their consequence, power and emolument by the establishment of the general government."[13] Furthermore, he worried that self-serving local elites would be susceptible to foreign meddling. As he explained in *Federalist* 85, "local factions and insurrections," spurred on by "the ambition of powerful individuals in single States, who may acquire credit and influence enough, from leaders and favorites, to become the despots of the people," would invite "opportunities to foreign intrigue" and the construction of "extensive military establishments, which could not fail to grow out of wars between the States in a disunited situation."[14]

Had the states of the Confederation Period not entered into tighter unity, the political and economic development of the United States would have looked more like that of South America. There, in the collapse of Bolívar's grand project, fragmented and weak states, dominated by entrenched rural elites and financially and militarily compromised by meddling foreign powers (namely Britain and the United States), remained underdeveloped and prone to domestic insurrection, foreign intervention, and occasional interstate warfare.[15]

Hamilton's Plan to Liquidate the States

Unusually quiet during the convention, Hamilton, as part of the New York delegation, represented a state government that was hostile to the project of creating a strong central government. Being a large state with an international border, major port, huge navigable river, major city, and demagogic governor, New York political leaders were jealous of their prerogatives. New York's delegation eventually walked out of the convention, leaving Hamilton as a participant without a vote.

On June 18, Hamilton presented his plan of government in a marathon speech of six hours. Already three plans had been proposed; two of them had traction, the Virginia Plan and the New Jersey Plan. Neither was as centralizing as Hamilton's.

Disparaged as crypto-monarchist, or sometimes just plain monarchist, Hamilton's plan nonetheless had much to recommend it. Hamilton's central concern was the dangerous, centrifugal power of the states. His solution? Abolish the states. "The general power whatever be its form if it preserves itself, must swallow up the State powers. Otherwise it will be swallowed up by them." For, as he put it, "Two Sovereignties can not co-exist within the same limits."[16]

For Hamilton, states were entropic laboratories of corruption, provincialism, and military crisis. "They constantly pursue internal interests adverse to those of the whole. They have their particular debts—their particular plans of finance &c. All these when opposed to, invariably prevail over the requisitions & plans of Congress." Just as "Men love power," so, too, had state political elites "constantly shewn a disposition rather to regain the powers delegated by them than to part with more, or to give effect to what they had parted with. The ambition of their demagogues is known to hate the controul of the Genl. Government."[17]

Then there was the dangerous sentimental attachment that Americans had toward their state governments, which were, after all, the governments they most often engaged with. As long as state governments existed, "the Citizens have not that anxiety to prevent a dissolution of" the national government because states "would still leave the purposes of Govt. attainable to a considerable degree." Hamilton wanted the widespread desire for government attached to the national project only. If state governments could serve as political escape vehicles, then fewer people would work to preserve the central state.

Nor were states equal to one another or static; they would only grow stronger and more unequal. He used Virginia as an example: "In a few years ... How strongly will it feel its importance & self-sufficiency?" Here the questions of force and violence, which are central to the nature of state power, become key to his argument. "A certain portion of military force is absolutely necessary in large communities," he explained. Referring to Shays's Rebellion, he noted that Massachusetts "is now feeling this necessity & making provision for it." But if this power were left to each state, how could it "be exerted on the States collectively?" It could not. Such a diffusion of military sovereignty would almost guarantee interstate warfare. "Foreign powers also will not be idle spectators. They will interpose, the confusion will increase, and a dissolution of the Union ensue."

Hamilton's solution, shocking even today: *liquidate the states.* He called for "the States to be divided into election districts."[18]

Hamilton disliked the states, regardless of their democratic or undemocratic features, because he feared their competing claims of sovereignty would destroy the larger national project. Hamilton was less concerned with *how* the states operated. He disliked *that* they operated. When New York started trade wars with its neighbors and contemplated a real war with Vermont, the manner of New York's deliberations was of less concern to Hamilton than was the larger question: Why should this destabilizing political subunit of government even exist?

In retrospect, the abolition of states would have avoided some rather major problems, such as the Civil War. Without state governments, their fragmented micro-sovereignties and their gray-clad state militias, Southern secession would have been far more difficult. Without states, there would have been no state control of elections, thus no Electoral College, thus no minority rule by presidents like George W. Bush and Donald Trump, men who lost the popular vote yet won majorities in the Electoral College.

Other aspects of Hamilton's plan are less appealing—in particular, lifetime terms for the president and for senators: "We ought to go as far in order to attain stability and permanency, as republican principles will admit. Let one branch of the Legislature hold their places for life or at least during good behaviour. Let the Executive also be for life."[19]

While some at the convention likely agreed with Hamilton's critique, his proposal was out of touch with the convention's overall mood. Hamilton's proposal was too autocratic and centralized. He was naïve in thinking that lifetime tenures would create disinterested and wise government. Some Hamilton defenders surmise that his plan was mostly a ruse, a provocation, an "intervention" intended to shake up the conversation by setting new outer boundaries. Perhaps. Whatever the case, Hamilton's plan was dead on arrival.

Slavery's Constitution

The question of states and their rights was closely linked to the emerging sectional conflict over slavery. This struggle would also influence the course of America's dirigiste industrialization. Developmentalist policy in the nineteenth century would proceed in fits and starts, often in the face of explicit Southern opposition, and in the South, when adopted, such policies were often ineffective due to the larger dynamics of underdevelopment imposed by slavery.[20]

As already mentioned, Vermont's 1777 state constitution had abolished bondage for adults.[21] Pennsylvania passed a law ending slavery in 1780. Litigation ended slavery in Massachusetts in 1783. Connecticut began gradual emancipation in 1784. New York passed a similar law in 1785. In the face of these changes, slaveholding Southern elites feared that the more populous, prosperous, commercial, and increasingly manufacturing-oriented states of the Northeast might use federal power to encroach upon slavery.

Speaking at the Constitutional Convention, James Madison identified slavery as a key source of instability, saying: "We have seen the mere distinction of colour made in the most enlightened period of time, a ground of the most oppressive dominion ever exercised by man over man."[22] John Rutledge of South Carolina, also speaking at the convention, embodied that potential instability. Rutledge essentially threatened secession! Speaking in defense of the slave trade, he argued: "Religion & humanity had nothing to do with this question—Interest alone is the governing principle with Nations—The true question at present is whether the Southn. States shall or shall not be parties to the Union. If the Northern States consult their interests they will not oppose the increase of Slaves which will increase the commodities of which they will become the carriers."[23]

Ultimately, the Constitution, produced in the spirit of compromise, would appease Rutledge and his ilk. Although the words "slave" and "slavery" were never used, six of the Constitution's eighty-four clauses directly address slavery. The Constitution limited the slave trade while significantly protecting slavery. As David Waldstreicher explains, "the Constitution enacted mechanisms that empowered slaveholders politically," and prevented "the national government from becoming an immediate or likely impediment to the institution."[24]

Most infamous among these was Article I, Section 2, the "three-fifths clause," which for the purposes of apportioning congressional seats counted every five enslaved people as equal to the existence of three free voters. This gave Southern voters disproportionately more power than Northern voters and thus boosted Southern (pro-slavery) political representation in the House of Representatives. Article I, Section 9 prevented Congressional interference with the slave trade until 1808: a clear protection, but also an admission of the controls that were on their way. This was further supported by Article V, which prohibited any amendment to Article I, Section 9 for twenty years.

The Constitution also protected slavery by forcing free states to honor the laws of slave states. The "fugitive slave clause" in Article IV, Section 2 forced free states to turn over anyone who had escaped slavery in a different state, just as they would extradite a criminal: "No person held to service or labor in one state, under the laws thereof, escaping into another, shall, in consequence of any law or regulation therein, be discharged from such service or labor, but shall be delivered up on claim of the party to whom such service or labor may be due."

The historian James Oakes asks, "Why was the Constitution so proslavery?" It was not the result of proslavery ideologues running the show. "A historian could count on the fingers of two hands all of the zealous partisans of slavery (and of abolition) who were known in the late 1780s. They occupied the extremes of a debate over a Constitution that in the end neither extreme produced. The men responsible were the men in the middle—those who considered themselves progressives but who compromised with proslavery extremists for the sake of ratification, and thereby secured a Constitution that resisted much of the Revolution's anti-slavery impulse."[25]

Thus, we find the slave owner George Washington, president of the Convention, silent on slavery. Alexander Hamilton, who was also an active member of the New York Society for Promoting the

Manumission of Slaves (despite seeming to have inherited two slaves through his wife's family), brought to the Convention a petition to end the slave trade, yet, in that spirit of compromise, did not present it. Likewise, Benjamin Franklin, member of the Pennsylvania Abolition Society, had a similar petition but also failed to bring it forward.[26]

The issue of Native Americans' role in the new nation was less controversial. Article I, Section 2, Clause 3 states, "Representatives and direct Taxes shall be apportioned among the several States ... excluding Indians not taxed." And in Article I, Section 8, we find that "Congress shall have the power to regulate Commerce with foreign nations and among the several states, and with the Indian tribes." This implies that Indian tribes were separate from the federal government, the states, and foreign nations and that their "regulation" was a federal rather than state matter. The phrase "with the Indian tribes" has been the legal basis for asserting and sometimes winning limited native sovereignty.[27] In short, Native Americans were foreigners when that worked, and subjects of the federal state when convenient. The central issue here, quite obviously, was land. The Native Americans possessed it and the new nation would have it, morality, sentiment, and legality notwithstanding.

The Federalist Papers as State Theory

Ratification of the new Constitution required approval by nine of the thirteen states. Such approval, however, was not immediately forthcoming. To promote ratification in New York, where the powerful governor, George Clinton, opposed it, Hamilton organized and along with John Jay and Madison authored The Federalist Papers: eighty-five essays published over the course of eight months from October 1787 to May 1788.

Hamilton's Federalist essays feel haunted by the author's political-economic experience of the war. They carry the rational paranoia of the long, hungry winter cantonments, and the shadow of Hamilton's 1777 mission up the west bank of the Hudson to intercept and contain the dangerous, centrifugal egotism of generals Gates and Putnam, and subsequent collapse into that "nervous fever" requiring a two-month-long convalescence at the home of Kennedy. Hamilton never lost his perhaps overdeveloped awareness of national vulnerability. For him, state failure loomed ever-present.

Charles Beard, who called Hamilton "the colossal genius of the new system," praised *The Federalist Papers* as "the finest study in the economic interpretation of politics, which exists in any language."[28] In Hamilton's fifty-one contributions we see most explicitly his theory of the state. At the heart of the matter was a dialectic relationship between military considerations and economic transformation, each supporting or undermining the other.

If his fear was disintegration, his wish for a fiscal military developmentalist state ran as follows: create a strong central state; use it to drive economic transformation and growth; tax that economic activity to fund the expansion and deepening of the state's military and administrative capacities; and with these powers harness the national territory's biophysical natural endowments of human labor power, the work energy of nature, and the organic properties of the soil, sediment, and rock. States and economies are at one level just specific configurations of the earth's metabolic processes.[29]

Simply stated, Hamilton's project was the developmentalist state as both means and ends. He wanted to develop the state so as to secure the state. Hamilton begins the arguments in *Federalist* 1, posing the question whether "societies of men are really capable or not of establishing good government from reflection and choice, or whether they are forever destined to depend for their political constitutions on accident and force." He dismissed critics of the Constitution as disingenuous populists: "An enlightened zeal for the energy and efficiency of government will be stigmatized as the offspring of a temper fond of despotic power and hostile to the principles of liberty." He warned readers that "a dangerous ambition more often lurks behind the specious mask of zeal for the rights of the people," whereas "the forbidden appearance of zeal for the firmness and efficiency of government" tended to be more honest, because its ambitions were clearly stated. In Hamilton's reading of history, "of those men who have overturned the liberties of republics, the greatest number have begun their career by paying an obsequious court to the people; commencing demagogues, and ending tyrants."[30]

At times Hamilton almost sounds like Lenin in *"Left-Wing" Communism: An Infantile Disorder*, in which the Russian revolutionary criticizes the ultra-left for "mistaking *their desire*, their political ideological attitude, for objective reality." Hamilton would likely have agreed with Lenin that such a miscalculation "is the most dangerous mistake for revolutionaries." He probably also would have agreed with Lenin's pronouncement that "our theory is not a dogma, but a *guide to action*."[31]

But at other times Hamilton in *The Federalist Papers* reads almost like a latter-day American pragmatist or postmodern cultural relativist: he acknowledges the darker side of the human will while maintaining that a correct set of rules could effectively contain and channel human action regardless of motivation: "Ambition, avarice, personal animosity, party opposition, and many other motives not more laudable than these, are apt to operate as well upon those who support as those who oppose the right side of a question."

In *Federalist 6*, Hamilton sets out to "delineate dangers of a different and, perhaps, still more alarming kind—those which will in all probability flow from dissensions between the States themselves, and from domestic factions and convulsions." Hamilton was certain the new states would make war on one another if not subordinated by a superior political force and absorbed into a common economy. After all, land grabs and territorial disputes were at the root of many centuries of war. "Perhaps the greatest proportion of wars that have desolated the earth have sprung from this origin," Hamilton cautioned. "This cause would exist among us in full force. We have a vast tract of unsettled territory within the boundaries of the United States. There still are discordant and undecided claims between several of them, and the dissolution of the Union would lay a foundation for similar claims between them all."[32]

To those who saw strong government and a standing army as invitations to despotism, Hamilton inverted their argument in *Federalist* 8. It was, he argued, *weak government* that led to war, and war that led to despotism: "Standing armies, it may be replied, must inevitably result from a dissolution of the Confederacy. Frequent war and constant apprehension, which require a state of as constant preparation, will infallibly produce them [that is, standing armies]. The weaker States or confederacies would first have recourse to them, to put themselves upon an equality with their more potent neighbors. They would endeavor to supply the inferiority of population and resources by a more regular and effective system of defense, by disciplined troops, and by fortifications. They would, at the same time, be necessitated to strengthen the executive arm of government, in doing which their constitutions would acquire a progressive direction toward monarchy. It is of the nature of war to increase the executive at the expense of the legislative authority."[33]

Hamilton's somewhat counterintuitive argument was that a small, volunteer-based standing army would actually serve as a defense against militarism. Small states that constantly threaten one another must constantly arm themselves, thereby distorting the social and political balance within each. "The continual necessity for their services enhances the importance of the soldier, and proportionably degrades the condition of the citizen. The military state becomes elevated above the civil. The inhabitants of territories, often the theatre of war, are unavoidably subjected to frequent infringements on their rights, which serve to weaken their sense of those rights; and by degrees the people are brought to consider the soldiery not only as their protectors, but as their superiors."[34]

The Federalist Papers as Political Economy

For Hamilton, a strong central state was not only a counterintuitive check on militarism and a better guarantor of liberty; it was also essential for economic development, which was essential for successful sovereignty. Hamilton takes up this theme in *Federalist*

11, 12, and 13. A weak and disunited government, he argued, would invite economic domination. As he put it in *Federalist* 11: "If we continue united, we may counteract a policy so unfriendly to our prosperity in a variety of ways. By prohibitory regulations … we may oblige foreign countries to bid against each other, for the privileges of our markets." But if the states were to fall into disunion: "It would be in the power of the maritime nations, availing themselves of our universal impotence, to prescribe the conditions of our political existence … We should then be compelled to content ourselves with the first price of our commodities, and to see the profits of our trade snatched from us to enrich our enemies and prosecutors." Then, "poverty and disgrace would overspread a country which, with wisdom, might make herself the admiration and envy of the world."[35]

Furthermore, national integration would create a large, diversified market, which would deliver powerful economies of scale and positive synergies. The states would benefit from easier trade with one another and from more opportunities abroad. As Hamilton put it: "An unrestrained intercourse between the States themselves will advance the trade of each by an interchange of their respective productions, not only for the supply of reciprocal wants at home, but for exportation to foreign markets. The veins of commerce in every part will be replenished, and will acquire additional motion and vigor from a free circulation of the commodities of every part."

Hamilton gave special attention to the benefits of economic diversification, the linking together of regional comparative advantages within a single national economy. "When the staple of one [state] fails from a bad harvest or unproductive crop, it can call to its aid the staple of another. The variety, not less than the value, of products for exportation contributes to the activity of foreign commerce. It can be conducted upon much better terms with a large number of materials of a given value than with a small number of materials of the same value." Strength through unity, cooperation, and economic diversification. These are admirable ideas.

For Hamilton, the state's ends (existence) and its means (strength) were one and the same. All hinged on the state's administrative, fiscal, and military capacities. He wanted a government that could check Europe, and "teach that assuming brother, moderation." The means? "Union will enable us to do it. Disunion will add another victim to his triumphs."

Throughout *The Federalist Papers*, Hamilton outlined the central mechanism of developmentalist nationalism: the state creates economic conditions; it does not merely react to them. For Hamilton, the fundamental problem with the Articles of Confederation was not so much an excess of democracy as an excess of economic disorganization. Or, as he put it in *Federalist* 22, "the want of a power to regulate commerce."

Bad Hamilton

There is no denying that Hamilton's faith in the utility of coercion was also ugly and dangerous. In *Federalist* 84, Hamilton supported the writ of habeas corpus but also sought to limit that right. "I go further, and affirm that bills of rights ... are not only unnecessary in the proposed Constitution but would even be dangerous. They would contain various exceptions to powers not granted; and, on this very account, would afford a colorable pretext to claim more than were granted."[36]

Incorrectly, Hamilton asserted that the Constitution was itself a Bill of Rights. However, neither was Hamilton totally wrong in worrying that positively stated rights might "afford a colorable pretext to claim more than were granted." After all, modern neoliberalism has wrapped itself in the discourse of "rights" and "choice" and "voice" even as it overrides real democracy. For example, consider the modern Supreme Court ruling *Citizens United v. Federal Election Commission*, which in the name of the First Amendment classified corporate campaign donations as protected "speech" and thus overturned decades of campaign finance laws that had limited the power of the rich to influence elections.

On September 20, 1787, the Constitution was "laid before the United States in Congress assembled." For two days Congress debated not adoption of the new document but rather whether to censure the Convention delegates for having exceeded their authority! They were, after all, to have met merely to *revise* the Articles of Confederation, not scrap them and start anew.[37]

As state-level debates proceeded, votes for ratification passed by only slim majorities, or failed altogether. Two of the largest and most important states, Virginia and New York, barely managed to ratify. By 1788 it became clear that the new, potentially very powerful centralized state being proposed could only meet public approval if a proper Bill of Rights was added to the Constitution. Only in 1789, when a Bill of Rights was brought forth in Congress, did North Carolina finally ratify. Rhode Island, which had rejected the Constitution in referendum and now risked being treated as a semi-hostile foreign state, finally ratified on May 29, 1790.[38] With that, the current political structure of the United States of America was finally formed. Today, for better and for worse, the document stands as the world's oldest operating written and codified national constitution.

10

A Dirigiste Interpretation
of the Constitution

This chapter continues the focus on *what* the new government was empowered to do, particularly in the economic realm. What functions did this powerful new central government give itself? The most important in this regard is Article I, Section 8, which enumerates the powers of Congress in relation not to other branches of government but in relation to the world.

Surprisingly, most literature on the Constitution does not directly address Article I, Section 8. Michael Klarman's *The Framers' Coup*, a masterful 880-page work published in 2016, does not mention it—though to be fair, many key clauses in Article I, Section 8 are discussed, as is Article I, Section 10, which enumerates the powers states are *prohibited* from exercising.[1] Charles Beard's much-debated *An Economic Interpretation of the Constitution* also ignores the significance of Article I, Section 8. Beard wrote, "The powers for positive action conferred upon the new government were few, but they were adequate to the purposes of the framers."[2]

Rather, the powers granted were numerous, sweeping, and economically transformative. Along with the regularly discussed War Powers Clause, granting Congress the power to make war, and the Necessary and Proper Clause, granting it the power to make any and all laws needed to execute its larger mission, Article I, Section 8 contains seemingly prosaic powers that are actually potent tools of economic policy. In summary, these are: the power to lay and collect taxes, pay debts, provide for the common defense and general welfare, borrow money, regulate commerce, control foreign relations, establish bankruptcy laws, coin money (and regulate its value), fix standards of weights and measures, suppress counterfeiting, establish post offices and post roads, punish piracies at sea, declare war, create and equip the Army and Navy, and exercise exclusive governing control over the geographical seat of government, military establishments, and all other lands owned by the federal government. And, finally, there is the power to "make all Laws which shall be necessary and proper for carrying into Execution the foregoing Powers, and all other Powers vested by this Constitution in the Government of the United States, or in any Department or Officer thereof."

Article I, Section 10, Clause 1 explicitly strips many of these same powers from the states.[3] And in case any doubt remained, Article VI, the Supremacy Clause, subordinates all other levels of government to federal power: "This Constitution, and the Laws of the United States which shall be made in Pursuance thereof; and all Treaties made, or which shall be made, under the Authority of the United States, shall be the supreme Law of the Land; and the Judges in every State shall be bound thereby, any Thing in the Constitution or Laws of any State to the Contrary notwithstanding." Only the "Reserved Powers" of the Tenth Amendment offer an abstract and feeble protest against the Constitution's mass allocation of power to the federal government.

Returning to the issue of economic development, Article I, Section 8 is so clearly the developmental state in outline that it is worth quoting in full before delving into details:

> The Congress shall have Power To lay and collect Taxes, Duties, Imposts and Excises, to pay the Debts and provide for the common Defence and general Welfare of the United States; but all Duties, Imposts and Excises shall be uniform throughout the United States;
>
> To borrow Money on the credit of the United States;
>
> To regulate Commerce with foreign Nations, and among the several States, and with the Indian Tribes;

To establish an uniform Rule of Naturalization, and uniform Laws on the subject of Bankruptcies throughout the United States;

To coin Money, regulate the Value thereof, and of foreign Coin, and fix the Standard of Weights and Measures;

To provide for the Punishment of counterfeiting the Securities and current Coin of the United States;

To establish Post Offices and post Roads;

To promote the Progress of Science and useful Arts, by securing for limited Times to Authors and Inventors the exclusive Right to their respective Writings and Discoveries;

To constitute Tribunals inferior to the supreme Court;

To define and punish Piracies and Felonies committed on the high Seas, and Offences against the Law of Nations;

To declare War, grant Letters of Marque and Reprisal, and make Rules concerning Captures on Land and Water;

To raise and support Armies, but no Appropriation of Money to that Use shall be for a longer Term than two Years;

To provide and maintain a Navy;

To make Rules for the Government and Regulation of the land and naval Forces;

To provide for calling forth the Militia to execute the Laws of the Union, suppress Insurrections and repel Invasions;

To provide for organizing, arming, and disciplining, the Militia, and for governing such Part of them as may be employed in the Service of the United States, reserving to the States respectively, the Appointment of the Officers, and the Authority of training the Militia according to the discipline prescribed by Congress;

To exercise exclusive Legislation in all Cases whatsoever, over such District (not exceeding ten Miles square) as may, by Cession of particular States, and the Acceptance of Congress, become the Seat of the Government of the United States, and to exercise like Authority over all Places purchased by the Consent of the Legislature of the State in which the Same shall be, for the Erection of Forts, Magazines, Arsenals, dock-Yards, and other needful Buildings;—And

To make all Laws which shall be necessary and proper for carrying into Execution the foregoing Powers, and all other Powers vested by this Constitution in the Government of the United States, or in any Department or Officer thereof.

Let us now explore this dirigiste toolbox.

Taxing, Spending, and the General Welfare

Foremost in this list of powers is the Taxing and Spending Clause. It permits taxation and spending for only three purposes: paying federal debts, providing for the common defense, and for the "general welfare" of the United States.

The government's ability to use tax revenue to service its debts is the most important element in creating a national credit system. This power is, in effect, a type of political alchemy by which coercive power becomes money. It goes like this: the state's monopoly on the legitimate use of violence underwrites its economic promises; this creates economic confidence (we know the state will pay, because we know it has the power to forcibly commandeer resources). Then, this confidence, in a moment of political economic transubstantiation, allows the state (within limits) to credibly create money and credit. This ability to issue credit is one of the most powerful macroeconomic tools in the dirigiste toolbox. This power, however, is not infinite. It exists in the messy context of political reality and class struggle. States have remarkable powers when they control a central bank, but every state faces internal and external constraints on its operations.

Next in the spending clause is the "common defense," a potentially very broad category. This power allows the federal government to build fleets, bases, and later roads, and indeed to manage whole military-related landscapes.[4] Like modern defense procurements, early U.S. investment in forts, weapons, ships, and provisions functioned as economic stimulus and veiled industrial policy that helped drive basic technological innovations. For example, the government-owned armory at Springfield, Massachusetts, established in 1778, pioneered manufacturing innovations including interchangeable parts, assembly line–style mass production, and hourly wages.[5] As Fred Block, put it: "The history of the United States is no different from that of other modern countries; fighting wars and preparing for wars have been an absolutely critical spur to economic growth and development. ... The government began to invest in technological expertise for military purposes in the first years of the republic."[6] In an early address to the joint houses, George Washington told the lawmakers that the American people's "safety and interest require that they should promote such manufactories, as tend to render them independent on others, for essential, particularly for military supplies."[7]

The Mighty Loophole

More important for Hamilton's project was the third category, "the general welfare," an idea so broad as to include almost anything. At the convention, Benjamin Franklin proposed giving the federal government an explicit power to build internal improvements, specifically canals. Madison, when still in the Federalist camp, put it well: "the political obstacles being removed, a removal of the natural ones, as far as possible, ought to follow."[8] Franklin's proposal was defeated, for fear that while all states would pay, only a few would benefit from such projects. However, the developmentalist effort did get a loophole in the form of that phrase the "general Welfare of the United States," words Hamilton would interpret in a most expansive fashion.

Four years after the convention, in the *Report on Manufactures*, Hamilton would argue that "the National Legislature has express authority 'To lay and Collect taxes, duties, imposts and excises, to pay the debts and provide for the Common defence and general welfare' with no other qualifications" than respecting certain constitutionally outlined state prerogatives regarding uniform taxation. Otherwise, contended Hamilton, "the power to *raise money* is *plenary*, and *indefinite;* and the objects to which it may be *appropriated* are no less comprehensive."[9]

Why was this? Because, as Hamilton saw it, the term *general welfare* "is as comprehensive as any that could have been used." And for a great nation in the making, the phrase "necessarily embraces a vast variety of particulars, which are susceptible neither of specification nor of definition."

Shortly after ratification, Jefferson and Madison, fearing encroachment upon the patrimonial powers of the slave-owning Virginia elite, began vigorous protestation of Hamilton's expansive interpretation. In Hamilton's reading of "the general welfare" they saw an emerging threat: federal power strong enough to destroy slavery and with it the whole social order of the South.[10]

Banks, Borrowing, Corporations, and Trade

Another important part of Hamilton's developmentalist toolbox is the power to "borrow Money on the credit of the United States." This clause laid the groundwork for the First Bank of the United States, which helped create a national financial system where none had previously existed. The power to borrow allowed the federal government to issue debt instruments that circulated like money and passed through independent regional banks. This helped stimulate commerce, build a national market, and drive the economic transformation toward industrialization.

During Washington's presidency, there was widespread support for the government buying back and retiring all the devalued debt left from the Revolutionary War. But as we shall see in a coming chapter, the federal government instead assumed all state debts, consolidated them into new federal debt instruments, and then paid creditors the face value of what had been badly devalued debt. By these means, the federal government maintained its creditworthiness among lenders at home and abroad and, very importantly, established itself as the center of a national credit system. Credit-worthiness, in turn, allowed the federal government to borrow more, and at lower interest rates. That borrowed income, in turn, allowed the central bank to lend and invest. The stimulus this provided did much to help revive the economy. As the economy grew, so, too, did federal tax revenue, allowing the government to service its debts and borrow more in a (hopefully) virtuous cycle of symbiotically public- and private-sector development.

The Constitution, however, did not expressly authorize Congress to charter corporations, a power that many states, when they were still colonies, had long engaged in.[11] During Washington's first term, Hamilton pushed an interpretation of the Borrowing Clause as authorizing Congress to charter the First Bank of the United States. Like building canals, that power was proposed and shot down. However, its residue could be seen in the Commerce Clause, which allows Congress the power to "regulate Commerce with foreign Nations, and among the several States, and with the Indian Tribes." This gave the federal government final internal and external control of the national economy.

Bankruptcy

The Bankruptcy Clause, allowing Congress to establish "uniform Laws on the subject of Bankruptcies throughout the United States," provided for a federally managed process for the liquidation of failed businesses. Business failure being an inevitable part of capitalist growth, a common national process greatly reduced transition costs, increased business confidence, and helped move the various regional economies toward national integration. Recall how the bad debts of the Critical Period fueled political conflict and even military clashes.

Military Clauses as Economic

The various military clauses also had economic effects. The clauses governing military installations and military regulations, the

Militia Clause, and the Navy Clause all establish federal power over military forces and allowed the government to act as an economic agent in the name of equipping and maintaining these forces. The role of military procurement as a force for driving economic growth seems to have been clear to Hamilton.

On the international front, American shipping, which was both a form of commerce and a manufacturing sector in the form of shipbuilding, was only as secure as the U.S. Navy could make it.[12] In *Federalist* 24, Hamilton noted the link between commerce and war, and hinted at how military procurement creates backward linkages into the rest of the domestic economy: "If we mean to be a commercial people, or even to be secure on our Atlantic side, we must endeavor, as soon as possible, to have a navy. To this purpose there must be dock-yards and arsenals; and for the defense of these, fortifications, and probably garrisons."[13]

Perhaps the best summary of the military's central role in early U.S. economic development is offered by William D. Adler and Andrew J. Polsky: "The Army spurred economic development through two distinct lines of activity, the 'traditional' military application of coercive force and the socioeconomic tasks that provided vital collective goods. Military force supported the assertion of national authority that was a precondition for a national market. Force also became a key mechanism through which the nation acquired new land. Meanwhile, the technical and non-combat branches of the Army—civil engineers, topographical engineers, explosives experts, bureaucrats, and quartermasters— offered expertise otherwise unavailable, built an infrastructure to support a national economy, drove technological innovation, and introduced new methods of administration for large-scale, multi-location organizations."[14] Toward such ends, in 1794 Congress provided $81,865 "for the erecting and repairing of Arsenals and Magazines." Soon three national armories were built or refurbished from pre-existing, makeshift, wartime works.[15]

Congress was also granted the right to make war, suppress "Insurrections and repel Invasions." This is not merely defensive war, connected to the territory of the United States; it is global and offensive war "on the high Seas," and not only in the name of the United States, but also in the name of international law, as in: "Offences against the Law of Nations. ... To declare War, grant Letters of Marque and Reprisal, and make Rules concerning Captures on Land and Water." Toward these expansionist ends the new state gave itself the right to "to raise and support Armies ... and maintain a Navy." All of which is to say, to industrialize and impose its economic vision as widely as possible.

Of Weights and Measures and Money

Among the most deceptively simple yet profound powers in Article I, Section 8 is the power to "coin Money, regulate the Value thereof, and of foreign Coin, and fix the Standard of Weights and Measures." It is no coincidence that money and measurement are side by side. The power to quantify is central to both political governance and modern economic development. In *Magna Carta Manifesto*, Peter Linebaugh traces the connections between standardized measurement, the emergence of modern economic exchange value, and thus the value form, and the slow modernization of statecraft all the way back to 1217 and the *Magna Carta* and *Charter of the Forest*. Linebaugh notes that "weights and measures" are "the basis of the commodity form."[16]

To "fix the Standard of Weights and Measures" is an invitation to subtly but powerfully regulate all of time and space. And these are two of the most essential measures of economic value: hours worked, yards of cloth produced, acres of land owned, etc. For the modern economy of industry, commerce, finance, and ubiquitous technology to function, there must be a culture of measurement in place. If money is to function as the "universal equivalent," quantification in general must be normal, easy, and widespread. The modern quantification of weight, area, time, and distance helps make legible the infinite variety of forms that are reality. Once legible, they are more easily controllable, exploitable, and exchangeable. Quantification is key to the epistemological framework upon which the money economy and value form of modern capitalism depends. However, markets alone do not create universal and uniform standards; through history they have depended on rulemaking and rule-enforcing umpires. The valorization process, whereby use values become exchange values, takes place through the rationalizing, juridical, political membrane of state-sanctioned meanings. For prices to be clear, underlying categories of quantification must be stable. The power of the dollar rests invisibly upon the standardization of an inch, a mile, an acre, a gallon, and so on.[17]

Hamilton's developmentalist vision sought to create a nationwide, government-centered money system that could facilitate the growth of a robust manufacturing-based economy. A nationally coherent system of standardized measurements was an essential techno-bureaucratic means toward that end.

Although traders, merchants, and financiers had for centuries been creating money in the form of private coinage, cowrie shells, wampum, bills of exchange, private bank scrip, etc., the unifying, rationalizing role of state-issued fiat money was instrumental in creating modern industrial and financial capitalism. Even many of the older forms of money, for example, wampum in seventeenth-century New England, had state sanction and were recognized as legal currency. Wampum, though private and decentralized in its production and organic in its form (beads ground from quahog shells), was nonetheless embedded in layers of state-anchored social relations. The contracts, claims on property, taxes, debts, interest, etc. that used wampum depended on state-centered systems of domination and coercion: courts for lawsuits; fines; sheriffs, to effect arrest; stocks for corporal punishment.[18]

The Articles of Confederation, drawn up in 1781, had left standardization of weights and measures to the states. But the states all used different standards, and this created growth-retarding friction. In Boston a hogshead of beer contained sixty-four gallons but in Baltimore only sixty-three.[19]

In January 1790, President Washington gave the new Congress a list of suggested tasks, and prominent among these was establishing a uniform system for measurement. In response, Thomas Jefferson prepared a system for measures of weight, volume, and length that mixed traditional English units with something like a proto-decimal system.[20] Two years later, a Senate committee appointed to investigate the subject recommended adopting this proto-metric system. However, Congress took no action.

In fact, creating a standardized system of weights and measures was taken up by the First, Second, and Third Congresses, yet no conclusive decisions were made. In practice, agreeing on standardized weights and measures was strangely elusive. One author called it "perhaps the most difficult problem which the early Congresses of the United States had to solve."[21] Customary and locally regulated standards remained the norm, and, as local economies remained relatively isolated from each other, there was no pressing need for standardization.[22] The new government did manage to impose standardized quantification when and where it had to, and that was most important in the question of land. A national standard bushel or gallon could wait for the creation of an actually integrated national market. However, controlling the territory upon which such a market would be built required a nationally consistent system of land survey, registration, and disposal. Thus, the weights-and-measures clause of Article I, Section 8 pertains also to lands, because for land to be politically controlled, commodified, collateralized, and distributed it must be known and, in the modern era, that means measured.

The Postal Clause, which allows for the construction of post roads, also had important implications for the geography of politics and state power. Roads are a crucial political economic tool; roads permit the extension of military power and thus the extension of legal power and thus the consolidation of market relations.

In summary, Article I, Section 8 brings to mind Karl Polanyi's argument about states creating markets: "Internal trade in Western Europe was actually created by the intervention of the state." Or, "There was nothing natural about laissez-faire; free markets could never have come into being merely by allowing things to take their course. Just as cotton manufactures, the leading free trade industry, were created by the help of protective tariffs, export bounties and indirect wage subsidies, laissez-faire itself was enforced by the state."[23]

11

Public Debt as Central Power

By early 1789 the Constitution had finally been ratified and Washington elected president. On September 11, Hamilton took up his post as secretary of the Treasury and began rolling out his developmentalist agenda. His plans came forth as a series of reports covering public credit, a national bank, a national mint, coastal revenue collection, the disposal of vacant lands, and finally, in 1791, the *Report on the Subject of Manufactures*.[1]

Each report was an effort to educate and persuade those who held the proverbial power of the purse. The reports built upon one another and together offered a blueprint for state-guided industrialization. Before he addressed manufacturing, Hamilton dealt with finance and, briefly, public lands. In his two financial reports, Hamilton engaged the leading political economists of his day, namely, Jacques Necker, David Hume, Malachy Postlethwayt, Adam Smith, and Sir James Steuart. But in the strange style of the eighteenth century, these thinkers were almost never named, even when they were directly quoted.[2]

It was in his *Report on the Public Credit* and *Report on a National Bank* that Hamilton proposed federal assumption of state debts and the creation of a central bank, both of which were indispensable prerequisites for the industrial plan laid out in *The Report on Manufactures*. Because Hamilton's efforts to create a national financial system have received far more attention than his efforts to develop manufacturing, this chapter and the next explores the financial reports only to the extent of providing context for *The Report on Manufactures*.

Dialectics of Debt

Upon arriving at the Treasury, Hamilton found that the United States had a foreign debt of about $10 million in principal, plus $1.6 million of unpaid interest. The domestic debt was estimated to be slightly over $27 million, plus roughly $13 million in unpaid interest. Thus, in Hamilton's exact calculation, the federal government's total debt was "54,124,464 dollars, and 56 cents."[3] The states also owed money, but how much was difficult to surmise. Neither Congress nor the states had kept perfect records of the myriad forms of IOUs issued, some of these having been handwritten notes from commissary officers. Adding to the confusion, many promissory notes had been recalled, consolidated, and reissued.[4]

The sums were formidable, and many politicians were confused about how to manage the burden. Most Southern states, having smaller per capita war debts than the Mid-Atlantic and New England states, had begun paying off their obligations. Virginia, most notably, paid down large portions of its debt by the somewhat circular means of issuing state currencies, paying creditors in that currency, and then imposing special state taxes that had to be paid in the same state currency.[5]

Hamilton had a radically different idea. Instead of eliminating the debt by paying it off or defaulting, he wanted to consolidate it all upon the books of an as yet nonexistent national bank, then reissue the debt anew to private lenders and pay those creditors regular interest, and then, by means of all this, use the national debt as money. His vision was driven by what he called the "decisive experience" of the Bank of England. There were indeed suggestive historical parallels: that bank was created just as England was emerging from a multidecade period of violent crisis that culminated in political revolution. It would go on to play a key role in both establishing domestic stability and fueling Britain's rise to world dominance.

The Bank of England's formation began in 1694 with a royal charter of incorporation and a pool of *private* investment of £1.2 million generated by selling shares in the bank. Next, that entire sum was loaned to the government, which had agreed in advance to pay 8 percent annual interest, tax-free, plus an annual management fee of £4,000 to the bank's directors. The bank's charter permitted it to accept deposits from the public and issue banknotes; essentially checks that circulated as privately issued paper currency. The government, in turn, would service its debts to the bank from its tax revenues. The Bank of England would thus maintain its liquidity by way of deposits and steady income from the government.[6]

The bank's strange mix of dependence on, and autonomy from, the state worked well, thanks to a form of divided government in which King William III shared power alongside Parliament, and thus could not unilaterally default without creating a major crisis. Parliament was very unlikely to condone default because it was full of men who had invested in the Bank.[7] Parasitic or symbiotic, whatever the case, the relationship was stable. Within two decades, the Bank of England was seen as so safe its notes were "as good as gold."[8]

The Report on Public Credit

Hamilton wanted something similar in the United States. The key to national survival was military strength, and the key to that was money. If this obvious fact needed theoretical justification, Hamilton could find it in the pages of Adam Smith's *Wealth of Nations*. Angelica Schuyler Church, Hamilton's sister-in-law but perhaps also one of his many lovers, had sent him a copy when she moved to London.[9]

"When war comes," Smith wrote, "there is no money in the treasury but what is necessary for carrying on the ordinary expense of the peace establishment. In war an establishment of three or four times that expense becomes necessary for the defence of the state, and consequently a revenue three or four times greater than the peace revenue." With the arrival of war "the army must be augmented, the fleet must be fitted out, the garrisoned towns must be put into a posture of defence; that army, that fleet, those garrisoned towns must be furnished with arms, ammunition, and provisions. An immediate and great expense must be incurred in that moment of immediate danger, which will not wait for the gradual and slow returns of the new taxes. In this exigency government can have no other resource but in borrowing."[10]

In that spirit, Hamilton began his 1790 *Report on Public Credit* by noting: "That exigencies are to be expected to occur, in the affairs of nations, in which there will be a necessity for borrowing." And "loans in times of public danger, especially from foreign war, are found an indispensable resource, even to the wealthiest of them." This was all the more true for the United States, a country with "little monied capital." Thus it was "essential that the credit of a nation should be well established."[11]

In the Critical Period, scarcity of money led to a classic deflationary trap of declining prices, hoarding, and stalled investment in the real economy. The *Report on Public Credit* put forth an expansionary logic rooted in cold military pragmatism. The public debt of the United States "was the price of liberty," and that gave "peculiar force to the obligation" for the central government to assume and manage these debts in a fashion that would facilitate economic growth. Hamilton maintained that the country *could not* default on its debts and still expect to survive. Any nation that would fight a war would be compelled to borrow. Thus, national security required that the United States establish and maintain good credit. "States, like individuals, who observe their engagements, are respected and trusted: while the reverse is the fate of those, who pursue an opposite conduct."

Already, formation of the new central state with its taxing powers was causing a recovery in the price of government IOUs. "A general belief," noted the *Report on Public Credit*, "prevails, that the credit of the United States will quickly be established on the firm foundation of an effectual provision for the existing debt." And "the intelligence from abroad announces effects proportionably favourable to our national credit and consequence." Then Hamilton made his request: the United States should remain, like the enemy Great Britain, a permanent debtor servicing its obligations with quarterly interest payments funded by tax revenues. As old debts were paid down, new loans would be taken.

How much interest should be paid on the national debt? Hamilton wanted 6 percent annually, which was 50 percent more than most European debt paid. This high rate of return for those who lent to the United States would effectively neutralize "foreign speculations" that might otherwise attempt to undermine the country's creditworthiness. A high rate of interest would harness foreign speculators to the aims of the state. Instead of stripping out the nation's assets, "their money laid out in this country, upon our agriculture, commerce and manufactures, will produce much more to us, than the income they will receive from it."

In other words, by way of Hamilton's so-called "funded debt" (that is, debt with a designated revenue source from which interest would be paid), faith in government could *literally* be turned into money. Hamilton was proposing a form of political alchemy: the coercive and administrative powers of the state—flowing from its files, ledgers, rules, courts, jails, and weapons—could produce from the minds of the population a type of confidence that would summon wealth into existence. In place of scarce specie money, paper representations of government debt could circulate as currency. Or, as Hamilton explained, "in countries in which the national debt is properly funded, and an object of established confidence, it answers most of the purposes of money." United States government debt could, also, be as good as gold.

For this to work, the debt had to pay quarterly interest so as to continually prove creditworthiness and thus attract more lenders. Here Hamilton drew on the writings of France's finance minister, Jacques Necker. For Necker, confidence in public debt turned not on the size of the principal but on "the amount of interest that the state pays annually." Necker even dismissed efforts to calculate the French national debt as "absolutely vain," akin to a geographer amusing "himself computing the time required for a cannon ball at constant speed to go from the earth to the sun."[12] Sounding almost like a proto–Modern Monetary Theory evangelist, Necker argued that the total amount of government debt was irrelevant, because all that mattered was the relationship between current obligations and current revenue. The more serious point, which Hamilton grasped, was that perpetually managing public liabilities rather than paying them off allowed government debt to function as a form of financial ballast for the national credit system as a whole. Gusts of speculation might fill the sails, but the system would not capsize thanks to safe public debt. Or, as Hamilton put it, the "good effects of a public debt are only to be looked for, when, by being well funded, it has acquired an *adequate* and *stable* value." If unfunded, it risked "fluctuation and insecurity," like a "mere commodity" and "a precarious one;" only if the debt was as good as gold could it "be rendered a *substitute* for money."[13]

In short, the funded debt was Hamilton's plan to hold close and harness potentially dangerous speculators and parasitic rentiers so that their self-interest could be made a catalyst of development.

The benefits of this debt-based, tax-backed credit system would be "various and obvious." First, "Trade is extended by it," because trade works better with adequate currency. Second, "Agriculture and manufactures" would also be "promoted by it," because "more capital can be commanded to be employed." And crucially, with growing confidence, demand for the public debt would increase and thus interest rates would ultimately *decrease* and "enable both the public [sector] and individuals to borrow on easier and cheaper terms." All of this would increase economic activity and, as a result, government tax revenues. By driving growth and increasing purchasing power, the funded debt would also increase the value of public lands, which along with taxes promised to be a significant source of government income. Thus would the virtuous cycle build.

To work well this plan would require a central bank. However, hostility to concentrated financial power being widespread, in the *First Report on Public Credit* Hamilton glided over the bank issue with a mere line: "The Secretary contemplates the application of this [borrowed] money, through the medium of a national bank, for which, with the permission of the House, he will submit a plan in the course of the session."

Assumption of State Debts

Having established the utility of a national debt, Hamilton turned to the issue of state debts. He wanted Congress to approve federal assumption of all outstanding state debts. And, even though these debts were trading at discounted values, Hamilton wanted Congress to buy up all the state debt at its full face value. If the funded debt was Hamilton's plan to hold the speculator class close and harness it to the federal government, his assumption plan similarly sought to bind the states, those fractious subunits of sovereignty, to the central government.

Federal assumption of state debts was, he argued, only fair. "Indeed a great part of the particular debts of the States has arisen from assumptions by them on account of the union." Thus the federal government, created by the generosity of the states, should repay the states. To sweeten the offer, Hamilton extended his plan to redeeming at face value "all sums of [nearly worthless] continental money now in the treasuries of the respective states, which shall be paid into the treasury of the United States."

Furthermore, the federal government should not attempt to discriminate between different classes of debt holders. In Hamilton's view "there ought to be no discrimination between the original holders of the debt, and present possessors by purchase." This proposal did not sit well with the many common soldiers, teamsters, farmers, and small contractors who had been paid with wartime IOUs but were then forced by poverty to sell at knocked-down prices. Recall that by 1779, Congress and the states had taken to paying soldiers and the vast web of suppliers with loan-office certificates, land warrants, and various state debt instruments like the Massachusetts Consolidated Note. Desperate for cash, many of the initial owners of such assets had sold them for a fraction of their face value to rich speculators offering hard currency. Now these new owners, who in many cases had risked little or nothing in the war, stood to reap fantastic profits.[14]

It was a totally unjust situation, reeking of inequality. "By 1790 only 2 percent of the adult white population held securities. Less than 0.5 percent held a fourth of all the nation's stock."[15] And recall the numbers from Massachusetts where almost "80 percent of the state debt made its way into the hands of speculators who lived in or near Boston, and nearly 40 percent into the hands of just thirty-five men."[16]

Forced to confront the unfairness of his plan, Hamilton fell back on the technical argument against "discrimination"—that is, sorting original owners from late-arriving speculators. Sadly, he had a point. Such a task was beyond the new government's bureaucratic capacities. Nor could such a project avoid being hijacked by schemers and grafters. If original debt holders were paid more than current debt holders, wealthy speculators facing discounted payouts could easily bribe penniless veterans to stand in at the moment of payout and thereby avoid any penalties aimed at speculators. The ensuing mess would be a bonanza for pettifogging lawyers, the courts would clog, sub rosa secondary markets in disputed debt would spread like mold, and government wealth would be sucked away from productive investment into endless adjudication. Worse yet, public mistrust and hostility toward the new government would metastasize into a culture of scamming. Faith in the soundness of government debt and currency would erode, and all of this would undermine the whole intention of the funded debt.

Another option was "repudiation," or default. That path was even more dangerous. If discrimination was administratively impossible and courted mass corruption, the second option promised international isolation. That would mean cripplingly high interest rates and economic torpor. Though the rich were few in number, the very concentration of their wealth made the risk of their coordinating to undermine the new government very real. To cancel their assets would invite a coup.

Thus, Hamilton saw the only feasible path forward as one that would harness the rich to the larger political project. As Ferguson put it in his classic *The Power of the Purse*, "the avarice of speculators was merely instrumental in Hamilton's mind to the creation of sound public policy. ... His scheme did not confirm maximum benefits on the creditors, but it offered enough, presumably to satisfy them and raise the value of securities."[17] The only solution, as the secretary saw it: all public debts should be paid at face value. It was unfair yet inescapable.

Viewed from the vantage point of state governments, Hamilton's assumption plan constituted a massive bailout. But it was also a financial power grab by the federal government. At the Constitutional Convention, Hamilton had proposed abolishing the states, and he knew that assumption would in the long run undermine their financial independence and establish the federal government as the center of a national credit system.[18]

Funding the Debt

How would the federal government afford to buy state debts? Hamilton's proposal: a massive foreign loan taken against the good name and vast, as yet uncolonized western lands of the United States. What about the country's outstanding foreign loans? "With regard to the installments of the foreign debt, these, in the opinion of the Secretary, ought to be paid by new loans abroad." The new loans would pay off old loans, thus maintaining the good credit of the nation and insuring lower interest rates, and, going forward, the new loans would be serviced with income from taxes "on wines, spirits, including those distilled within the United States, teas and coffee." Hamilton proposed that all stills be taxed. He justified his proto–sin taxes in familiar terms: the consumption of underpriced luxuries was "carried to an extreme, which is truly to be regretted," because such excess damaged "the health and the morals" and "the œconomy of the community." Taxes would be collected twice, once at ports (which is to say from shippers and merchants) and again by interior inspectors (which is to say from consumers). To enforce his tax regime, Hamilton convinced Congress to fund construction and operation of a fleet of ten swift coastal cutters to suppress the otherwise robust American pastime of smuggling.[19]

Crucial to Hamilton's argument was the idea that offering high interest rates would eventually create low interest rates. "The Secretary conceives, that there is good reason to believe, if effectual measures are taken to establish public credit, that the government rate of interest in the United States, will, in a very short time, fall at least as low as five per cent" and before long "will sink still lower, probably to four."[20]

Backlash and Compromise of 1790

For many Americans, this alchemical plan to transform administrative and military capacity into economic confidence and then into actual money was too much to fathom. The merchants in regional towns were happy if they owed public debt, but most did not. Southern farmers, large and small, shared a common problem: income arrived seasonally with the harvest, while expenditures were constant. Therefore, even the wealthy lived in debt. Due in part to slavery, the South had few banks. Slaves served not only as sources of labor power but also as stores of value—moveable, alienable, and to some extent, fungible repositories of wealth. As James Oakes put it in *The Ruling Race*, "As capital, slaves became useful instruments of barter in the economy of the colonial South." He goes on to cite advertisements offering land for sale by owners ready to accept "Money, or young Negroes"; or "tobacco, hogs, negroes, or money."[21] Storing wealth in, and clearing accounts with, human beings had the effect of retarding the growth of Southern banking. Thus, planters depended on Yankee and foreign banks, and that imbalance nurtured a bank phobia. Southern politicians tended to greet Hamilton's plans with deep suspicion.

The popular classes—urban craftsmen, mechanics, sailors, odd-jobbing laborers, and small farmers—still hurting from the tax-driven austerity, bailiff justice, and economic humiliations of the Critical Period, correctly saw Hamilton's plan to tax tea, coffee, and alcohol as very unfair.

To Hamilton's dismay, his plan was attacked from all sides. Even Madison, with whom Hamilton had collaborated so closely, now turned on him. In 1789, Virginia was under the control of anti-Federalists led by Henry Lee. Denied appointment to the U.S. Senate, Madison had to run for the House of Representatives, and in so doing pandered to the sentiments of Virginia voters.[22] As already noted, there were morally valid objections to the assumption plan, in particular its failure to remedy the injustice of the redistribution of debt from those who had earned it by wartime service to the rich who purchased it at knockdown prices as a means of speculation. But it seems Madison opposed assumption so as to curry favor with the bank-phobic freeholders of his home state.[23]

Hamilton's *Report on Public Credit* was introduced in early January 1790, but a decision on assumption was not immediately forthcoming, as the process in Congress appeared stuck as winter gave way to spring and then early summer. Federal assumption appeared doomed.

The deadlock was finally broken, thanks in part to a fortuitous encounter outside the president's house in New York City, the nation's temporary capital. Secretary of State Thomas Jefferson, who had been away from New York for most of the assumption controversy, happened upon the "somber, haggard & dejected" Treasury secretary.[24] Perhaps naïvely, Hamilton poured out his frustrations to Jefferson and bore down on him about the necessity of federal assumption of state debts. As the story goes, Jefferson agreed to arrange a dinner for Madison, Hamilton, and himself at which the three discussed solutions to the impasse. The dinner was held sometime in June 1790, or as a later revelation seems to suggest, maybe it was Hamilton's trusted assistant Tench Coxe who attended, and maybe it wasn't a dinner but rather an afternoon spent sailing in the harbor.[25] Regardless, a quid pro quo was agreed to: if Hamilton used his clout to push for the permanent federal capital to be constructed on the banks of the Potomac adjacent to Virginia, Madison and Jefferson would use their influence to force Congress to approve the assumption plan. In exchange for the votes of the Pennsylvania delegation, which were needed for assumption to pass, Philadelphia would host the national capital for ten years while the new federal district was under construction.[26]

Later, when the financial system was up and running, a very pleased Daniel Webster offered this joking appreciation of the secretary's work: "He smote the rock of the natural resources, and abundant streams of revenue gushed forth. He touched the dead corpse of Public Credit, and it sprang upon its feet. The fabled birth of Minerva from the brain of Jove was hardly more sudden or more perfect than the financial system of the United States as it burst forth from the conception of Alexander Hamilton."[27]

12

The Bank Uniting Sword and Purse

With assumption assured, Hamilton made his pitch for a national bank. On December 13, 1790, almost a year after proposing assumption, Hamilton presented the *Second Report on the Further Provision Necessary for Establishing Public Credit*, better known as the *Report on a National Bank*. In it, he explained the "principal advantages of a [central] Bank" and, by extension, of a banking system. The main advantage, essentially stated, was a banking system's ability to create a form of stable money that could be abundant yet not suffer rapid devaluation. Despite previous hyperinflation, the problem in 1790 was deflation. As Hamilton put it, "stagnation is a natural consequence of an inadequate medium."[1]

Hamilton's bank would unlock productive potential by making savings that would otherwise be hoarded as gold or silver available as currency. Circulating as paper currency, this wealth would help finance production and consumption. The *Report on the Bank* explained to a confused and suspicious Congress the basic functions of banking; that is, how banks safely store wealth while at the same time put wealth into circulation. Or how banks allow money to effectively exist in two places simultaneously. Put differently, he explained what modern economists now call fractional-reserve banking and the creation of so-called bank money. This is when banks hold only a fraction of their customers' deposits as reserves while loaning out the majority. Because both depositors (essentially, the lenders) and borrowers can write checks against the same sum, this style of banking creates new money. Hamilton explained it as follows: "Gold and Silver, when they are employed merely as the instruments of exchange and alienation, have been not improperly denominated dead Stock; but when deposited in Banks, to become the basis of a paper circulation, which takes their character and place, as the signs or representatives of value, they then acquire life, or, in other words, an active and productive quality."

To illustrate this "subtil and abstract" idea, Hamilton asked his readers to imagine "the money, which a merchant keeps in his chest." This hoard, awaiting an opportunity to be employed, "produces nothing 'till that opportunity arrives." But, if "instead of locking it up in this manner, he either deposits it in a Bank, or invests it in the Stock of a Bank, it yields a profit, during the interval." Meanwhile, the merchant's "money thus deposited or invested, is a fund, upon which himself and others can borrow." Thus, banks offered the same savings function of hoarding actual species coin, yet overcame the growth-killing impacts of actual hoarding. "The money of one individual, while he is waiting for an opportunity to employ it … [can] administer to the wants of others, without being put out of his own reach." This allows saving wealth without decreasing the money supply.

"It is a well established fact," Hamilton explained, "that Banks in good credit can circulate a far greater sum than the actual quantum of their capital in Gold & Silver." Because, as Hamilton explained, every "loan, which a Bank makes is, in its first shape, a credit given to the borrower" which the bank "stands ready to pay … in gold or silver … But, in a great number of cases, no actual payment is made … The borrower … transfers his credit to some other person, to whom he has a payment to make …" that person, "in his turn, is as often content with a similar credit, because he is satisfied, that he can, whenever he pleases, either convert it into cash, or pass it to some other hand, as an equivalent for it. And in this manner the credit keeps circulating, performing in every stage the office of money. … Thus large sums are lent and paid, frequently through a variety of hands, without the intervention of a single piece of coin." Here Hamilton anticipates by about a century the idea of endogenous money, or the idea that lending and borrowing creates money.

By introducing "greater plenty of money," a central bank would release the economy from deflationary stagnation and reduce the friction associated with clearing accounts by means of barter. It would also "facilitate the payment of taxes" and be of use "to business of every kind."

Why a central bank partially owned by the state rather than scattered private banks and a government-owned printing press for money? Because, as the second report explains, "the stamping of paper is an operation so much easier than the laying of taxes, that a government, in the practice of paper emissions, would rarely fail in any such emergency to indulge itself too far." Banknotes, essentially circulating bank checks or promissory notes from banks pledging to pay the owner of the note its value in gold or silver, offered a plentiful form of de facto money. Banknotes were a happy medium between two problems. The first problem avoided was that of hyperinflation—too much unbacked paper money, as had occurred with the overproduction of Continental dollars. The other problem avoided was that of deflation, or inadequate sums of money in circulation, which could cause falling prices and the hoarding of money rather than its investment and spending, which in turn can lead to economic contraction.

A central bank would also help the government in "obtaining pecuniary aids, especially in sudden emergencies." Adam Smith's insight on the link between war and borrowing got to the heart of this matter: state power rests on force, force costs money, and during military emergencies it costs lots of money, all at once. As Hamilton saw it, America's few existing private banks would be inadequate if and when military emergency arrived. There were, after all, only three banks: the Bank of North America, started by Robert Morris in Philadelphia; the Bank of New York; and the Bank of Massachusetts, in Boston. Only the largest of these, the Bank of North America, had direct relations with the federal government. And despite the continental scope of its name, it was merely a regional operation. By Hamilton's estimation, the Bank of North

America held no more than 20 percent of the capital required for a proper central bank. "So small a capital promises neither the requisite aid to government, nor the requisite security to the community. It may answer very well the purposes of local accommodation, but is an inadequate foundation for ... the United States" as a whole.

Furthermore, these private banks were designed to serve their investors, *not* some abstraction called "the national interest." Hamilton wanted a bank that, like the Bank of England, would be private enough to be autonomous of political meddling, yet public enough to serve purposes other than the immediate economic interests of its stockholders. "Public utility" explained Hamilton, "is more truly the object of public Banks, than private profit. And it is the business of Government, to constitute them on such principles."

Next, Hamilton explained why the central bank he envisioned had to hold its capital in the form of money rather than land, or why it had to be a "money bank" rather than a "land bank." "Land is alone an unfit fund for a bank circulation. If the notes issued upon it were not to be payable in coin, on demand, or at a short date; this would amount to nothing more than a repetition of the paper emissions, which are now exploded by the general voice. If the notes are to be payable in coin, the land must first be converted into it by sale, or mortgage." Land could "only be regarded as an additional security." In other words, public confidence in banknotes depended on their ready and immediate convertibility to gold or silver. Land as collateral was simply too clumsy, illiquid, and not fungible.

Bank Structure

Finally, Hamilton "respectfully submitted" his comprehensive plan for the bank. The core components were this: a capital stock of $10 million, divided into 25,000 shares, each worth $400. The federal government would buy 20 percent of the shares, with the rest offered to "Bodies politic as well as individuals." Each share would be paid to the bank as one-quarter gold and silver coin and three-quarters interest-paying United States debt. (If, as Hamilton surmised, the new consolidated federal debt paying 6 percent interest proved to be a popular investment, it would be easily converted into cash and thus be as good as cash at staving off any potential bank run.)

The bank would have a twenty-five-member board of directors, elected to one-year terms. A quarter of the directors would be required to rotate off the board every year. One of these directors would be elected president of the bank. Shareholder votes would be based on the amount of stock each shareholder owned. However, to prevent powerful cliques from hijacking bank governance, voting would be progressively weighted against the largest shareholders. This would work by way of a complex, multitiered formulation that began with one to two shares allowing a shareholder one vote, progressing through various ratios until "for every ten shares above one hundred," a shareholder would receive only one additional vote. Furthermore, no shareholding "person, copartnership, or body politic" would be allowed more than thirty votes no matter how much bank stock they owned.

To insure liquidity, the bank's ability "to hold real and personal estate" would be limited. Such "lands and tenements, which it shall be permitted to hold," would be tightly vetted, lest the bank become a dumping ground for low-value and illiquid real estate. Real estate could be sold for cash, but never traded for different real estate. The bank would be otherwise free to trade various types of "bills of exchange, gold and silver bullion." When it made loans, it was never to charge more than 6 percent per annum. The bank would not be permitted to loan out more than the total amount of its deposits plus original capital stock. If the bank did overextend itself and failed to meet its payment obligations, the bank's directors "shall be liable for it in their private or separate capacities." If any of the directors feared the bank was becoming insolvent, they would have the right to inform the U.S. president directly, compel a general meeting of the bank stockholders to air their concerns, and there, resign.

Crucially, the bank *did not* have the guarantee of a government bailout. While it could hold government debt issued by the

Treasury, its own borrowing was not to be considered government debt. Similarly, its dealings with "any foreign prince or State" would be strictly limited "unless previously authorized by a law of the United States." The bank would be allowed to open branches "wheresoever" the directors "shall think fit, within the United States, for the purposes of discount and deposit only."

The Treasury Department would have the right to inspect the bank's books once a week. And every three years, the directors would hold a general meeting at which they would open the books to the stockholders and give "an exact and particular statement of the debts ... and of the surplus of profit." The bank's profits, if there were any, would be paid to shareholders twice a year, unless the directors deemed that unwise. The "bills and notes of the Bank" would be considered "receivable in all payments to the United States," meaning taxes could be paid with its banknotes. Finally, "no similar institution shall be established by any future act of the United States, during the continuance of the one hereby proposed to be established."

Like assumption of state debts, the proposed bank faced immediate and fierce opposition. Jefferson and Madison, echoing the fears of Southern gentlemen who were rich in land and human beings but frequently carried debts until the sale of crops, labeled the bank as unconstitutional and claimed it would benefit Northeastern merchants at the expense of Southern farmers and planters.

Eventually, the state logic of high finance prevailed. On February 25, 1791, Hamilton's semipublic Bank of the United States was signed into law with a twenty-year charter, a main office in Philadelphia, and eight branches nationwide. The bank raised $10 million in capital—$8 million from the private sector, $2 million from the federal government. For comparison, recall that Hamilton calculated the entire national debt as $52 million. By 1796, there were five state-chartered banks and eight insurance companies; all together these were worth only about $3 million total.[2] Only the new Bank had the capacity to act in a truly national capacity.

The Mint

In the meantime, Hamilton sent Congress another lengthy report on the question of establishing a national mint. For lack of money, many Americans conducted business through barter. This introduced a host of avoidable forms of friction: unnecessary carrying costs (i.e., the costs of storage), time lost to negotiation of quantities (in place of prices), and the time and expense lost to verifying the actual quality of the quantities of the goods being exchanged. Readily available money in the correct denominations as the "universal equivalent" would remove these burdens. In the interest of creating abundant coins of low denomination, Hamilton endorsed bimetallism: coins of gold and coins of silver. Being tangible, familiar, and rooted in the seemingly "intrinsic" value of specie metal, the mint proposal generated little hubbub or opposition. It helped that the spiritual chieftain of the anti-Federalists, Jefferson—who self-identified as a commonsense country squire—was fascinated by coins and supported the national mint. The mint became law and was established in the spring of 1792.

Macroeconomic Effects

In retrospect, Hamilton's multipart plan—federal assumption of state debts, creation of an interest-paying federal debt (i.e., the "funded debt"), and creation of a central bank and the federal mint—did achieve its stated aim of improving economic conditions for the vast majority by lowering the overall tax burden and increasing economic growth. The new federally anchored credit system broke the vicious deflationary cycle of the Critical Period. The money supply expanded. Interest rates declined. The costs of debt servicing declined. All of this revived investment and economic growth. *As a result, the overall tax burden on common people declined significantly.*

Historians too often overlook the scale of this success. As Max Edling and Mark Kaplanoff have shown, "It is no exaggeration to say that the tax reduction that followed from Hamilton's funding and assumption plans remains a neglected aspect of Federalist policies and one that has not been systematically studied."[3]

Comparing the taxation rate in eight Northern states for the four-year period 1785 through 1788 versus that of 1792 through 1795, Edling and Kaplanoff found the *average rate of taxation across all eight states fell by 77 percent.*[4] The four Southern states they studied experienced similar though less drastic reductions. The Southern numbers are somewhat skewed by the fact that Virginia had already lowered its taxes in the late 1780s.

Lower taxes also had positive political effects. In most of the Southern states, poll taxes for white men were abolished or, in North Carolina, reduced by 90 percent. South Carolina and Georgia retained the poll tax on free African Americans, who, it is worth noting, actually had the right to vote.[5]

Meanwhile, income from customs duties sharply increased as state authorities relinquished customs services to federal authorities. Records from four major ports—New York, Philadelphia, Baltimore, and Charleston—show that total revenue increased by 600 percent.[6] If this was unfair (and it was), it was no more unfair than the less accountable, less rational system of rent-seeking parasitism that had bound moneyed men and women like Mrs. Adams to their state governments.

Be that as it may, real security and social stability required a deeper economic transformation. It required a wholesale economic transition to manufacturing. As Hamilton saw it, that could only occur if government drove the process.

13

The *Report*

In December 1791, Hamilton delivered his *Report on the Subject of Manufactures*. The most visionary of the papers he sent to Congress, it is also the most overlooked. The reasons the report is not more widely discussed are apparent from the outset: it opens with an attack on Adam Smith and the doctrine of laissez-faire. It goes on to advocate subordination of elite interests to the project of economic development and state building. The *Report* is an interventionist call to arms, an elaborate justification of state planning and regulation. As such, it is fundamentally at odds with the economic theories dominant in the English-speaking world.[1] In many ways, Hamilton's *Report* is the unacknowledged founding text of dirigiste developmentalism; an early blueprint of what Alice Amsden called "late industrialization."[2] Though it is rarely studied in the United States, the *Report*'s influence is appreciated throughout the developmentalist states of East Asia.[3] Fittingly, the *Report* also contains the earliest published use of the word "capitalist."[4]

Modern politicians tend to fawn over entrepreneurs and disparage state action. But once in power, even the most radical free-market ideologues practice a form of bastardized Hamiltonianism. This reflects an important historical truth: capitalism is produced and reproduced by the state.

For Hamilton, the state was both means and ends. Sovereignty would create the conditions of its own reproduction; government economic activity would provide "the means of promoting such as will tend to render the United States, independent on foreign nations, for military and other essential supplies." Hamilton called his specific recommendations for government economic action to jump-start and assist development of manufacturing "the Means proper." That phrase should be as ubiquitous in American history as "checks and balances," yet it has remained obscure.

Hamilton's means proper include protective tariffs, import bans, producer subsidies, export bans on key raw materials, import liberalization for strategic industrial inputs, prizes and patents for science and technological inventions, government regulation and inspection of product standards, development of transportation infrastructure, and a central bank. By the early nineteenth century these tools and the agenda of government-led industrialization were known as the American School, and then the American System. Michael Hudson has shown how an interventionist state drove nineteenth-century economic development. Fred Block and Mariana Mazzucato have documented how an interventionist state is still central to the continual reproduction of American capitalism.[5]

The real story of American economic growth, if honestly told, would diminish the role of individual action, competition, and self-interest while elevating the importance of cooperation, collective action, and planning. And the blunt truth offered by Ha-Joon Chang bears repeating: if Hamilton were "the finance Minister of a developing country today, the IMF and World Bank would certainly have refused to lend money to this country and would be lobbying for his removal from office."[6]

Sectional Interests and the Balanced Economy

The *Report*, like *The Federalist Papers*, was shaped by the fear of national disintegration. Foreign invasion and civil war lurk ever present in its subtext. Hamilton's solution was economic integration. Thus, the *Report*'s first line of attack addressed the relationship between agriculture and manufacturing. Its second line of attack targeted laissez-faire.

Hamilton began by casting manufacturing as offering "universally accepted" benefits for all. Southern anti-federalists, on the other hand, disagreed; they feared that "the promoting of manufactures" by government would elevate the North at the expense of the South. Hamilton thus allowed the existence of "respectable patrons of opinions, unfriendly to the encouragement of manufactures." These opponents claimed that "Agriculture is the most beneficial and productive object of human industry." And, that this applied "with peculiar emphasis to the United States, on account of their immense tracts of fertile territory, uninhabited and unimproved." It was said that nothing could "afford so advantageous an employment for capital and labour, as the conversion of this extensive wilderness into cultivated farms. Nothing equally with this, can contribute to the population, strength and real riches of the country."[7]

This argument fit well with the self-regarding prejudices of rural landlords. Those needing theoretical backup could turn to the Physiocrats, French political economists who in the early eighteenth century came up with the labor theory of value—the idea that economic value, as in material wealth, was the product of human labor. The Physiocrats, however, held that *only* agricultural labor produced value, because "in the productions of the soil, nature co-operates with man."[8] Other forms of labor, in the Physiocratic view, merely transferred value and changed its form. Adam Smith, then David Ricardo, and finally, Marx would all develop the labor theory of value beyond its early agricultural confines.

The Physiocrats were also ardent free traders. Hamilton disagreed but summarized the free trade argument as follows: "To endeavor by the extraordinary patronage of Government, to accelerate the growth of manufactures, is in fact, to endeavor, by force and art, to transfer the natural current of industry, from a more, to a less beneficial channel. Whatever has such a tendency must necessarily be unwise. Indeed it can hardly ever be wise in a government, to attempt to give a direction to the industry of its citizens."[9]

For Hamilton, debunking the Physiocrats' fixation on agriculture and free trade was an oblique way to address Southern political anxieties. Many Southern elites feared that if the North developed a strong manufacturing economy, its population and political power would grow, and the privileged place of the Southern slave economy would be threatened. These fears were not abstractions; laws against slavery were being passed, and among the Founding Fathers slavery was a divisive issue. As mentioned in Chapter 9, at the convention Madison identified slavery as a key source of instability. Recall his comments about "the mere distinction of colour" facilitating "the most oppressive dominion ever exercised by man over man."[10] Or the comments of South Carolinian John Rutledge's implicit threat of secession: "The true question at present is whether the Southn. States shall or shall not be parties to the Union."[11] These conflicts helped poison friendships, most notably the close bond between Jefferson and the Adamses.[12]

Increasingly defensive, Southern gentlemen masked their sectional self-interest with complex and high-minded theories. Jefferson epitomized this when he disparaged manufacturing for its supposedly corrupting influences: "While we have land to labor, let us never wish to see our citizens occupied at a workbench or twirling a distaff. Carpenters, masons, smiths, are wanting in husbandry; but for the general operations of manufacture, let our workshops remain in Europe. It is better to carry provisions and materials to workmen there than bring them to the provision and materials and with them their manners and principles." Such were the anti-industrial moral pronouncements of a man who later used enslaved boys—"a dozen little boys from 10 to 16 years of age"—in his nail factory, perhaps the most profitable operation at Monticello, and sold his nails in the urban markets of Baltimore and Philadelphia.[13]

In the face of Southern sensitivities, Hamilton offered a deft parsing of the Physiocrats. "It has been maintained, that Agriculture is, not only, the most productive, but the only productive species of industry." Hamilton rebuts this by singling out a central contradiction in the Physiocrats' argument: "Inasmuch as it is acknowledged, that manufacturing labour reproduces a value equal to that which is expended or consumed in carrying it on, and continues in existence the original Stock or capital employed—it ought on that account alone, to escape being considered as wholly unproductive." In fact, the claim that agriculture was "even more productive than every other branch of Industry requires more evidence, than has yet been given in support of the position."

Hamilton's engagement with the Physiocrats' arguments grows long and detailed, all the while leaning heavily on paraphrases of Adam Smith. Throughout the paper Hamilton engages deeply with Smith, yet never names him. Hamilton is reported to have written an extended, now lost commentary on *Wealth of Nations*.[14] Strange by today's standards, Hamilton's quotations of Smith, while presented in quotation marks, remain unattributed. And even as the quotations track passages from *Wealth of Nations*, Hamilton's wording is at times slightly different. Perhaps this is because Hamilton was working from hastily taken notes, both his own and those of his assistant Tench Coxe, and perhaps at times from bowdlerized and haphazardly bootlegged reprints and extracts of Smith.[15] Or perhaps this was just the style. As Samuel Fleischacker explains: "Circumstantial evidence figures prominently in scholarly work on early American intellectual history. The founders hardly ever discussed their intellectual heritage explicitly, and in their writings, they often failed to let the reader know whom they were quoting. The arguments for Hume's influence on Madison, Hutcheson's on Jefferson, and Reid's on Wilson have been supported almost entirely by identifying verbal echoes, coupled with evidence that the relevant Scottish writing was taught in colleges and owned by American libraries. By these evidentiary standards, the case for Smith's importance does very well."[16]

Thus, leaning on Smith, Hamilton attacked the Physiocratic theory that all profits are just other forms of agricultural rent. Against their core claim that "in the productions of the soil, nature co-operates with man; and that the effect of their joint labour must be greater than that of the labour of man alone," Hamilton makes a very Smithian argument about the division of labor, arguing that "the labor of man alone laid out upon a work, requiring great skill and art to bring it to perfection, may be more productive, *in value*, than the labour of nature and man combined, when directed towards more simple operations and objects." In other words, the complexity of manufacturing labor might add more value than even the free "work energy" of plants and animals. (For a modern discussion of such questions see Jason W. Moore's *Capital in the Web of Life*.)[17]

This very same dynamic, Hamilton argued, would also improve labor productivity in agriculture by freeing the farmer to specialize even more exclusively. Or as Hamilton put it: "The labour of the Artificer replaces to the farmer that portion of his labour, with which he provides the materials of exchange with the Artificer, and which he would otherwise have been compelled to apply to manufactures."

Stating it even more clearly, Hamilton writes: "If instead of a farmer and artificer, there were a farmer only, he would be under the necessity of devoting a part of his labour to the fabrication of cloathing and other articles ... and of course he would be able to devote less labor to the cultivation of his farm; and would draw from it a proportionably less product." At a larger level, manufacturing would provide new and stable markets for American agricultural products. Agriculture's "real interests ... will be advanced, rather than injured by the due encouragement of manufactures."

A common fear was that government encouragement of manufactures would "give a monopoly of advantages to particular classes at the expense of the rest of the community." More specifically, the fear was "that measures, which serve to abridge the free competition of foreign Articles, have a tendency to occasion an enhancement of prices." Hamilton conceded that "the immediate and certain effect of regulations controuling the competition of foreign with domestic fabrics was an increase of price." However, once "a domestic manufacture has attained to perfection ... it invariably becomes cheaper. Being free from the heavy charges, which attend the importation of foreign commodities, it can be afforded, and accordingly seldom or never fails to be sold Cheaper, in process of time, than was the foreign Article for which it is a substitute." Nor should the opposition fear monopoly: "The internal competition, which takes place, soon does away every thing like Monopoly, and by degrees reduces the price of the Article to the *minimum* of a reasonable profit on the Capital employed."[18]

And there would be other benefits. Manufacturing would provide markets for the raw materials of the countryside, be they from farm, quarry, wood lot, fisheries, or mine. A robust manufacturing base "enables the farmer, to procure with a smaller quantity of his labour, the manufactured produce of which he stands in need, and consequently increases the value of his income and property." Looking abroad, Hamilton asserted, the benefits were obvious: "A country which is both manufacturing and Agricultural will be more lucrative and prosperous, than that of a Country, which is, merely Agricultural."

For much of this discussion, agriculture is not framed as sectional, even though that is clearly the subtext. Eventually, Hamilton shifts to more explicit language: "The Northern & southern regions are sometimes represented as having adverse interests in this respect. Those are called Manufacturing, these Agricultural states; and a species of opposition is imagined to subsist between the Manufacturing and Agricultural interests."

Hamilton granted that his opponents might have a point, in some specific cases, but not if one took in the larger picture: "Particular encouragements of particular manufactures may be of a Nature to sacrifice the interests of landholders to those of manufacturers; But it is nevertheless a maxim well established by experience, and generally acknowledged, where there has been sufficient experience, that the *aggregate* prosperity of manufactures, and the *aggregate* prosperity of Agriculture are intimately connected. ... the superior steadiness of the demand of a domestic market for the surplus produce of the soil, is alone a convincing argument of its truth."

The notion of conflicting "interests between the Northern and southern regions of the Union, are in the Main as unfounded as they are mischievous." Because "Mutual wants constitute one of the strongest links of political connection"; and suggestions "of an opposite complexion are ever to be deplored, as unfriendly to the steady pursuit of one great common cause, and to the perfect harmony of all the parts" because Northern and middle states' manufacturing "would immediately benefit the more southern, by creating a demand for [southern] productions."

To make this perfectly clear, Hamilton then listed raw materials in which the Southern states held advantages: "Timber, flax, Hemp, Cotton, Wool, raw silk, Indigo, iron, lead, furs, hides, skins and coals. Of these articles Cotton & Indigo are peculiar to the southern states; as are hitherto Lead & Coal. Flax and Hemp are or may be raised in greater abundance there, than in the More Northern states; and the Wool of Virginia is said to be of better quality than that of any other state: a Circumstance rendered the more probable by the reflection that Virginia embraces the same latitudes with the finest Wool Countries of Europe. The Climate of the south is also better adapted to the production of silk." Indeed, a century and half later Schumpeter would agree with Hamilton's suggestions that industrialization was good for agriculture. "In the United States the production of agricultural raw materials in general followed rather than preceded the development of the industries that use them. This is especially true of wool, which, in spite of many efforts by manufacturers, of protection, of the impulses given by the English war and by the growing demand for mutton, and of the introduction of the Merino breed (1801), developed slowly until ... it temporarily became an article of export. Cotton continued to be imported and also to be an article of transit trade—net exports began in 1794—until a growing industry almost impelled its production on a larger scale. The great investment in cotton planting in the South [was] ... a typical example of an induced development or of what we have called expansion into new economic space created by previous innovation."

All of this would improve the United States' balance of trade. "The importations of manufactured supplies seem invariably to drain the merely Agricultural people of their wealth. Let the situation of the manufacturing countries of Europe be compared in this particular, with that of Countries which only cultivate, and the disparity will be striking." Hamilton is here almost groping toward a theory of uneven development.

The Benefits of Manufacturing

Next, Hamilton defended manufacturing in its own terms. "It is now proper to proceed a step further, and to enumerate the principal circumstances, from which it may be inferred—That manufacturing establishments not only occasion a possitive augmentation of the Produce and Revenue of the Society, but that they contribute essentially to rendering them greater than they could possibly be, without such establishments."

In Hamilton's view manufacturing helped create seven dynamics that would encourage growth: the further division of labor and thus increased efficiency; "an extension of the use of Machinery"; "additional employment to classes of the community not ordinarily engaged in the business"; "the promoting of emigration from foreign Countries"; opportunity for increased specialization and expertise, or as he put it, "greater scope for the diversity of talents and dispositions which discriminate men from each other"; economic diversification, or "more ample and various field for enterprize"; and, again, "more certain and steady demand for the surplus produce of the soil."

Hamilton was seeing economic synergies and linkages. "Each of these circumstances has a considerable influence upon the total mass of industrious effort in a community. Together, they add to it a degree of energy and effect, which are not easily conceived."

Each point is then detailed. Hamilton begins, as did Smith, with the division of labor. "The seperation of occupations," Hamilton writes, "causes each to be carried to a much greater perfection, than it could possible acquire, if they were blended." The three principal benefits that the division of labor facilitates are greater skill and dexterity; economy of time; and extension of the use of machinery. It is in this discussion that Hamilton commits what is seen as one of his great sins: advocating child labor. In explaining how manufacturing could offer "employment of persons who would otherwise be idle (and in many cases a burthen on the community), either from the byass of temper, habit, infirmity of body, or some other cause, indisposing, or disqualifying them for the toils of the Country," he makes special note that "in general, women and

Children are rendered more useful and the latter more early useful by manufacturing establishments, than they would otherwise be. Of the number of persons employed in the Cotton Manufactories of Great Britain, it is computed that 4/7 nearly are women and children; of whom the greatest proportion are children and many of them of a very tender age."

Brutal? Yes. But child labor and widespread child poverty were then accepted as facts of life. Hamilton himself had started full-time work at age twelve or thirteen. In Hamilton's view, waged work for children and paupers was better than the alternative, no work and hunger.

Against Laissez-Faire

Secure that he had shown the value of manufacturing in itself and the benefits it would offer rural and Southern interests, Hamilton next had to explain why government should promote it. Hamilton now addresses the issue that is perhaps most essential to us who live in this age of unfolding climate crisis: the false doctrine of laissez-faire. Or as Hamilton put it, the "proposition, that Industry, if left to itself, will naturally find its way to the most useful and profitable employment ... that manufactures without the aid of government will grow up as soon and as fast, as the natural state of things and the interest of the community may require."

Hamilton rejected this assumption that to "leave industry to itself," is "the soundest as well as the simplest policy." Instead, he wanted to "endeavor by the extraordinary patronage of Government, to accelerate the growth of manufactures."

Why should government do this? Because the international trade system was not a level playing field. Powerful states with strong economies took advantage of weaker ones. Such adversaries had already "obstructed the progress of our external trade." This made clear "the necessity of enlarging the sphere of our domestic commerce" as the "increasing surplus of our Agricultural produce" built up "a more extensive demand for that surplus."

Under different circumstances, perhaps government's role could be smaller. "If the system of perfect liberty to industry and commerce were the prevailing system of nations—the arguments which dissuade a country in the predicament of the United States, from the zealous pursuits of manufactures would doubtless have great force ... In such a state of things, each country would have the full benefit of its peculiar advantages to compensate for its deficiencies or disadvantages." But that was "far from characterising the general policy of Nations." Rather, the international system as it actually existed "has been regulated by an opposite spirit." The same holds true today amid the climate crisis—incumbent industries such as fossil fuels do not welcome competition. Rather, they actively suppress it by whatever means possible.[19]

Hamilton was here as elsewhere using an amoral, materialist framework. Never mind economic doctrine; look first and foremost at economic reality. Due to what we might call the uneven and colonial nature of the world system, the early United States was, as Hamilton put it, "to a certain extent in the situation of a country precluded from foreign Commerce." Like many developing economies today, the U.S. was free to "obtain from abroad the manufactured supplies" it needed, but experienced "numerous and very injurious impediments to the emission and vent of their own commodities."[20]

This problem went beyond the question of British commercial power. "The regulations of several countries, with which we have the most extensive intercourse, throw serious obstructions in the way of the principal staples of the United States." And "the greatest obstacle of all to the successful prosecution of a new branch of industry in a country, in which it was before unknown, consists, as far as the instances apply, in the bounties premiums and other aids which are granted, in a variety of cases, by the nations, in which the establishments to be imitated are previously introduced."

In other words, laissez-faire was for dupes. Powerful states used political, legal, and military might to shape their economies. Hamilton's solution: Do the same. Use state power to bend, mold, and transform economic conditions. As the *Report* puts it: "To maintain between the recent establishments of one country and the long matured establishments of another country, a competition upon equal terms, both as to quality and price, is in most cases impracticable. The disparity in the one, or in the other, or in both, must necessarily be so considerable as to forbid a successful rivalship, without the extraordinary aid and protection of government."

All states used their legal and military power to shape economic outcomes. "It is well known," Hamilton wrote, "that certain nations grant bounties on the exportation of particular commodities, to enable their own workmen to undersell and supplant all competitors." These were the facts. "Hence the undertakers of a new manufacture have to contend not only with the natural disadvantages of a new undertaking, but with the gratuities and remunerations which other governments bestow. To be enabled to contend with success, it is evident, that the interference and aid of their own government are indispensible."

Crucially, government aid had to encourage entrepreneurial experimentation. As Hamilton explained, "the simplest and most obvious improvements, in ... ordinary occupations, are adopted with hesitation, reluctance and by slow gradations." Important economic innovation would not occur fast enough without exogenous incentive. Waiting passively meant technological and organizational innovations risked being "more tardy than might consist with the interest either of individuals or of the Society." The truth was, "To produce the desireable changes, as early as may be expedient, may therefore require the incitement and patronage of government." Entrepreneurs and investors had to be encouraged to experiment; "the confidence of cautious sagacious capitalists both citizens and foreigners, should be excited." To "inspire this description of persons with confidence ... a degree of countenance and support from government" was needed.[21]

Providing Labor and Capital

Among the objections to Hamilton's plan was a set of seemingly technical concerns. Even if manufacturing was beneficial, the United States, it was said, lacked key ingredients; the country's development would be held back by "scarcity of hands—dearness of labour—want of capital."[22]

"With regard to scarcity of hands," Hamilton argued, this applied only "to certain parts of the United States" because in other areas, there were "large districts, which may be considered as pretty fully peopled" and "thickly interspersed with flourishing and increasing towns." These areas already had "fewer attractions to agriculture, than some other parts of the Union," and showed a "stronger tendency towards other kinds of industry." In these urbanizing zones, the *Report* notes there existed "a vast scene of household manufacturing." Hamilton suggested that "scarcity of hands" could be overcome by means of increased deployment of woman and children, foreign migrants, and, critically, increased use of machinery. This was, after all, what was happening in England, where textile-manufacturing tasks were "performed by means of Machines, which are put in motion by water, and attended chiefly by women and Children."

These mills were even starting to break free of waterpower. As Hamilton noted, "late improvements to the employment of Machines, which substituting the Agency of fire and water, has prodigiously lessened the necessity for manual labor." Another "resource for obviating the scarcity of hands" was "the attraction of foreign emigrants."

As for investment capital, Hamilton had already laid the groundwork: a functioning national credit system that could entice, summon, create, and allocate capital on a scale not previously known in the United States. The "want of Capital for the prosecution of manufactures" was addressed by "the introduction of Banks," the recruitment "of foreign Capital," and the ultimate source, "a species of Capital actually existing within the United States ... the funded Debt ... This operation of public funds as capital is too obvious to be denied." Key to Hamilton's scheme was the publicly controlled, partly publicly owned central bank. Around this would arise a national credit system.

"Public Funds answer the purpose of Capital, from the estimation in which they are usually held by Monied men; and consequently from the Ease and dispatch with which they can be turned into money. This capacity of prompt convertibility into money causes a transfer of stock to be in a great number of Cases equivalent to a payment in coin." In other words, investors could use public debt as money. Though not stated explicitly, such investors could include government itself. Hamilton insisted that this "operation of public funds as capital is too obvious to be denied."

Then, in an oblique swipe at Smith, who in *The Wealth of Nations* asserted that such public funding was predicated on "the *destruction* of some other capital to an equal amount," Hamilton explained. "Though a funded debt is not in the first instance, an absolute increase of Capital, or an augmentation of real wealth; yet by serving as a New power in the operation of industry, it has within certain bounds a tendency to increase the real wealth of a Community." That said, Hamilton acknowledged that too much debt, and debt misused, could be toxic: "The debt ... may be swelled to such a size, as that the greatest part of it may cease to be useful as a Capital, serving only to pamper the dissipation of idle and dissolute individuals: as that the sums required to pay the Interest upon it may become oppressive, and beyond the means, which a government can employ."

Here Hamilton's argument foreshadows Ricardo, Marx, Keynes, and a plethora of later economic thinkers who grappled with the "realization problem." Put very simply, "the realization problem amounts to this: is there sufficient monetary demand for the commodities which have been produced to be sold, and sold at their value?" Or can all use values (in the form of useful commodities) be sold and their costs recouped, or "realized" as money? Linked to this is the problem variously described as overproduction, underconsumption, and overinvestment or overaccumulation. This occurs when the reinvestment of capital no longer produces returns because too much has been produced and markets are glutted, or because consumers (workers) are simply too poor to buy all the products on offer. In either case there is, by definition, too much capital stock relative to the opportunities for profitable outlet. Under such conditions a crash is likely: prices will plummet, investment seizes up, unemployment rises, consumption contracts, and the whole economy slides into recession. Various answers have been given to these problems, and most hinge on the question of filling the demand gap; i.e., creating enough effective demand to absorb all the potential output.[23]

In 1791, as a top official in a largely agrarian and still war-ravaged nation, Hamilton's solution was simple: invest in, and legislate for, a manufacturing revolution.

Manufacturing as It Was

About halfway through the *Report*, Hamilton turned to a survey of actually existing manufacturing, organized by raw materials. For example, "of Skins. ... Tanned and tawed leather dressed skins, shoes, boots and Slippers, harness and sadlery of all kinds. Portmanteau's and trunks, leather breeches, gloves, muffs and tippets, parchment and Glue." Then, "II of Iron ... Barr and Sheet Iron, Steel, Nail-rods & Nails," etc. The list encompasses eighteen categories ending with gunpowder.[24]

This survey, largely the result of Tench Coxe's efforts, revealed a plethora of workshops and small proto-factories that had attained "a considerable degree of maturity." But there was also "a vast scene of household manufacturing, which contributes more largely to the supply of the Community, than could be imagined." Robust household production existed in all regions, including the South, and from it flowed a great quantity of textiles. Again, an exhaustive list followed: "coarse cloths, coatings, serges, and flannels, linsey Woolseys, hosiery of Wool, cotton & thread, coarse fustians, jeans and Muslins, checked and striped cotton and linen goods, bed ticks, Coverlets and Counterpanes, Tow linens, coarse shirtings, sheetings, toweling and table linen, and various mixtures of wool and cotton, and of Cotton & flax ..."

This household-based production was not only "sufficient for the supply of the families" but also produced "for sale, and (even in some cases) for exportation." *The Report* estimated that in some areas up to "4/5 of all the clothing of the Inhabitants are made by themselves."

Nor was this household-based petty commodity production restricted to textiles. Household manufacturing also turned out "flour, pot & pearl ash, Pitch, tar, turpentine and the like." Thus, the doubters who would "question the probability of success" in manufacturing efforts need only look at what was already underway. In all of this, Hamilton was attempting to show that manufacturing was indigenous to the American economy and could coexist harmoniously with agriculture.

Hamilton's focus on an economic transition to manufacturing was, ultimately, a means to "the independence and security" of the new state. For Hamilton, national security was "materially connected with the prosperity of manufactures." A well-developed manufacturing base would offer "all the essentials of national supply." And it would produce the wealth "necessary to the perfection of the body politic, to the safety as well as to the welfare of the society." Failure to develop the economy would invite catastrophe, because "in the various crises which await a state, it must severely feel the effects of any such [economic] deficiency."

To illustrate, Hamilton reminded Congress of the "extreme embarrassments of ... the late War" caused by "an incapacity of supplying" American forces. A "future war might be expected again to exemplify" such "mischiefs and dangers." Action was imperative. The country needed "timely and vigorous exertion" involving "all the attention and all the Zeal of our Public Councils." In particular, he noted, the lack of "a Navy to protect our external commerce."

The Means Enumerated

The remedy was for government to exercise its legal and administrative powers so as to unleash the nation's latent economic potential. Then, buried in a rather clotted sentence, came the phrase that should be famous: "the means proper to be resorted to by the United states..." These means were "those which have been employed with success in other Countries." There followed an enumeration of the means proper, a list of dirigiste tactics, eleven in all, starting with:

"I. Protecting duties ... on those foreign articles which are the rivals of the domestic ones." Because America's "infant manufactures" faced higher production costs due to higher labor, capital, and transportation costs, duties of around 10 percent, "by enhancing the charges on foreign Articles," would "enable the National Manufacturers to undersell all their foreign Competitors." These tariffs offered "the additional recommendation of ... being a resource of revenue." A protective tariff would be legal, Hamilton reminded Congress, because it was "sanctioned by the laws of the United states in a variety of instances."

"II. Prohibitions of rival articles or duties equivalent to prohibitions." This "mean of encouraging national manufactures" was only fit to be employed when a sector had developed to the point that it was "in so many hands as to insure a due competition, and an adequate supply on reasonable terms." He reminded readers that the "taxation clause" of the Constitution's robustly developmentalist Article I, Section 8 gave Congress the power to "collect taxes, duties, imposts and excises."

"III. Prohibitions of the exportation of the materials of manufactures." If some imports could be outright blocked, or de facto blocked, by special taxes, then so, too, could exports of key raw materials be blocked. If used wisely, this type of law could secure "a cheap and plentiful supply" of rare and necessary inputs "for the national workmen." This measure was only appropriate for materials that might be "peculiar to" an exporting region, "or of peculiar quality there." The goal in such cases would be to "keep down the price" of strategic inputs. While this might help manufactures, this would hurt "some other branch of industry, generally speaking, [that] of Agriculture." Therefore, export prohibitions should be used only when "essential to the prosperity of" a "very important national Manufacture." Even if "those who are injured in the first instance, may be eventually indemnified, by the superior steadiness of an extensive domestic market," in the meantime their incomes would suffer. Thus, export bans "ought to be adopted with great circumspection."

"IV. Pecuniary bounties," or direct subsidies, were in Hamilton's view "the most efficacious means of encouraging manufactures," because among other things they helped diminish "the risks of loss, in the first attempts." If failure was a normal part of experimentation and innovation that later delivered positive outcomes for society as a whole, then the costs of such risk-taking should be lowered. Unlike import tariffs, subsidies to domestic manufacture avoided "the inconvenience of a temporary augmentation [increase] of price." Excessive tariffs could even lead to shortages of essential imported inputs, and that could have the perverse effect of undermining domestic manufactures by "destroying the requisite supply, or raising the price of the article, beyond what can be afforded ... by the Conductor of an infant manufacture." Alternately, if tariffs were too protective or poorly managed, they might allow monopolization, snuff out competition, or permit the survival of inefficient firms producing high-cost, low-quality goods. Hamilton wanted robust state aid for industry, but he was Smithian enough to see the heuristic effects of market competition in driving innovation and efficiency.

In *Federalist* 35, Hamilton had written about the dangers of overreliance on tariffs: "Suppose, as has been contended for, the fœderal power of taxation were to be confined to duties on imports, it is evident that the government, for want of being able to command other resources, would frequently be tempted to extend these duties to an injurious excess. There are persons who imagine that this can never be carried to too great a length; since the higher they are, the more it is alleged they will tend to discourage an extravagant consumption, to produce a favourable balance of trade, and to promote domestic manufactures. But all extremes are pernicious in various ways. Exorbitant duties on imported articles would beget a general spirit of smuggling; which is always prejudicial to the fair trader, and eventually to the revenue itself: They tend to render other classes of the community tributary in an improper degree to the manufacturing classes to whom they give a premature monopoly of the markets: They sometimes force industry out of its more natural channels into others in which it flows with less advantage. And in the last place they oppress the merchant, who is often obliged to pay them himself without any retribution from the consumer."

In other words, Hamilton urged cautious and intelligent taxation policies: "There is no part of the administration of government that requires extensive information and a thorough knowledge of the principles of political economy so much as the business of taxation. The man who understands those principles best will be least likely to resort to oppressive expedients, or to sacrifice any particular class of citizens to the procurement of revenue."[25]

The correct path was "to lay a duty on foreign *manufactures*" in strategic industrial sectors, "the growth of which is desired," and then "apply the produce of that duty" as a bounty to assist the competing homegrown firms.

Bounties could also unite "the encouragement of a new object of agriculture, with that of a new object of manufacture." For it was "the Interest of the farmer to have the production of the raw material promoted," and "the interest of the manufacturer to have the material abundant and cheap."

Opponents feared that bounties would lead to corruption, or what we might call corporate welfare. Thus, Hamilton made clear that he saw limits to the "continuance of bounties on manufactures long established." Assisting infant industry was "justifiable" and "oftentimes necessary," but coddling grown ones was "questionable policy." To those who charged that bounties were a waste of public money, Hamilton countered: "There is no purpose, to which public money can be more beneficially applied, than to the acquisition of a new and useful branch of industry; no Consideration more valuable than a permanent addition to the general stock of productive labour." In Hamilton's view, subsidies were essential because they were targeted and thus less market-distorting than tariffs. Throughout the *Report*, Hamilton sounds proto-Schumpeterian in recognizing "creative destruction" as helpful in spurring on economic development. Hamilton wanted neither to suppress competition nor let markets run wild; rather, he sought to manage and use creative destruction as a means toward the political project of building an autonomous and sovereign state.

Even today there is a common misunderstanding of this bounties-vs.-tariffs point. Following in the path of a remarkably weak article by John R. Nelson that cast Hamilton as not really a supporter of manufacturing, some writers point to Hamilton's desire to use both bounties and tariffs as proof of his pro-merchant subterfuge.[26]

"V. Premiums" were "allied to bounties, though distinguishable" from them. While bounties applied to whole classes of goods, premiums were targeted "to reward some particular excellence or superiority, some extraordinary exertion or skill, and are dispensed only in a small number of cases." Unlike tariffs, narrowly targeted premiums would not produce price spikes or shortages. As one writer put it, bounties and premiums offered "protection without protective duties."[27]

As for legality, Hamilton again reminded Congress of its new powers: "The National Legislature has express authority 'To lay and Collect taxes, duties, imposts and excises, to pay the debts and provide for the Common defence and general welfare.'" The term *general welfare* was, as Hamilton explained, "intended" to be "as comprehensive as any that could have been used." Readers may recall from the chapter on Article I, Section 8 how more explicit mention of canals and roads, wanted by Franklin, Hamilton, and others, was dropped on the grounds that "general welfare" plus "necessary and proper" implicitly empowered public investment in transportation infrastructure.

"VI. The Exemption of the Materials of manufactures from duty." The logic here was that it was "hardly ever adviseable to add" costs "to the difficulties which naturally embarrass a new manufacture." The one illustrative example Hamilton offers was of an existing "regulation which exempts from duty the tools and implements, as well as the books, cloths and household furniture of foreign artists, who come to reside in the United states." But his argument continued in the next section.

"VII. Drawbacks of the duties which are imposed on the Materials of Manufactures." These were tax breaks on otherwise duty-laden imports. Hamilton illustrated his thinking with this example: "Cottons and linens in their White state fall under" this description. A duty upon imported cloth was "proper to promote the domestic Manufacture of similar articles"; while a "drawback of that duty is proper to encourage the printing and staining at home." And once these manufactures "attained sufficient maturity" and were capable of furnishing what was needed, "the utility of the drawback ceases." Drawbacks were essentially small, strategically sited openings in the wall of protective tariffs.

"VIII. The encouragement of new inventions and discoveries, at home, and of the introduction into the United States of such as may have been made in other countries; particularly those, which relate to machinery." Hamilton called this "among the most useful and unexceptionable of the aids, which can be given to manufactures." Delicately worded, this section suggests legal protection for those committing industrial espionage: "it is desireable in regard to improvements and secrets of extraordinary value, to be able to extend the same benefit to Introducers, as well as Authors and Inventors." Meaning: never mind the property rights—get the technology. As always, the defense was a resort to *realpolitik*. Protection and patents for stolen knowledge "has been practiced with advantage in other countries." In fact, Hamilton and Tench Coxe were even then secretly and, under British law, illegally attempting to acquire plans for state-of-the-art, water-powered Arkwright spinning looms.[28]

"IX. Judicious regulations for the inspection of manufactured commodities." This, too, was "one of the most essential" forms of state action for the promotion of industry. It would help "prevent frauds upon consumers at home," and in the realm of exports it would "improve the quality & preserve the character of the national manufactures." Better-quality domestic products would help expand market share, or, as Hamilton put it, "aid the expeditious and advantageous Sale of" exported finished products and "guard against successful competition from other quarters." To illustrate, Hamilton pointed to the good "reputation of the flour and lumber of some states, and of the Pot ash of others" that had "been established by an attention to this point."[29]

Logically, "a judicious and uniform system of Inspection; throughout the ports of the United States" would confer the advantage of a quality reputation "to other commodities." Embedded in this argument is the simple acknowledgment of "the free rider problem" and "the prisoner's dilemma": capitalists will cheat unless prevented from doing so.[30]

"X. The facilitating of pecuniary remittances from place to place." This was an effort to create more integrated regional markets and even a national market. It had already been aided with the creation of the Bank of the United States and of the United States Mint to produce small coins and bills. However, more was needed.

Facilitating payment would reduce friction, thus "rendering more easy the purchase of raw materials and provisions and the payment for manufactured supplies." The "general circulation of Bank paper" thanks to the bank would help. "But much good would also accrue from some additional provisions respecting inland bills of exchange." These "inland bills of exchange" were promissory notes produced by a merchant or business, recognized as exchangeable within a given jurisdiction—essentially IOUs or private money. Hamilton wanted a nationally organized market for these instruments: "If those drawn in one state payable in another were made negotiable, everywhere, and interest and damages allowed in case of protest, it would greatly promote negotiations between the Citizens of different states" much to the "advantage of the Merchants and manufacturers of each."[31]

"XI. The facilitating of the transportation of commodities." This provision had perhaps the most far-reaching implications for U.S. development; functioning transportation systems "concern all the domestic interests of a community" but had an especially "important relation to manufactures." Again, foreign competitors warranted imitation. "There is perhaps scarcely any thing, which has been better calculated to assist the manufactures of Great Britain, than the ameliorations of the public roads of that Kingdom, and the great progress which has been of late made in opening canals." Meanwhile, the United States was "much in need" of roads, and though it had no canals to speak of, it did have "uncommon facilities" for their development.

Hamilton hoped that the few attempts at canal building then underway would "stimulate the exertions of the Government and the Citizens of every state." Anticipating the failure of private canal making, Hamilton offers the vision of a largely socialized, nationally coordinated, locally executed and managed transportation system. "There can certainly be no object, more worthy of the cares of the local administrations; and it were to be wished, that there was no doubt of the power of the national Government to lend its direct aid, on a comprehensive plan. This is one of those improvements, which could be prosecuted with more efficacy by the whole, than by any part or parts of the Union." Then Hamilton quotes Smith: "Good roads, canals, and navigable rivers, by diminishing the expence of carriage, put the *remote parts of a country* more nearly upon a level with those in the neighborhood of the town. They are *upon that account* the greatest of all improvements."[32]

Taxes

Clearly, Hamilton wanted the state to take in, borrow, and spend lots of money. Yet he was not insensitive to the danger of strangling demand by means of too much taxation and by regressive taxation that fell hardest upon the working and consuming masses that formed the base of the economic pyramid. "There are certain species of taxes, which are apt to be oppressive to different parts of the community, and among other ill effects have a very unfriendly aspect towards manufactures. All Poll or Capitation taxes are of this nature. They either proceed, according to a fixed rate, which operates unequally, and injuriously to the industrious poor." Hamilton was also weary of corrupt officials. As he saw it, tax laws too often "vest a discretion in certain officers, to make estimates and assessments which are necessarily vague, conjectural and liable to abuse. They ought therefore to be abstained from, in all but cases of distressing emergency."

Hamilton also worried for the investor class and saw taxes "on the amount of capital supposed to be employed in a business, or of profits supposed to be made in it" as "unavoidably hurtful to industry." Assessing taxes locally was open to corruption. But arbitrary taxes were also hurtful. What to do?

There followed a "selection of objects," that were subject to "five circumstances" that in Hamilton's view made them appropriate targets for taxation. His five parameters were: "the capacity of the Country to furnish the raw material," "the degree in which the nature of the manufacture admits of a substitute for manual labour in machinery," "the facility of execution" of the taxation, "the extensiveness of the uses, to which the article can be applied," and finally, a consideration of the articles' "subserviency to other interests, particularly the great one of national defence."

There follows a long and detailed enumeration of what should be taxed and why. Hamilton's list is organized by types of basic commodities but his discussion of them hints at what we might call leading sectors and commodity chains. The list goes: iron, copper, lead, fossil coal, wood, skins, grain, flax and hemp, sugar, cotton, wool, silk, glass, gunpowder, paper, printed books, and finally (as if for dessert), refined sugar and chocolate. Hamilton discusses all these in detail and suggests tariff increases that would move the target tax rate from 5 or 7 percent to 10 percent.

Ugo Rabbeno, a late-nineteenth-century progressive economist, described the *Report*'s tax discussion as follows: while "American protectionists demanded protection almost exclusively in the shape of duties upon the importation of foreign goods [...] Hamilton, although he accepted such duties as proper means to the end, and even recommended them to Congress, still attached much greater importance to bounties and premiums to be granted directly to the various branches of industry, and insisted on the adoption of them either exclusively or conjointly with the customs duties."[33] Congress accepted a small part of Hamilton's proposed measures. By one estimate the average duty *ad valorem* in 1789 was around 8 percent. By 1792, after the *Report* and two alterations of the rate, the average tariff was around 13 percent.[34]

Overall, Rabbeno characterizes the *Report* as having a limited immediate impact: "The theory of protectionism contained in it is truly remarkable, but it seems to us that the vigour with which Hamilton advocated its application in the United States was not consistent with the very mild nature of the practical proposals which he presented to Congress, and which were only to a small extent approved. Hamilton's *Report* has been the foundation and authority upon which afterwards were laid the arguments of all the American protectionists ... which proves further that it had more scientific and historical importance than influence in the commercial policy of his country."[35] As we shall see in the concluding chapters, even Rabbeno, a fan of the *Report*, somewhat underestimates its afterlife.

Final Proposal

In the last paragraphs of the *Report*, Hamilton requests creation of a government-funded "Board, to be established, for promoting Arts, Agriculture, Manufactures and Commerce." This board would invest in the development of science and the recruitment of skilled labor and "defray the expenses of the emigration of Artists, and Manufacturers in particular branches of extraordinary importance." It would also "induce the prosecution and introduction of useful discoveries, inventions and improvements, by proportionate rewards, judiciously held out and applied." The board would "encourage by premiums both honorable and lucrative the exertions of individuals, And of classes, in relation to the several objects, they are charged with promoting"; and it would "afford such other aids ... as may be generally designated by law."

Here at the end of the report, Hamilton was, rather sneakily, proposing a massively powerful Board of Economic Planning. Though not as statist as the USSR's *Gosplan* (State Planning Committee), Hamilton's proposed board sounds a lot like one of the greatest developmentalist bureaucracies in world history: postwar Japan's famously effective Ministry of International Trade and Industry (MITI).[36]

In his closing lines, Hamilton made one last, pragmatic pitch for public investment: "In countries where there is great private wealth much may be effected by the voluntary contributions of patriotic individuals, but in a community situated like that of the United States, the public purse must supply the deficiency of private resource. In what can it be so useful as in prompting and improving the efforts of industry?"

While key parts of Hamilton's vision were achieved during his lifetime—foremost among these, the Constitution's strong federal government serving a broadly defined "general welfare," the federal acquisition of state-claimed public lands, the funded debt, the U.S. Mint, the First Bank of the United States—the more extensive implications of the *Report* were embraced only partially and haphazardly. Congress increased tariffs but rejected bounties. And for a long time to come, most development of internal improvements was carried out by the states.

And yet, ultimately, the *Report*'s logic would prevail.

14

Small-Government Apocalypse: Tax Cuts, Austerity, and Enemy Invasion

Opposition to the *Report* was immediate. In late February 1792, Jefferson complained to President Washington that "the Report on manufactures which, under colour of giving *bounties* for the encouragement of particular manufactures, meant to establish the doctrine that the power given by the Constitution to collect taxes to provide for the *general welfare* of the U.S. permitted Congress to take every thing under their management which *they* should deem for the *public welfare*."[1] Jefferson was not incorrect. Hamilton's economic designs were expansive and, viewed from the heights of Monticello, posed a threat to existing property arrangements. Ever since the Convention, developmentalist framers like Hamilton had indeed seen the General Welfare Clause as the crucial loophole through which they would drive total economic transformation.

Madison—stung by electoral defeat in Virginia and now an increasingly hostile, small-government partisan—joined the attack. In March 1792, he sent a copy of the *Report* to Henry Lee III, father of Robert E. Lee. "What think you of the commentary ... on the terms 'general welfare'?" asked a worried Madison. "The federal Govt. has been hitherto limited to the Specified powers. ... If not only the means, but the objects are unlimited, the parchment had better be thrown into the fire at once."[2]

Around the same time, Abigail Adams summed up the growing

hostility toward the idea of government from within the government as decidedly sectional: "there are Grumblers and antifeadelist,
but very few from the North. The old dominion is in a Rage,
because they could not carry the point of getting more than there
share of Representation in the Government all the attacks upon
the Secretary of the Treasury and upon the Goverment come from
that Quarter."[3]

As John C. Miller explained, in the *Report* Hamilton had recommended twenty-one increases in the existing tariff rates, five
reductions in rates on raw materials, and four specific subsidies
to industry. In February and March 1792, Congress incorporated
eighteen of Hamilton's proposed tariff increases and three of his
suggested tariff reductions on raw materials. Protective tariffs
covered Northern industries like the whaling and cod fisheries, and
the middle states' steel and iron production, but also the Southern
staples of hemp and cotton.[4]

There was, however, little after that. The board "for promoting
Arts, Agriculture, Manufactures and Commerce" never material-
ized. Nor was there a major campaign of road and canal building.
The developmentalist agenda moved slowly. It was hurt not only
by agrarian opposition but also by the Federalists' slide into
authoritarianism.

Responding to the Whiskey Rebellion of 1794, Washington
and Hamilton asserted overwhelming federal power against poor
frontier farmers who were shirking their taxes and beating up tax
collectors. It had to be stopped, but the massive federal reaction
carried the stench of despotism.

The second administration, which Hamilton was not part of,
was even worse, for it bore the character of its central figure, the
mean-spirited, begrudging, and self-regarding John Adams. As
tensions with both Britain and France mounted, Adams signed
into law the loathsome Alien and Sedition Acts of 1789. Though
Hamilton never formally supported these laws, he did call for the
deportation of Irish immigrants, whom he saw as blanket supporters of the excessively radical French Revolution.[5] Meanwhile, the
Adams administration grew increasingly paranoid and punitive,
going as far as ordering Republican editors and politicians jailed

for their critiques of the government! Shamefully, Hamilton, from the sidelines of private life, endorsed this repression.

Failure of the SEUM

Another blemish on the Federalist record was the failure of the Society for the Establishment of Useful Manufactures. Even before *The Report on Manufactures* was sent to Congress, Hamilton and Assistant Secretary of the Treasury Tench Coxe helped initiate a public-private partnership known as the Society for the Establishment of Useful Manufactures (SEUM). Planned as a complex of mills, the project was established at what is now Paterson, New Jersey, where the Passaic River spills over a cliff in a set of mighty waterfalls.

Societies for promoting industry were common in the 1780s; some were created by moneyed inventors and some by working-class "mechanics" or artisans. And like the SEUM, many of these efforts were not particularly effective. The idea for the SEUM is often traced to Tench Coxe, who, in the late summer of 1787, had helped found a similar venture called The Pennsylvania Society for the Encouragement of Manufactures and the Useful Arts. This Philadelphia-based society had a twofold mission: it was part profitable venture, part business laboratory. It was, in other words, something like a modern startup incubator.[6] Most manufacturing societies operated in this mixed, or maybe even mixed-up, fashion.

Tench Coxe was president of the Pennsylvania organization. Among its managers was the Irish immigrant and journalist Mathew Carey. Like his son Henry, the elder Carey's pen was a major force in American developmentalist political economy. Gathering funds through subscriptions of £10 or more per person, the Pennsylvania Society, or rather a subset of it called "the manufacturing committee," began textile production in the winter of 1787–88. At first, work was done using a putting-out system, in which women spun flax and wool at home. Then, in the early spring of 1788, the society built a cotton mill at Ninth and Market streets, complete with horse-driven spinning jennies for turning fiber into thread, and handlooms for weaving the thread into cloth.[7] The 1780s being in the midst of an abominably bad economic depression, the Philadelphia Society struggled. On March 24, 1790, calamity struck. The dry, dusty, fiber-filled environment of the mill somehow ignited, and the conflagration destroyed much of the factory, "causing a great abridgement of the means of the committee."[8] The loss of capital was devastating, and operations were suspended.[9]

A year and a half later, on October 25, 1791, Coxe helped found the Society for the Establishment of Useful Manufactures in New Jersey. Like its Philadelphia predecessor, the SEUM also faced difficulties, most notably a failed speculative stunt perpetrated by the organization's incompetent and unscrupulous governor, William Duer.

Though mostly privately owned, the SEUM received generous tax breaks (for example, all its property was exempt from state tax for ten years). It was chartered by the State of New Jersey and given the right to build canals, locks and dams, and to establish and control an industrial town—actually the origin of Paterson, New Jersey. Thanks to Duer's connections, the SEUM raised $600,000 by selling shares; the state of New Jersey bought $10,000, a Dutch Bank bought $25,000, and New York City speculators bought much of the rest. The SEUM hired a number of talented manufacturers, including one Thomas Marshall, who had superintended the operation of one of Richard Arkwright's mills in Britain. The famous Pierre Charles L'Enfant designed the town and waterworks.[10] As construction began, most of the society's capital was invested in government debt. When ready, the SEUM intended to sell its government bonds and invest the money in production.[11]

But the scheme faced immediate opposition. As Lawrence Peskin put it in *Manufacturing Revolution: The Intellectual Origins of Early American Industry*: "What most frightened the opponents of the [SEUM] was its proposed size. Such a large project could gain unfair advantages by wielding inordinate influence over the market for raw materials and through its power in the halls of government." Indeed, mechanics and smaller manufactures wrote letters often complaining, as one correspondent from Connecticut put it, that "building large manufactories at the expense of government … will create an influx of wares to our detriment."[12]

Before operations could even begin, the SEUM's governor, William Duer, ravaged the society's finances in a failed gambit involving U.S. government debt. To gather the capital for this campaign, Duer borrowed widely, including a $50,000 loan from the society itself.

Heavily leveraged, Duer and a small crew of allies calling themselves the 6 Per Cent Club tried to corner the market for government securities. This drove up the price of government debt to the point that many investors thought it was overvalued. Then Duer defaulted on one of his many loans, and suddenly market confidence evaporated. In March 1792, desperate selling began and lasted five weeks. The only good news from this economically and politically harmful debacle was that the Treasury Department managed to quickly right the capsized market by providing hundreds of thousands of dollars to banks across the Northeast. The banks in turn bought up beleaguered securities on the open market, forcing prices to recover, and allowing calm to return.[13]

The finances and reputation of the SEUM were badly damaged. As one author put it, "Duer's failure cost the SEUM $15,000 directly; indirectly, it cost at least $50,000."[14] Duer never repaid the loan he had taken, was sent to debtor's prison, and died there in 1799. The SEUM's manufacturing effort failed, but the society survived for many decades as a hydropower utility, real estate developer, and industrial landlord, leasing locations to independent manufactures. "Paterson reportedly had a remarkable 11 cotton mills in 1814, although few of the enterprises were able to survive the economic flood of cheap British textiles that entered the country in 1815."[15]

Ultimately the story of the SEUM lives on mostly as the whipping boy of small-government partisans, alleged proof that big plans always fail. More correctly, it is a story about the dangerous and parasitic nature of excessive speculation in relation to the real economy.

The Federalists were rewarded for their political bullying and economic incompetence with a massive electoral defeat in the so-called "Revolution of 1800." Jefferson became president and served two terms. His protégé and fellow slave-owning Virginian, James Madison, was elected in 1808 and carried the Revolution to its catastrophic, fiery, conclusion.

The View from Monticello

With the arrival of Jefferson, the idea of big government leading national economic transformation was out. As Jefferson had put it, "Let our work-shops remain in Europe." Of Smith, Jefferson wrote, "In political oeconomy I think Smith's wealth of nations the best book extant."[16]

The Jeffersonian vision imagined the U.S. economy to be fundamentally agrarian. According to that view, exporting agricultural surplus and supplementing imports with small-household–based manufacturing would allow for a prosperous and harmonious social order marked by low taxes, small government, limited federal power, and pronounced local political control. Jefferson, though not all his followers, was in sentiment a hard-money man, casting paper currency "as oak leaves."[17]

In Jefferson's letters, America often appears much like a great plantation, like Monticello, seemingly separate from civilization, looking down upon it, self-contained, backed by wilderness. As he explained in a later letter: "what might be wise and good for a nation essentially commercial, and entangled in complicated intercourse with numerous and powerful neighbors, might not be so for one essentially agricultural, & insulated by nature from the abusive governments of the old world."

In Jefferson's view, trade should be limited. It "may suffice to exchange our superfluities, for our wants," but it did "not follow that, with a territory so boundless ... to become a mere city of London, to carry on the business of one half the world at the expence of eternal war with the other half." More to the point, "the agricultural capacities of our country constitute its distinguishing feature: and the adapting our policy & pursuits to that, is more likely to make us a numerous and happy people than the mimicry of an Amsterdam, a Hamburg, or a city of London. ... such is the situation of our country. we have most abundant resources of happiness within ourselves, which we may enjoy in peace and safety, without permitting a few citizens, infected with the Mania of rambling & gambling, to bring danger on the great mass engaged in innocent and safe pursuits at home." The choices were "licentious commerce, & gambling speculations for a few, with eternal war for the many" or "restricted commerce, peace, and steady occupations for all."[18]

It was this essentially autarkic, patrician, Southern vision that led Jefferson to endorse the idea of breaking up the union: "every society has a right to fix the fundamental principles of it's association, & to say to all individuals that, if they contemplate pursuits beyond the limits of these principles, and involving dangers which the society chuses to avoid, they must go somewhere else for their exercise; that we want no citizens, & still less ephemeral & Pseudo-citizens on such terms. we may exclude them from our territory, as we do persons infected with disease." And, "if any state in the union will declare that it prefers separation ... to a continuance in union without it, I have no hesitation in saying 'let us separate.' I would rather the states should withdraw, which are for unlimited commerce & war, and confederate with those alone which are for peace & agriculture."

Even though this ideology of small-government Republicanism produced its own forms of tyranny and crisis, it is, even today, typically cast as more democratic than the centralized fiscal-military state of Hamiltonianism.

Despite the new administration's worldview, Jefferson's treasury secretary, Albert Gallatin, issued his own developmentalist *Report on Manufactures* that largely echoed Hamilton, and laid out an ambitious plan for federal investment in national transportation infrastructure. Jefferson, alas, did not support the vision. Gallatin's grand and admirable plan of eight major and several minor transportation projects at an estimated cost of only $25 million fell victim to a pandering, myopic, electioneering politics of localism. While many politicians approved of Gallatin's vision, few were willing to pay for it. They worried that federal taxes taken from their districts would be spent elsewhere, for the benefit of other people in distant locations.

Sovereignty on the Cheap

In his first address to Congress, Jefferson explained his plan: "We may now safely dispense with all the internal taxes, comprehending excises, stamps, auctions, licenses, carriages and refined sugars." Taxes on land, houses, and slaves were also eliminated.[19] Indeed, Jefferson eliminated all internal taxes while also reducing the national debt from $83 million to $57 million, and he did so despite spending $15 million on the Louisiana Purchase.[20]

Under these conditions, internal improvements fell to the state governments and private efforts. The private efforts mostly failed, but states using dirigisme in miniature made some headway. The federal government sometimes gave crucial donations of public land, but the bold vision of transformation was off the agenda. In 1807, when New York boosters made their first serious pitch for the Erie Canal, Jefferson declined all federal funding and called the idea of "making a canal 350 miles through the wilderness ... little short of madness."[21] But Gallatin managed to provide the project with a huge, essential gift of public land and, crucially, *water*. More generally, however, under Jefferson federal developmentalism stalled. The economic historian Richard Sylla summed it up with blunt accuracy: "Most of the Jeffersonian vision, based as it was on the misreading of U.S. interests, capabilities, and prospects, proved to be illusory. As implemented it led to a period of weakness and drift in U.S. public affairs."[22]

Jefferson explained his hostility toward developmentalist government in an 1802 letter to Gallatin: "You know my doubts or rather convictions about the unconstitutionality of the act for building piers in the Delaware, and the fears that it will lead to a bottomless expence, & to the greatest abuses." Jefferson was, in terms of political economy, a strict constructionist. He contended that "the power to regulate commerce does not give a power to build piers, wharfs, open ports, clear the beds of rivers, dig canals, build warehouses, build manufacturing machines, set up manufactories, cultivate the earth."[23] But of course, it did! The General Welfare Clause, the Necessary and Proper Clause, and all the seemingly prosaic details of Article I, Section 8 were then, and still are, the catalysts of the state's means proper. The terrible, awesome, and at times profoundly humane and just power of the U.S. Government is testament to this truth.

John Joseph Wallis has shown how after 1800, as the national government in the hands of the Jeffersonians turned away from development, state governments picked up the slack. "It was at the state, not the national, level that the critical interplay between political and economic development, between democracy and capitalism if you will, occurred. ... The states led the process of political and economic development." In fact, "Nine out of every ten dollars spent on public transportation investment came from state and local governments."[24]

Hamilton died in his 1804 duel against Aaron Burr, halfway through Jefferson's two terms. Hamilton had by that point retired from public life. Much like his close friend and possible one-time lover, John Laurens, Hamilton seemed to seek death. John Laurens had pointlessly charged British defenses rather than wait for reinforcements. During the duel, Hamilton *deloped*; that is, he threw away his shot, allowing Burr to kill him.

War of 1812

The period of Jeffersonian drift, encompassing Jefferson's terms and that of Madison, culminated in the catastrophic War of 1812. Still largely overlooked and misunderstood in the United States, the War of 1812 is one of American history's most squalid and shameful indictments of small government and states' rights ideology. It was, in retrospect, when the entire American experiment momentarily fell apart. Only the globe-spanning burdens of empire and years of war against Napoleonic France prevented Great Britain from re-subjugating her errant American colonies; or at least breaking the United States into nominally sovereign fragments that could be informally ruled as temperate-latitude banana republics, minus the bananas.

All lovers of small government ideology should be made to rub their faces in the excruciating and unflattering details of Alan Taylor's masterful book *The Civil War of 1812*. The war, started by the Jeffersonians, was a debacle from start to finish.[25] A brief account is in order. Under Jefferson, the economy was badly mismanaged, and rising tensions with both Britain and France hammered U.S. exports, shipping, and fishing. In his first annual message to Congress, Jefferson proposed switching the military to a "body of neighboring citizens, as formed into a militia." A radical reduction of the professional military followed. When Jefferson took office, the Army consisted of 4,436 men. During his first year, Jefferson reduced that by almost a quarter to 3,287, cut funding for the Navy by two-thirds, and dismissed over three hundred naval officers.[26]

With fewer American ships at sea, the British exerted even greater control of shipping routes. In retaliation, Jefferson imposed a total embargo on trade with Britain. The embargo damaged U.S. exporters, including Republican-leaning agricultural interests like Southern tobacco and Mid-Atlantic wheat farmers and merchants. Income from customs plummeted. To be fair, the embargo had some developmentalist effects: stranded capital now flowed into manufacturing. As Gordon Woods points out, "Before 1808 only fifteen cotton mills existed in the United States; by the end of 1809 eighty-seven mills had been added."[27]

The embargo, failing to deter the British, was repealed in March 1809. But the British continued to patrol American waters, search American vessels, and impress sailors—about 6,000 of them by 1812.[28] Meanwhile, American military preparations stagnated. For the militia, the "average number of training days dropped from six to four per year. In some states the militia became more a money game than a training program. These states commenced to charge fees against many persons whom state laws exempted from duty, and to collect fines with more vigor."[29]

With the defenses in disarray and little more than light coastal cutters for a navy, the menacing British presence grew closer. Soon

British ships were landing at U.S. ports for supplies and seizing sailors within U.S. coastal waters. A brief, disastrously lopsided fight between a British frigate and the U.S. ship *Chesapeake* was the final straw. Patriotic mobs rioted, Madison called for war, and on June 18, 1812, Congress obliged.

Now the nightmare warnings of the *Federalist Papers* leapt from the page. Weak, disorganized, and poorly led, American forces invaded Canada three times, viciously burning towns and abusing civilians as they went, and were repelled three times. A British naval squadron cruised the Virginia and Carolina coasts, landing to provoke sabotage and to encourage slaves to escape to refuge and freedom among the British. Once united with British troops, many African-American escapees from bondage were trained, armed, and then sent against the Southern master class. At Washington, D.C., American forces broke and ran, as did Madison and the entire government. British soldiers took the capital, looting and torching public buildings, including the Capitol and the White House.

The pillage of Washington was vividly recounted by George Robert Gleig, a Scottish seminary dropout turned army officer. The destruction began when a British detachment entered the city under a flag of truce to discuss terms of surrender. An American sniper opened fire, killing the British general's horse. With that, Gleig, explains, "Every thought of accommodation was instantly laid aside; the troops advanced forthwith into the town, and having first put to the sword all who were found in the house from which the shots were fired, and reduced it to ashes, they proceeded, without a moment's delay, to burn and destroy every thing in the most distant degree connected with Government." That included "the Senate-house, the President's palace, an extensive dock-yard and arsenal, barracks for two or three thousand men, several large store-houses filled with naval and military stores, some hundreds of cannon of different descriptions, and nearly twenty thousand stand of small arms."[30]

Also burnt were two publicly owned rope manufacturers or "rope-walks," a sixty-gun frigate, several brigs, armed schooners, and numerous small craft. Government powder magazines were blown up, destroying "many houses in their vicinity ... whilst quantities of shot, shell, and hand-grenades, which could not otherwise be rendered useless, were cast into the river."[31]

Through this devastation the British forces moved. The "blazing of houses, ships, and stores, the report of exploding magazines, and the crash of falling roofs, informed them, as they proceeded, of what was going forward. It would be difficult to conceive a finer spectacle than that which presented itself as they approached the town. The sky was brilliantly illumined by the different conflagrations; and a dark red light was thrown upon the road, sufficient to permit each man to view distinctly his comrade's face ... towards morning, a violent storm of rain, accompanied with thunder and lightning, came on. ... The ashes of lightning vied in brilliancy with the flames which burst from the roofs of burning houses, whilst the thunder drowned, for a time, the noise of crumbling walls, and was only interrupted by the occasional roar of cannon, and of large depôts of gunpowder, as they one by one exploded."[32]

Cockburn's Vengeance

When the detachment sent to destroy the White House arrived, "they found a dinner table spread, and covers laid for forty guests." In the kitchen, "Spits, loaded with joints of various sorts, turned before the fire; pots, saucepans, and other culinary utensils, stood upon the grate; and all the other requisites for an elegant and substantial repast, were in the exact state which indicated that they had been lately and precipitately abandoned." For the "party of hungry soldiers" this "elegant dinner ... after the dangers and fatigues of the day, appeared peculiarly inviting. They sat down to it, therefore, not indeed in the most orderly manner, but with countenances which would not have disgraced a party of aldermen at a civic feast; and having satisfied their appetites with fewer complaints than would have probably escaped their rival *gourmands*, and partaken pretty freely of the wines, they finished by setting fire to the house which had so liberally entertained them."[33]

Admiral George Cockburn (forefather of the modern clan of radical journalists who carry his name and of the actress Olivia

Wilde) was on land that night to oversee the destruction. In the Capitol building Admiral Cockburn is said to have mounted the Speaker's chair as if convening, and mockingly put forth a motion to the British troops on the floor: "Shall this harbor of Yankee democracy be burned? All for it say aye." The motion passed unanimously and the building was set ablaze.[34]

As one contemporary American chronicler described it: "The admiral was merry in his grotesque rambles about Washington, laughing at the terrified women imploring him not to destroy their homes." At the offices of the *National Intelligencer*, the nation's semi-official newspaper, Cockburn, presiding with what the writer called "characteristic brutality" and "Mongolian vengeance," ordered his men to destroy "all the C's" in the paper's collections of lead type "so that the rascals can have no further means of abusing my name."[35]

At the White House, which had not properly ignited on the first try, Cockburn—whose views on race had quickly evolved from typical to genuinely advanced—added a bit of justice and insult to the injury. He sent in the Colonial Marines, a unit of battled-hardened African Americans who had escaped slavery, to insure that the Madisons' mansion was properly immolated.[36] In the morning "nothing could be seen, except heaps of smoking ruins." Even the one bridge spanning the Potomac was destroyed.[37]

Such was the culmination of Jeffersonian small-government ideology. Lack of preparation led to calamitous outcomes. Luckily for the American nation-building project, decades of almost constant warfare with France had left Britain victorious but militarily exhausted; thus a proper reconquest of the United States was beyond its reach though it would not at all have been impossible.

My point is not that such a reconquest would have been good or bad. In many ways, it might well have been far better for the common American than continued independence; for one thing, it would have led to an earlier abolition of slavery.[38] Rather, my point is technical: the founders, be they Federalist or Republican, did not desire a British invasion. Yet that it is exactly what the small-government policies of Jefferson and Madison delivered.[39] Morality and ethics aside, by their own standards the Jeffersonian

Republicans failed. The nation was only saved from dismember-
ment and re-colonization thanks to external factors, namely British
imperial exhaustion.

If the lesson of this history for the era of climate change is
unclear, in your mind's eye replace the "Mongolian vengeance" of
the young Admiral Cockburn, the flames illuminating his manic
laughter, with ferocious tree-toppling winds, surging street-flooding
tides, floating cars, and a government response in chaotic default
and ruin. Then imagine the next day, sweltering hot, sodden, soggy,
and starting to stink of rotting garbage and the occasional corpse.

15

The *Report*'s Long Impact

Because Congress did not immediately embrace all of the *Report*'s recommendations there is a tendency to dismiss its impact. Frank Taussig wrote that the "famous document had little, if any, effect on legislation." Jacob Cooke argued "it was the only one of his major reports that Congress failed to adopt and that its subsequent influence (particularly on a protective tariff) is indeterminable." Stanley Elkins and Eric McKittrick wrote that the Report "was not acted upon at all."[1] But these assessments are too harsh.

Over the long run, most of the Hamiltonian agenda was implemented. Michael Lind was correct when he wrote: "What is good about the American economy is largely the result of the Hamiltonian developmental tradition, and what is bad about it is largely the result of the Jeffersonian producerist school. To the developmental tradition ... we owe the Internet and the national rail and highway and aviation systems ... federally enforced civil rights laws and minimum-wage laws. ... To the Jeffersonian tradition ... the United States owes the balkanization of the economy by states' rights and localism, underinvestment in infrastructure ... the neglect of manufacturing."[2]

During most of the nineteenth century, America was governed by, broadly defined, Jeffersonians. Prior to the Civil War, the developmentalist agenda was followed piecemeal by the states, which funded projects with state-level borrowing. After the Panic of 1837, eight states and the territory of Florida defaulted on their debts to primarily European creditors. After that, developmentalist efforts shifted to municipalities and local government.[3] But ultimately, the majority of Hamilton's proposals became national policy over the course of American history, largely due to the recurring crucible of war. Even many Jeffersonian anti-Federalists, once in national office, embraced elements of the developmentalist agenda, particularly protectionism.

The American System

The catastrophe of the War of 1812 forced the question of national economic capacity back to center stage. In 1811, the small-government Jeffersonian crew had allowed the Bank of the United States to pass out of existence. But in 1816, only a year after the war's completion, "the same political party and even the same persons who had refused to recharter the Bank of the United States ... voted to establish an even larger institution."[4] The bitter lessons of war financing, and the urging of wealthy creditors like the German-born fur trader John Jacob Astor, forced Congress and the Madison administration to tack back toward developmentalism. As one summary put it, "Between 1816 and 1820, Congress enacted high tariffs to discourage foreign imports and to encourage domestic manufactures, rechartered a national bank to facilitate commerce and credit and more reliable paper currencies, and championed road and canal construction."[5]

The Kentuckian Henry Clay was now emerging as a prominent champion of developmentalist political economy. Influenced by Hamilton's American School, Clay advocated for government-led developmentalism at the state level. In Kentucky, Clay's agenda was known as the Bluegrass system.[6] Others included the journalist Matthew Carey and, after him and with more elaboration, his son Henry Carey; also, the now largely forgotten economist Daniel Raymond.[7] In his 1820 book, *Thoughts on Political Economy*, Raymond praised Hamilton's reports as, "The only American book that has the semblance of a treatise on political economy." Placing his own book in that tradition, Raymond saw it as "a humble effort to break loose from the fetters of foreign authority—from foreign theories and systems of political economy." By "foreign" Raymond meant British. He saw the ideas generated in the fast-industrializing imperial core as "unsuited to our country," which was essentially trying to catch up with its opponent.[8]

Under Carey, Hamilton's "American School" morphed into the "American System." In Carey's work, national development also took on an environmental aspect. The economist Michael Perelman called Carey, "an important, although ambiguous, forerunner of modern ecological economics." Carey worried that lack of a sufficiently robust American manufacturing base and a consequent dependence upon agricultural exports would amount to an export of the country's fertility. Being the son of an Irish immigrant, Carey had a special loathing of the British Empire. He portrayed the British advocacy of laissez-faire in the name of comparative advantage as an invitation to underdevelopment and ecological ruin.[9]

The British, Carey argued sarcastically, were in effect saying to the farmers of the United States: "Cultivate your rich soils, and leave us to our poor ones. Labor being cheap with us, we can manufacture more cheaply than you do. *Do not*, therefore, *once and for all* build mills or furnaces; continue year after year to expend your labors in carrying goods back and forth; continue to exhaust your land; continue to have no combination of effort among yourselves. ... The time, however, will arrive when you will be forced to cultivate the poor soils, and then you will be troubled with overpopulation. Wages falling *you may then be enabled to accumulate the capital required for entering into competition with us*; that is, the poorer you become, the greater will be your power."

Unfortunately, Carey was also an apologist for slavery. His developmentalist vision combined an all-too-common blending of democratic republicanism and white supremacy.[10] One of his most important books, *The Olive Branch*, picked up on the *Report*'s themes of a balanced economy and direct appeal to Southern agrarian interests, but with the added twist of horrible racism and an explicit defense of slavery.[11] Karl Marx read Carey and detested his reactionary politics. However, as Perelman relays, although Marx "was strongly critical of Carey's theories, he still acknowledged that Carey was 'the only American economist of importance.'"[12] More specifically, Marx saw value in Carey's critique of laissez-faire economists. Prefiguring Karl Polanyi, Marx's summary of Carey's critique of the free traders was that they were guilty of "tearing society apart, and of paving the way for civil war."[13]

As Perelman points out, "Carey was not alone among U.S. thinkers in developing these ideas, which emerged in a larger constellation" that included the economist E. Peshine Smith, the agronomist George Waring, and the soil chemist Justus von Liebig.[14] The German political economist Friedrich List, during his exile in Pennsylvania, soaked up the statist ideas of Clay, Carey, and other economic nationalists. List would build upon Hamilton's formulation of "infant manufactures" as described in the *Report,* and from it build his developmentalist theory of "infant industry" protection. During the 1830s, the "American System" in the pages of List morphed into the more detailed "National System." List returned to Germany where he influenced the first generation of the dirigiste German Historical School of Economics and the course of German industrialization.[15] Against Smith's implicit methodological individualism, List argued for economic policies based on the collective interests of nations, even when such a path would inevitably harm short-term elite interests. He argued for German national unification, somewhat in the style of how early American Federalists had pushed for the Constitution and opposed states' rights. List pushed for national economic development, and what we might call a proto-Schumpeterian creative destruction, even when this meant harming powerful incumbent interests. "Canals and railroads," List wrote, "may do great good to a nation, but all waggoners will complain of this improvement. Every new invention has some inconvenience for a number of individuals, and is nevertheless a public blessing."[16]

Only during the administration of John Quincy Adams (1824–29) were such ideas briefly in the saddle. In fact, during Adams's tenure "more than four times as much money would be appropriated for [Internal Improvements] than in any earlier comparable period."[17] In his December 1825 Message to Congress, Adams

returned to the sweeping scope of the *Report*. Along with sketching a bold program of action by the Army's engineers, Adams
"extended his definition of internal improvements to cultural and
moral progress," including in his vision a national university, an
astronomical observatory, and an exploratory expedition to the far
Northwest. Alas, even supporters like the ardent developmentalist and now Secretary of State Henry Clay "thought the country
would find such forays too radical." The cabinet succeeded in
reining in the president's ambitions.

Post Roads

Nevertheless, during the Quincy Adams presidency, developmentalist intervention made progress, through the combined efforts of
federal, state, and local government. Internal improvements, for a
moment, again received federal aid.

Central in this effort was one of those generally overlooked yet
profoundly transformative clauses from Article I, Section 8. The
humble Postal Clause gives Congress the power to "establish Post
Offices and post Roads." As Richard John has explained, thanks to
that last word, "roads," the post office became a robust developmentalist force.[18] During the early decades of the Republic, the post
office was one of the most important institutions in the economy;
it moved the mail, lifeblood of commerce, and led a federal road-
building program. This road building helped open the interior to
settlement and investment and catalyzed the emerging capitalist
environmental regime.

The Postal Clause was operationalized by the powerful
Postal Act of 1792. This law facilitated three important forms
of economic intervention. First, it subsidized the movement of
newspapers, which encouraged the production, circulation, and
consumption of a popular press. Second, the Act prohibited postal
officials from opening letters, meaning postal officials could not
use their positions to conduct surveillance, which built confidence
in and business use of the system. Third, and most importantly,
the Postal Act expanded the postal road network deep into the

trans-Appalachian West. A follow-up act in 1794 perpetuated the
Post Office indefinitely. Early debates about the Post Office provided "arguments and precedents" that shaped all later struggles
around "internal improvements" and the role of the public sector
in economic development.[19] In 1790, the Postal Service had only
75 post offices and 1,875 miles of post roads. By 1828, there were
8,004 post offices and 115,000 miles of post roads.[20]

The government did not build these post roads itself but rather
solicited bids from local contractors who organized construction
crews and sourced materials. This sort of contracting not only
created landscapes and ecologies; it also created social relations.
In the massive and ongoing construction of postal roads, we have
an example of the state conjuring forth classes of employers and
employees. The carrying of mail was likewise a public–private
partnership; the Post Office did not own and run stagecoaches but
largely contracted with private companies and individuals, with
strict regulations, to carry and manage the mail.

In making roads, the Post Office also made, or remade, the environment.[21] Roads brought settlers and the biophysical metabolism
of market social relations. Alexis de Tocqueville marveled at the
post road system when he traveled with it across the Michigan
territory in 1831: "I traveled along a portion of the frontier of
the United States in a sort of cart, which was termed the mail.
Day and night we passed with great rapidity along the roads,
which were scarcely marked out through immense forests. When
the gloom of the woods became impenetrable, the driver lighted
branches of pine, and we journeyed along by the light they cast."[22]
As interesting as his description of the diligent service is Tocqueville's description of what else the roads brought to "the pioneer."
While his surroundings were "primitive and wild," the settler was
"a very civilized man prepared for time to face life in the forest,
plunging into the wilderness of the new world with his Bible, ax,
and newspapers."[23]

Yes, the ax. The postal roads followed settlement, but also
encouraged it. Just as in today's Amazonia, new roads inevitably
lead to logging, forest fragmentation, settlement, poaching, and
then more roads; so, too, were early American roads the agents of

massive self-compounding environmental transformation. Down roads and improved rivers came the settler with his ax, cattle, and diseases. As arteries of commerce, these transportation links delivered radical ecological transformation. Roads and improved rivers meant the final displacement of various Native American versions of nature, which used regular burning to create grassland and edge habitat. In came clear-cutting, mono-cropping, very often slavery, and soil erosion. Down the roads and rivers came grain, or grain converted into whiskey, and the quantifying logic of money.

Tocqueville noted this rapacious metabolism: "It is unusual for an American farmer to settle forever on the land he occupies; especially in the provinces of the West, fields are cleared to be sold again, not to be cultivated. The farm is built in the anticipation that since the state of the country will soon be changing with the increase of population, one will be able to sell it for a good price."[24]

Speculation, surveying, clearing, road building, and then migration repeated a constant throbbing pattern along the frontier. Again, Tocqueville: "Every year a swarm of people arrive from the North in the southern states and settle in the lands where cotton and sugarcane grow. These men cultivate the land in order to make it produce enough to reach them within a few years … in such a fashion the Americans carry over into agriculture the spirit of a trading venture, and their passion for industry is manifest there as elsewhere."

Roads increased the value of land, inducing speculators and their representatives in Congress to lobby for construction of ever more post roads. Where post roads could not be had, land companies sometimes went it alone. The Holland Land Company built roads where it had holdings in western New York, the idea being that rising land values would subsidize unprofitable roads. Some heavily used turnpike roads were privately owned and maintained, but it was very difficult to profit from such ventures.[25] Most roads in America were built by state, local, and, through the Post Office, federal government.

Newspapers, too, were an indirect product of federal subsidy, because the Post Office carried them at steeply discounted rates.

More precisely they were subsidized by merchants whose many and constant letters and documents made up the bulk of the mail. The central government was in effect redistributing wealth from merchants, surveyors, speculators, and slaveholders to journalists, readers, and citizens. According to one postal official cited by John, had newspapers moved at the same price as letters, their price would have increased by 700 percent![26]

Tocqueville declared it "hard to imagine quite how incredibly quickly ideas circulate in these empty spaces," even asserting, "I do not believe that there is so much intellectual activity in the most enlightened and populist districts of France." Later Tocqueville reflected on the unifying and state-making role of the Post Office in the nation that otherwise had so much tearing it apart. "The patriotism attaching each American to his state has become less exclusive. By getting to know each other better the various parts of the union have drawn closer. The post, that general link between minds now penetrates into the heart of the wilderness, and steamships provide daily connections between all points on the coast. Trade flows up and down the rivers of the interior with unexampled rapidity. To these facilities due to nature and to art may be added the insatiability of desires, cravings of a restless mind, and the love of wealth, which constantly drive the American from his home and put him in contact with many of his fellow citizens."

As John put it, "No other branch of the central government penetrated so deeply into the hinterland or played such a conspicuous role in shaping the pattern of everyday life. Indeed it would hardly be an exaggeration to suggest that for the vast majority of Americans the postal system *was* the central government."[27]

By the mid 1820s, John Quincy Adams and Secretary of State Henry Clay would almost turn the Post Office into "the headquarters of a national program of internal improvements."[28] Furthermore, the Post Office earned money for the federal government. It was in essence, publicly owned big business, a type of crypto-socialism midwifing the birth of American capitalism.

DeWitt Clinton's "Hydraulic State"

Although the American System was defeated at the national level, mainly by the same Southern interests that would later start the Civil War, much of the vision was operationalized by the states. New York State's construction of the Erie Canal is perhaps the best example, but there were many such projects during the canal-building mania of the 1820s and 1830s.

The story of the Erie Canal not only illustrates the critical role of the state in developing and continually reproducing capitalism, but also how that role turns on the management of nature. That is, the canal reveals the connections among nature's use values, state geo-power, and accumulation.[29] The Erie Canal connected Atlantic trade circuits via New York City to the Great Lakes, and thus the whole interior Old Northwest. New York City became the pivot point of a huge international network of financial and biological flows, and as such became the capital of American finance and, later, world finance.

The rise of New York City was, however, merely the urban manifestation of a primarily rural process; the radical transformation of a huge swath of interior territory. Great swaths of previously Iroquois-controlled land were opened to white settlers and their environmental practices. In this sense, the Erie Canal was a revolutionary moment, a massive rupture, a great leap forward in American capitalism's production of nature.

The role of government in all this was central. At the physical and financial heart of this de facto national project was a massive gift of public land, and with it public water. By one count, no less than 4.5 million acres of federal land were given to canal companies.[30] This land provided the territory and water for the canals, as well as land to be developed along the right of ways. The land grants also functioned as collateral against which to finance the canals. There was something else about the canals that made them state-centric—*the unwieldy properties of water.*

Few things in history seem to "call forth the state" so consistently as water. The peculiar link between water management and state power was not lost on eighteenth-century European observers.

The fact that water management is difficult and thus requires collective rather than individual action would of course later play a role in Marx's conception of an "Asiatic mode of production" and Wittfogel's concept of "hydraulic societies" and his problematically associated notion of "Oriental Despotism."[31] Without getting into the critiques of these ideas, it is worth acknowledging that water management demands collective action. This was the key political insight that allowed American canal-building mania. Only when the general cause of canals was taken up by the public sector, that is, by various U.S. states with federal support, did the dream of canals come to fruition.

Interestingly, written accounts of Chinese canals played an important role in exciting the imagination of American canal proponents.[32] Some of what they learned from reading about China's 1,000-mile-long, north–south Grand Canal linking Beijing to the southeastern coast at Hangzhou was technical, but just as important were the *political lessons* about the essential role of government in producing and maintaining this amazing waterway.

In 1797, the British diplomat Sir George Staunton wrote one of the most widely read investigations of China's Grand Canal. Staunton noted that China's Grand Canal was not the product of private investment but rather the result of state planning and investment. "This canal," Staunton wrote, "is not nor indeed is any in China, a private concern, carried on at the expense and for the profit of individuals but is under the regulation and immediate inspection of the government, whose policy it is to maintain an easy communication between the several parts of the empire, as tending to promote the commerce and agriculture of the country, thereby increasing the revenues of the state and the comforts of the people."[33]

As early as 1777, Gouverneur Morris "predicted the eventual union of the waters of the Great Lakes with those of the Hudson." He said this even as most of what is now upstate New York was still controlled by the Iroquois, most of whom sided with the British during the American Revolution. After the Revolution, about two-thirds of the Iroquois decamped to lands on the Grand River in British Upper Canada. In the United States, conflicting land claims between New York and Massachusetts were resolved in the mid-1780s. Huge tracts of land were given to land speculators, who in turn tried to encourage settlement. But they had limited success.

In 1792, the New York State Legislature chartered (the mostly privately funded) Western Inland Company and passed an "Act for establishing and opening lock navigation within the state."[34] Like many other private experimentations with canal building, the Western Inland Company failed spectacularly; one of its principals was even jailed. Jefferson denied New York's request for federal money, calling "talk of making a canal of 350 miles through the wilderness … little short of madness."[35] Similarly, Madison, though once the principal co-author with Hamilton of *The Federalist Papers*, soon reverted to type by defending planter privilege and states' rights—which is to say, the path toward *underdevelopment* —in the name of Jeffersonian democracy.

In 1817, New York State finally allocated money to start building the canal. Gallatin, though unable to provide federal money, committed plenty of adjacent federal land to the canal.[36] In all, the canal would cost $6 million; its primary contractor was the Canal Commission, a not-for-profit public entity, which in turn doled out work to local for-profit contractors.

According to Hanyan, the state-centric political lessons from China were as important or more important than any technological vision:

> During the next decade many states made efforts in this direction, building canals in profusion. These projects were carried out under government control, following the pattern set by New York State's well-known Canal Commission and Canal Fund. Drawing more heavily from legislative allotments, rather than private shareholders and controlled more by state commissions than corporate directors, these new waterways indicated that the day of the [private] canal company was passing. If not providing new methods of building, then, the oriental example played a part in this change. This was, indeed, but one aspect of a pervasive influence. G. F. Hudson has pointed out that China provided a model for European theories of enlightened despotism and influenced the French Physiocrats. During the Enlightenment, moreover, Ralph

Linton has suggested there was a burst of interest in Chinese philosophy and culture—an interest which subtly formed part of the background to the French Revolution. The Chinese ideas which percolated the experience of New York's canal builders worked with equal subtlety, but with equal force. To a New York provided only with the inadequate works of the Western Company, China gave the vision of a government-built Grand Canal.[37]

Completed in 1825, the economic effect of the Erie Canal was massive; the cost of moving a ton of freight dropped by up to 95 percent. As one classic book on the history of New York agriculture explains: "The canal reduced travel from Buffalo to New York from 20 days to 10, and the cost of moving a ton of freight fell from $100 to $5. All the farm products of western New York at once poured eastward instead of southward. ... Western New York flour could be shipped via the canal and the Atlantic to southern markets in the West Indies at less than $1.50 a barrel for freight."[38] Conversely, as the West opened, New England began its long, slow reforestation. Its old and increasingly worn-out farms were steadily abandoned in the face of Erie Canal competition. New York State, ranked second in agriculture after Pennsylvania, soon took first place and stayed there until after the Civil War.[39]

The historian Daniel Walker Howe noted that "the Erie Canal represented the first step in the transportation revolution that would turn an aggregate of local economies into a nationwide market economy."[40] Before long, the Erie Canal was carrying twice as much cargo as flowed down the Mississippi to New Orleans. Historians refer to the period from 1815 to 1848 as the "market revolution." In his excellent book on that era, *What Hath God Wrought: The Transformation of America, 1815 to 1848,* Howe prefers the term "communications revolution," partly because market relations were more extensive and more important to colonial society than once realized, and partly because the most important technological and economic innovations of the market revolution in early-nineteenth-century America were mostly focused on communication and transportation: canals, the telegraph, and railroads.[41]

Either way, the state was the crucial but often overlooked economic director of this drama, and the state-led market revolution
was also an environmental revolution. The famous canal-triggered
growth of New York City was only one side of a broader spatial
transformation, the rest of which was going on throughout the
Midwest. The Iroquois, like other Indigenous peoples in the East,
had practiced burning as a method of creating what we now call
"edge habitat," which is preferred by deer and other game. Burning
also facilitated food gathering and returned nutrients to the soil to
facilitate the farming of corn, squash, and beans.

Adriaen van der Donck, a Dutch chronicler of life in New
Amsterdam writing in the 1640s, described the practice. "The
Indians are in the habit—and we Christians have also adopted it
—once a year in the fall to burn the woods, plains, and those
marshlands that are not too wet as soon as the leaves have dropped
and the herbage has withered. Portions that were missed, as may
happen, get their turn later in the months of March and April. This
is known among our people as well as the Indians there as bush
burning."[42]

After the American Revolution, while a substantial number
of Iroquois remained on lands reserved in New York and Pennsylvania, a majority withdrew to land grants in Canada. On the
American side of the border, some white settlers moved in and
cleared land for subsistence farming. But it was the canal that
really opened this region and tied the settlers into broader markets.
Gone was selective burning; in came forest clearing and mono-
cropping of wheat and other grains. Isolated subsistence farmers
became wheat exporters, and in the process developed new types
of "natures." Mono-cropping would later invite fungal disease
and pests like the midge and Hessian fly.[43] To remain competitive,
Hudson Valley farmers had to put "all available land under cultivation, some of it inferior land that had been previously depleted."[44]
Ultimately, Hudson Valley agriculture converted from wheat to
dairy production. At the same time, Hudson Valley farmers intensified household-based manufacturing of barrels and coarse cloth,
drawing in and transforming resources from further afield.

Canals, as a development of the means of production, facilitated the extension and intensification of agriculture, which is to say they facilitated (*pace* Neil Smith) the capitalist production of nature. Much of the Erie Canal's freight, therefore, can be seen as not merely carried by the new waterway, but in a fashion conjured and created by it.

As Howe notes: "Wheat flour from the Midwest was stored in New York alongside the cotton that the city obtained from the South through its domination of the coastal trade; both could then be exported across the Atlantic. New York merchants began to buy wheat and cotton from their producers before shipping them to the New York warehouses. Soon the merchants learned to buy the crops before they were even grown; that is they could advance the grower money on the security of his harvest. Thus the city's power in commercial markets fostered its development as a financial center."[45] As such, New York was merely one spatial expression in an emerging "regime of nature" that had as a central mechanism the administrative power of the state, which built the canal, and helped create the agricultural economy of the Midwest.

The River-Making State

As soon as relatively swift steamboats began navigating American rivers, the central government decreed that they must also carry the mail. "Beginning in 1815, operators of steamboats and other craft had to deliver the letters and packets they carried to local postmasters within three hours of docking in daylight or two hours after sunrise the following day." Five years later, Congress established more regular and better-paying contracts to these mail-carrying vessels, and in 1823 "Congress declared waterways to be post roads."[46]

Far from being passive "natural" features, the rivers of the Midwest required significant public investment and acts of transformation to be made safe for commerce and accumulation. Once again it was the federal government that did this. Among the greatest dangers steamboats and flatboats faced on American rivers were sunken trees called snags. "Some snags were trees left standing when the water changed course, while others were whole trees, their roots still clinging in a mass of earth, that were washed into the river. As the heavy root mass absorbed water they sank and embedded themselves in the river bottom." Riverboat pilots divided these obstacles into so-called "planters" that were firmly rooted in the riverbed and "sawyers" that floated half submerged, bobbing up and down.

One notorious logjam on the Red River was 150 miles long, solid enough to climb on, and known simply as "the great raft." Described as a "snake infested jungle," "stagnant log jam, a tangle of vines and uprooted trees," the Great Raft was just the largest of many such obstacles.[47]

A year after these waterways were declared postal routes, the federal government held a contest for the invention of a boat to remove snags. In 1829, Henry Shreve built the first successful snag boat. "Shreve designed and built it with federal money but assumed financial risk in case it flopped." But as Robert Gudmestad relays, "The *Heliopolis* did not disappoint." Built like a steamboat catamaran, it had two hulls, each with its own engine and paddlewheel. A twenty-foot-high windlass for ripping up snags bridged the two hulls, as did rollers over which the snags could be pulled. The *Heliopolis* became the prototype for a fleet of government-funded and sometimes government-operated snag boats. In a seven-month stretch of work, the *Heliopolis* ripped up 1,548 snags. Areas of river that had been dangerous were made so safe that riverboats could pass at night.[48]

Shreve's environment-making did not stop at the water's edge. Because snag boats could work only when the water was high, Shreve found himself cooped up on land for months at a time. While stuck on the banks waiting, it became clear to Shreve that the snag problem could best be solved on land "by cutting down all the timber from off the banks of the river, at all places where they are liable to fall in, from three to four hundred feet from the margin of the river."[49] Like some land-stranded, manic, riparian Ahab, Shreve started making war on trees. Up and down the banks his crews assaulted the forests with ruthless determination. Shreve directed the action and documented his progress in detailed reports. "In the last quarter of 1832 and the first quarter of 1833 his workers felled 10,000 trees. ... Shreve's workers reached full speed between September 1842 and June 1845 when they removed almost 75,000 trees."

And yet, as is so often the case, these radical methods had very serious unanticipated consequences. As the felled trees' root structures died and rotted, whole chunks of the bank began collapsing into the river, silting up the channels. Nor did the state attack trees only in a direct form. As the environment-making state opened the rivers to steamboats, it thereby unleashed commerce, made markets, and converted mere things and use values into exchange values. With steamboats plying the waters, riverbank forests acquired economic utility, or exchange value. Private interests joined the assault. Trees were felled to feed the fires in the steamboat engines. Thus, when the state opened the rivers, the forests became fuel, which is to say a means to money, and thus extended the social relation that Marx called "capital."[50] In Marx, capital is the noun that acts like a verb. As a social relation, it expands like a self-replicating prion, but always the state assists.

Railroads

Another absolutely essential piece in this narrative of the American capitalist state as manager of nature is the story of railroads. The 1830s marked the beginning of the railroad boom. As with the story of canals, its fundamental sine qua non was 130 million acres of free federal land. The railroads were built upon these grants, but they were also financed from the development of the lands and the many use values that lay in and upon these terrains. Not a single railroad in the United States was built without massive public subsidies. One estimate has it that Congress transferred "approximately seven per cent of the continental United States to aid in the construction of railroads in the western and southern states."[51] Railroad grants were so substantial that as late as the 1970s there were still legal efforts underway to take back some of those lost public lands.[52]

Section 3 of the 1862 Pacific Railroad Act granted the railroads 10 square miles of public land for every mile of track completed. This amount was later doubled to 20 square miles per mile of track. Sections 5 and 11 of the Act allowed for the issue of federal government bonds of 30 years with an annual rate of 6 percent, doled out at a rate of $16,000 per mile of track completed in flatlands, "doubled" (to $32,000) per mile of completed grade laid between the two mountain ranges, and bonds of "treble the number per mile" ($48,000) for track laid over the two mountain ranges. An amendment of the Pacific Railroad Act authorized the company to issue its own private bonds and gave these company-issued securities priority in repayment over the original government bonds.

The collateral for these bonds was the railroad's assets, but the majority of the assets were, of course, those public land grants. As Heywood Fleisig put it: "When the Federal government gave land to the Central Pacific, it gave as well control over the disposal of the land, control over people working the land, an enhanced interest in influencing state and local government policies on taxation of the land, on zoning, on urban land use, and on a variety of other decisions in which the Central Pacific would not have had a pecuniary interest had it not owned the land. It was the exercise of these rights, some legitimate and some dubious, that earned for the Central Pacific the sobriquets of 'The Curse of California' and 'The Octopus.'"[53]

Successful railroad operations depended upon developing their land grants. If there were no farms, factories, mines, and population, then there would be no freight and passengers. In the post–Civil War drive west, settlement of the arid American plains was justified with the idea that "rain follows the plow." And for much of the 1860s and 1870s, during a spate of particularly rainy years, this seemed to be true.

But a series of El Niño–linked droughts and economic depressions caused railroad traffic to fall by roughly a third for several years after 1877. "Freight and passenger traffic, the principal source of the railroad's income, was of course directly related to the population and economy of the state, as was the value and marketability of the railroad's extensive land grant, scattered throughout the

Central Valley, the foothills of the Sierra, and the southern deserts. Financing the expansion of the Central and Southern Pacific lines ... was also based upon such factors as traffic revenues, land-grant sales, and the general economy of California."[54]

Thus by "the 1880s railway land, advertising, and agricultural departments, through extensive interchange of personnel and information on effective land policies, had become largely professionalized and standardized. ... From the 1880s well into the twentieth century the Southern Pacific and its allied companies were aggressively engaged in the Capay Valley in subdividing large tracts of low-value real estate into small farms, introducing new specialty crops, and sponsoring compact settlement ... In addition, other subsidiary land companies were subdividing and improving railroad lands in the Northern Sacramento Valley, the Sonoma Valley, Southern Alameda County, the Monterey Bay region, the coastal plain near Santa Barbara, and elsewhere."

Other railroads faced similar dilemmas and took similar action. "The Southern Pacific engaged in an intensive advertising campaign and supported agents in the United States and abroad. Its promotion plans affected the distribution of population and the development of certain specific localities. There are no statistics to show how many people came to southern California as a direct result of the company's propaganda, but the success of the program is evident in the more than two hundred and fifty percent increase in population in the region between 1880 and 1890."[55]

A typical railroad land grant was that received by the Northern Pacific, which connected St. Paul, Minnesota, to the Pacific coast at Seattle, and in doing so opened massive swaths of rangeland, forest, mineral mines, and future wheat field to exploitation. The land was given in "ten alternate sections on either side of the track in the states and twenty in the territories for every mile constructed. The area in which lands might be selected extended fifty miles on either side of the track. In Montana this gave the company a total of 14,000,000 acres of land. Specifically excluded from the grant, however, were mineral lands except those containing iron or coal."[56]

Clearly, at one level railroad interests clashed badly with "the public good." Even Andrew Jackson Sparks, commissioner of the

General Land Office in 1885, was critical: "I found that the mag-
nificent estate of the nation in its public lands had been to a wide
extent wasted under defective and improvident laws, and through
a laxity of public administration astonishing in a business sense if
not culpable in recklessness of official responsibility."

But at the same time, due to their ownership of massive amounts
of land, railroads became promoters of capitalist development; i.e.,
coordinators, investors, and planners of a type of social nature that
is the California landscape and agribusiness.

The geographer Richard Walker's *The Conquest of Bread* shows
how California agriculture was from early on "organized around
economies of scope, not just simple economies of scale."[57] Thus,
"the smaller grower has some things going for her, especially
paying close attention to the production process from planting
to harvest. In agriculture there is still no substitute for hands-on
know-how and personal attentiveness to problems as they arise."
In other words, it is not the size of the farm that determines its cap-
italistic qualities, it is the intensity of the capitalist social relations:
using technology, hiring wage labor, borrowing money from credit
markets, deploying capital-intensive technology in the realm of
irrigation, fertilization, and pest management, and subcontracting
expertise specialists. Walker shows that all these "industrial features" can and do happen on small farms in California.

Yankee Leviathan

In many ways the Civil War marked the second arrival of the American developmental state. Two factors summoned the economically
active state: the economic demands of the war, and the political
latitude allowed by the departure of Southern politicians. Southern
secession left the developmentalist element in the Republican Party
able to pass previously blocked legislation. Long outvoted, the
developmentalists' legislative math suddenly changed, and finally,
the "Hamiltonian-Whig-Republican measures for government promotion of socioeconomic development" came to fruition.[58]

The 37th Congress (March 4, 1861 to March 4, 1863), some-times called the most productive in American history, passed the Homestead Act of May 20, 1862. It provided 160 acres of unoc-cupied public land to each homesteader (regardless of their race or gender) who paid a nominal fee and occupied the land for five years. This proposal had been a national issue at least as early as 1848, when the Free Soil Party first proposed it, but slaveholding elites consistently blocked passage. Southern secession briefly removed this obstacle. Over the 123 years of its existence, the Homestead Act transferred fully 10 percent of the land in the United States, or about 270 million acres, to 4 million homesteaders.[59]

There was indeed some corruption and elite manipulation of this scheme. And more significantly, the Act subsidized a renewed onslaught of white settler invasion upon both unconquered and reservation-confined Native American nations. Although nothing justifies that, my point is narrower. It is that the Homestead Act did constitute a progressive victory over elite class interests—primarily, elite interests found "at the South."

Next came the Pacific Railroad Act, a huge program of govern-ment subsidy to build a transcontinental railroad. This law gave companies, at first, 6,400 acres of public land per mile of track completed, and later twice that amount. In all the federal govern-ment transferred 120 million acres of public land to construct the rail system. It also offered cheap government loans of $16,000 per mile on the plains and $48,000 per mile in the Rocky Moun-tains.[60] The transcontinental railroad laid the groundwork for a truly national market and truly national firms.

The third big program was the Morrill Act of July 2, 1862. The eponymous Representative Justin Morrill of Vermont had, for many years, been proposing a bill to grant public lands to the states for the promotion of higher education. With the evacua-tion of Southern opposition, his bill passed. Under the law, each state was given 30,000 acres of public land for each senator and representative it had, to use in funding the creation of land-grant universities. Those universities still operate today, and the vast majority of them are public.

Deutschland Developmentalist

The American experience with state-fostered development as a rejection of laissez-faire economics proved influential abroad. The Industrial Revolution in Britain, which was never as laissez-faire as conventional wisdom maintained it to be, only strengthened its imperial dominance.[61]

By the early nineteenth century, rivals like Germany were falling behind.[62] To correct this, the governments of Germany's many small independent states—practicing what is often called Cameralism, a smaller, landlocked Germanic variety of mercantilism—offered financing, management, and subsidies; established firms; created producer cooperatives; and made extensive public investments in transportation.[63] Friedrich List brought his understanding of Clay's American System with him when he returned to Germany, and was said thenceforth to have "shouted his message of national strength, national independence, and national survival, not so much as a rabble-rouser, but rather as a man who thinks he is addressing the deaf."[64]

German unification, emerging from Prussia's victory over France in 1871, kicked this decentralized developmentalism into high gear. With more than thirty small states federated under the strong leadership of Chancellor Otto Von Bismarck, a whole new level of state support for industry became available. The global economic crash of 1873 made such intervention essential, and the advocates of free trade were sidelined. The ensuing "Great Depression" cemented Germany's "marriage of iron and rye," in which heavy industry and the large agriculturalists (the Junkers) united around a tariff policy for both industry and agriculture.[65]

In 1879, Germany imposed heavy protective tariffs, but many private railroad companies disagreed with this policy. As one stilted old government history explained: "Up to the period which opens with the year 1878, the private lines in Germany still held the paramount position, but with the growth of their power and influence the feeling of opposition against them grew also. The practical monopoly which they had of all the great traffic routes, the prominence given to the financial interests of their shareholders, the opposition they showed to the tariff policy of the State, and to a uniform regulation of the railway systems of the country, made it evident that their power must be broken and all the important railway lines united under the control of the State. Military reasons had, however, also a most decisive influence upon the bringing of the Prussian lines into the possession of the State."[66]

Thus began the nationalization of German railroads. Under the same rationale, the state forced consolidation of small firms into larger companies and pushed the cartelization of whole industries.[67] That last policy was supported by German social democrats, who viewed cartelization as a step toward a planned and fully socialized economy.

The overall result was significant growth in railroads, steel, petrochemicals, and weapons. By 1913, Germany had the largest chemical industry and the second-largest rail system and steel industry in the world. Like Hamilton's agenda, Germany's industrial statecraft was fundamentally defensive. The threat abroad was Britain; at home it was socialism. To be strong, Germany had to be wealthy. Orchestrating the necessary industrial leap forward was simply too much for the fragmented capitalist class. The guidance of government was essential.

Meiji Japan

Around the same time, a similar process of defensively imitating rivals in order to catch up with them began in Japan. In 1853, Commodore Perry of the U.S. Navy sailed into Tokyo Harbor, gave a bloodless show of force, and demanded that Japan open its economy to American merchants. Under the Tokugawa Shogunate's policy of *Sakoku*, or "closed country," contact with foreigners had been almost entirely prohibited, feudal social relations were deliberately preserved, and with that, Japanese industrial and military development became increasingly antiquated. When the modern gunboats of British, French, Dutch, Russian, and American fleets arrived, Japan was forced to sign a series of humiliating and concessionary treaties.[68]

This deepening crisis led to revolution. In 1868, the self-secluding Tokugawa Shogunate was overthrown by an alliance of modernizing interests that used restoration of the Meiji imperial line as their traditionalist political cover. With national defense as motivation they began a crash program of top-down societal modernization. This meant mandatory secularization and Westernization of education and dress, dissolution of feudal privileges, and creation of a constitutional democracy. The government imposed land reform, which helped break the political power of conservative agrarian elites and facilitated a capitalist innovation of agriculture, which boosted production.[69]

Numerous Japanese writers advocated a Hamiltonian agenda of wholesale economic transformation. Earliest among them was Wakayama Norikazu, who was heavily influenced by H. C. Carey. Chuhei Sugiyama describes Wakayama's thinking as follows: "As early as 1871, only three years after the Restoration, he wrote on protective duties. Free trade, he asserted, was good enough in theory but not in practice. Although it was claimed that free trade brought about the wealth and strength of a nation, it was not practical to adopt the principle in such a country as Japan." Sounding much like the proto-ecological Carey, Wakayama maintained that it was necessary "to prohibit the export of agricultural products and thereby to recover the fertility of the soil, to prevent the activities of cunning merchants and thereby to rescue trade from decay, to prohibit the import of, or levy heavy duties on, foreign goods, and thereby to encourage useful industries."[70]

Other advocates of "means proper"–style policies included Nishimura Shigeki, who noted how the U.S., which had forced Japan to open its markets, was itself protectionist vis-à-vis Great Britain. By 1874, H. C. Carey's work had been translated into Japanese. List and other representatives of the early German Historical School of Economics advocating the National System were first translated in 1889.[71]

Most importantly, the new government of the Meiji Restoration began the process of state-led industrialization. The goal was summed up in the phrase *fukoku kyohei*, or "wealthy country, strong military."[72] To jump-start the necessary economic growth, Japanese officials were sent to study in the West, while some 3,000

European and American managers, scientists, engineers, economists, and military experts were recruited to work in Japan on limited contracts. Patents were introduced and innovation rewarded.[73]

The government created a powerful ministry of industry to drive and coordinate the economic transformation with planning and a robust program of nationalization and public works. Numerous mines were partially or completely taken over by the state, while the ministry built government-owned railroads, shipyards, iron, steel, glass, cement, and textile factories. Ministry agents acquired and copied cutting-edge technology, such as the newly invented telephone.

As local engineering and management expertise increased, imported equipment and know-how were steadily replaced with homegrown replacements in a pattern that would become known as import-substitution industrialization (ISI).[74] There are, of course, very many other such stories of state-led industrialization and planned transformation. However, that is a topic for another book.

Green Hamilton?

What does the Hamiltonian tradition have to say to the present and the climate crisis? The unprecedented challenge of climate change requires, at a minimum, that we euthanize the fossil-fuel industry and build out a vast clean-energy sector. This energy transformation, already underway but going too slowly, involves a simultaneous *deindustrialization*, putting an end to fossil-fuel use, and a *green reindustrialization*, building the new energy economy.

The United States has already faced the prospect of collapse and disintegration several times—the Critical Period, the War of 1812, the Civil War, the Great Depression. In all these crises, part of the solution was a return to economic planning. If we're serious about the climate crisis and the reindustrialization it demands, we could do worse than consulting templates from our own history. In that regard, the *Report on Manufactures* has something to say to the present. It offers reference points, proven practices, the half-faded sketch of a plan. Call it a greener means proper.

Acknowledgements

I owe deep thanks to my wife, Marcie Smith, for her patience and kindness as she stuck by me during the long and not always pleasant process of writing this book. My friend and colleague Josh Mason read parts of the manuscript and gave helpful feedback. John Jay colleagues Jay Hamilton and Geert Dhondt have been very supportive and welcoming as I settled into a new institutional home. Forrest Hylton commiserated from afar and offered some key sources and insights for this project. Andy Hsiao has been an excellent editor and comrade. Jeff Klein gave the book a truly deft copy-edit, catching and fixing some very important flaws in the process. Taylor Lloyd was kind enough to copy-edit my dyslexic first drafts. My good friend Dante Dallavalle read the text and caught important mistakes. My mother, Susan, and my Aunt Jeanne gave me love and support throughout, and for that I am very grateful. And finally a salute to the generally sweet and hard-working students of John Jay, who by their curiosity and good nature unknowingly helped motivate me through this long process.

Notes

1. Do We Know Hamilton

1 Ron Chernow, *Alexander Hamilton* (Penguin: New York, 2004), p. 377.
2 Richard Brookshire, *Alexander Hamilton, American* (Touchstone: New York, 1999), pp. 93–7.
3 Douglas C. North, *The Economic Growth of the United States, 1790–1860* (New York: W.W. Norton, 1966), p. 18, note 3; and p. 46.
4 Andrew Shankman, *Original Intents: Hamilton, Jefferson, Madison, and the American Founding* (New York: Oxford University Press, 2018), p. 116. Discussion of duties in *Report on the Subject of Manufactures*, Chapter 13.
5 Shankman, *Original Intents*, pp. 114–17.
6 John C. Miller, *Alexander Hamilton and the Growth of the New Nation* (New Brunswick: Transaction Publishers, 2004).
7 Ha-Joon Chang, *Kicking Away the Ladder: Development Strategy in Historical Perspective* (New York: Anthem Press, 2002); Ha-Joon Chang, *Bad Samaritans: The Myth of Free Trade and the Secret History of Capitalism* (New York: Bloomsbury, 2009).
8 Fred L. Block and Matthew R. Keller, eds., *State of Innovation: The U.S. Government's Role in Technology Development* (Boulder: Paradigm Publishers, 2011), for Hamilton, p. 34.
9 Michael Hudson, *America's Protectionist Takeoff, 1815–1914* (Dresden: ISLET-Verlag, 2010), p. vii.
10 John Lynch, *Simon Bolívar: A Life* (New Haven, Yale University Press, 2006); Janet Burke and Ted Humphrey, eds., *Nineteenth-Century Nation Building and the Latin-American Intellectual Tradition: A*

Reader (Indianapolis: Hackett, 2007); Matthew Brown, ed., *Simon Bolívar: The Bolivarian Revolution,* (New York: Verso, 2007); Marie Arana, *Bolívar: American Liberator* (New York: Simon & Schuster, 2013).

11 Joshua Simon, "Simon Bolívar's Republican Imperialism: Another Ideology of the American Revolution," *History of Political Thought,* vol. 33, no. 2, p. 282.

12 Charles Austin Beard, *An Economic Interpretation of the Constitution* (New York: McMillan Publishers, 1913), pp. 106–7.

13 Peter B. Evans, Dietrich Rueschemeyer, Theda Skocpol, eds., *Bringing the State Back In* (New York: Cambridge University Press, 1985).

14 Looking backward, the globe-spanning American Empire can appear inevitable, but in reality it had to be produced and continually reproduced, often in the face of crisis, through policy. It took a full century of independence for the U.S. economy to match the size of the British economy, and then another fifty years before the dollar displaced the pound sterling as the world's primary reserve currency. See Sam Gindin and Leo Panitch, *The Making of Global Capitalism: The Political Economy of American Empire* (New York: Verso, 2013); Timothy Mitchell, *Carbon Democracy: Political Power in the Age of Oil* (New York: Verso, 2013).

15 Michael Grunwald, *The New New Deal: The Hidden Story of Change in the Obama Era* (New York: Simon & Schuster, 2013).

16 Karl Polanyi, *The Great Transformation: The Political and Economic Origins of Our Time* (Boston: Beacon Press, 1944 / 2001), p. 3. Next two quotes, pp. 145–7.

17 Quoted in Daniel Walker Howe, *What Hath God Wrought: The Transformation of America, 1815–1848* (New York: Oxford University Press, 2007), p. 222.

18 Bhaskar Sunkara, "The 'Anarcho-Liberal,'" *Dissent,* Sept. 27, 2011; Doug Henwood, Liza Featherstone, and Christian Parenti, "Action Will Be Taken," *Left Business Observer,* 2002.

19 For example, see Arturo Escobar, *Encountering Development: The Making and Unmaking of the Third World* (Princeton: Princeton University Press, 2012 [1995]).

20 For a lucid discussion of such contradictions, see Michael E. Latham, *The Right Kind of Revolution: Modernization, Development, and U.S. Foreign Policy From the Cold War to the Present* (Ithaca: Cornell University Press, 2010).

2. Cometh the Hour, Cometh the Man

1 This is suggested in Ron Chernow, *Alexander Hamilton* (New York: Penguin, 2005).

2 "From John Adams to Benjamin Rush, 25 January 1806," *Founders Online*, National Archives.

3 "From George Washington to William Crawford, 17 September 1767," W. W. Abbot and Dorothy Twohig, eds., *The Papers of George Washington*, Colonial Series, vol. 8, *24 June 1767–25 December 1771* (Charlottesville: University Press of Virginia, 1993), pp. 26–32. For a complete history of how the Proclamation Line came to be, see Fred Anderson, *The War That Made America: A Short History of the French and Indian War* (New York: Penguin, 2006). To put the Proclamation Line in a larger "frontier" context, Greg Grandin, *The End of the Myth: From the Frontier to the Border Wall in the Mind of America* (New York: Metropolitan Books, 2019).

4 To be fair, Horne was not the first to make this case. See William M. Wiecek, "Somerset: Lord Mansfield and the Legitimacy of Slavery in the Anglo-American World," *University of Chicago Law Review*, vol. 42, no. 1, Autumn 1974: 86–146; Alfred W. Blumrosen, et al., *Slave Nation: How Slavery United the Colonies and Sparked the American Revolution* (Naperville: Sourcebooks, 2005); Gerald Horne, *The Counter-Revolution of 1776: Slave Resistance and the Origins of the United States of America* (New York: New York University Press, 2014).

5 A book that brilliantly illustrates the centrality of "western lands" to American politics and economics in the nineteenth century is Alasdair Roberts, *America's First Great Depression: Economic Crisis and Political Disorder after the Panic of 1837* (Ithaca: Cornell University Press, 2013).

6 Terms like "company" and "battalion" had no clear meaning in eighteenth-century America, in fact all units of measurements for soldiers or grain were chaotically irregular. Steuben, who would reorganize the Army for Washington, explained, "There was consequently no regularity in military formation." Quoted in John W. Wright, "Some Notes on the Continental Army, Part 2," *The William and Mary Quarterly*, vol. 11, no. 2 (July 1931), p. 187.

7 For example, in this letter he protested a pay reduction: "From Alexander Hamilton to the Provincial Congress of the Colony of New-York, [26 May 1776]," Harold C. Syrett, ed., *The Papers of Alexander Hamilton*, vol. 1, 1768–78, (New York: Columbia University Press, 1961), pp. 183–5.

8 Chernow, p. 73.

9 Anderson, p. vii.

10 "From Alexander Hamilton to the Convention of the Representatives of the State of New-York [6 March 1777]," Syrett, ed., *The Papers of Alexander Hamilton*, vol. 1, pp. 199–201.

11 Brian N. Morton, "Beaumarchais, Francy, Steuben, and Lafayette: An Unpublished Correspondence or 'Feux de joye' at Valley Forge," *The French Review*, vol. 49, no. 6, (May 1976), pp. 943–59.

12 Paul Lockhart, *The Drillmaster of Valley Forge: The Baron de Steuben and the Making of the American Army* (New York: HarperCollins, 2008).

13 "*The Farmer Refuted* [23 February 1775]," Syrett, ed., *The Papers of Alexander Hamilton*, vol. 1, pp. 81–165. Next two quotations, pp. 254–6.

14 "To George Washington from Colonel Hugh Hughes, 20 November 1777," Frank E. Grizzard Jr. and David R. Hoth, eds., *The Papers of George Washington, Revolutionary War Series*, vol. 12, (Charlottesville: University Press of Virginia, 2002), p. 329.

15 David Hackett Fischer, *Washington's Crossing* (New York: Oxford University Press, 2006).

16 "*The Farmer Refuted.*"

17 Thomas J. McGuire, *The Philadelphia Campaign: vol. 1: Brandywine and the Fall of Philadelphia* (Mechanicsburg: Stackpole Books, 2006), p. 269.

18 Quoted in Chernow, p. 99.

19 "John Adams to Abigail Adams, 8 October 1776," L. H. Butterfield, ed., *The Adams Papers, Adams Family Correspondence*, vol. 2 (Cambridge, MA: Harvard University Press, 1963), pp. 139–41.

20 Matthew Moten, *Presidents and Their Generals: An American History of Command in War* (Cambridge, MA: Harvard University Press, 2014), p. 30.

21 Benjamin H. Newcomb, "Washington's Generals and the Decision to Quarter at Valley Forge," *The Pennsylvania Magazine of History and Biography*, vol. 117, no. 4 (1993), pp. 309–29.

22 Richard M. Ketchum, *Saratoga: Turning Point of America's Revolutionary War* (New York: Henry Holt, 1997), p. 395; John F. Luzader, *Saratoga: A Military History of the Decisive Campaign of the American Revolution* (El Dorado Hills: Savas Beatie, 2008), p. 230.

23 Ketchum, pp. 368–9.

24 William A. Griswold and Donald W. Linebaugh, eds., *The Saratoga Campaign: Uncovering an Embattled Landscape* (Hanover: University Press of New England, 2016), p. 167.

25 John Ferling, "Myths of the American Revolution: A noted historian debunks the conventional wisdom about America's War of Independence," *Smithsonian Magazine*, January 2010.

26 "To Alexander Hamilton from George Washington, 30 October 1777," Syrett, ed., *The Papers of Alexander Hamilton*, vol. 1, pp. 347–9.

27 "Account of Expenses of Lieutenant Colonel Alexander Hamilton and Captain Caleb Gibbs, 30 October 1777–20 January 1778," Syrett, ed., *The Papers of Alexander Hamilton*, vol. 1, pp. 412–13.

28 "From Alexander Hamilton to George Washington [6 November 1777]," Syrett, ed., *The Papers of Alexander Hamilton*, vol. 1, pp. 353–6.

29 John C. Miller, *Alexander Hamilton and the Growth of the New Nation* (New York: Harper and Brothers, 1959), pp. 23–5.

30 "From Alexander Hamilton to Major General Israel Putnam, 9 November 1777," Syrett, ed., vol. 1, pp. 356–7.

31 "From Alexander Hamilton to George Washington, 2 November 1777," Syrett, ed., vol. 1, pp. 349–51.

32 "From Alexander Hamilton to George Washington, 12 November 1777," Syrett, ed., vol. 1, pp. 360–2.

33 "To George Washington from Colonel Hugh Hughes, 20 November 1777," Frank E. Grizzard Jr. and David R. Hoth, eds., *The Papers of George Washington, Revolutionary War Series*, vol. 12 (Charlottesville: University Press of Virginia, 2002), p. 329.

34 "To George Washington from Captain Caleb Gibbs, 23 November 1777," Grizzard Jr. and Hoth, eds., vol. 12, pp. 360–1.

35 "From Alexander Hamilton to George Clinton, 22 December 1777," Syrett, ed., pp. 368–9.

36 The exact date of the Pay Book notes is unclear. The National Archives dates them simply as 1777. Back in 1957, E. P. Panagopoulos noted that clear "internal evidence of the precise period when Hamilton made these notes is lacking" and places their writing sometime "after 1776 and before 1779" because in the fall of 1779, Hamilton seems to have used these notes in his "Letter on the National Bank." Philip Stadter dates the notes as "probably made in the winter of 1777–1778 at Valley Forge." Chernow dates them as "during the winter encampments." See "Pay Book of the State Company of Artillery [1777]," Syrett, ed., vol. 1, pp. 373–412; Also see Panagopoulos, "Hamilton's Notes in His Pay Book of the New York State Artillery Company," *The American Historical Review*, vol. 62, no. 2, 1957, pp. 310–25; Stadter, "Alexander Hamilton's Notes on Plutarch in His Pay Book," *The Review of Politics*, vol. 73, no. 2 (Spring 2011), pp. 199–217; and Chernow, p. 110.

37 For Hamilton's low opinion of Conway, see Miller, p. 28; For understated report of the duel, see "To George Washington from Major David Salisbury Franks, 4 July 1778," David R. Hoth, ed., *The Papers of George Washington, Revolutionary War Series*, vol. 16, p. 21.

38 "Henry Lawrence to James Grant, October 13, 1767," George C. Rogers, ed., *The Papers of Henry Laurens*, vol. 5 (Columbia: University of South Carolina Press, 1976), p. 359.

39 Chernow, pp. 94–5; Also see "From Alexander Hamilton to Lieutenant Colonel John Laurens [April 1779]," Syrett, ed., vol. 2, pp. 34–8.

40 For Lafayette quote, see Gregory D. Massey, *John Laurens and the American Revolution* (Columbia: University of South Carolina Press, 2000), p. 75.

41 There is a long tradition of mythologizing the suffering of the soldiers who wintered at Valley Forge in 1777–78. Some have argued that

Washington exaggerated the crisis and used conditions at Valley Forge to pressure Congress to provide a steady flow of supplies. Washington may have emphasized or even played up the crisis in his letters, but he did not invent. See Wayne Bodle, *The Valley Forge Winter: Civilians and Soldiers in War* (University Park: Pennsylvania State University Press, 2002). As one author put it: "Only four of every five hundred soldiers inoculated died, and Washington had all of his non-immune troops inoculated during the winter of 1778 at Valley Forge. Though the mortality rate was low, between three and four hundred soldiers must have died from inoculation in 1777 alone, as nearly forty thousand soldiers underwent the procedure." See Ann M. Becker, "Smallpox in Washington's Army: Strategic Implications of the Disease During the American Revolutionary War," *The Journal of Military History*, vol. 68, no. 2 (April 2004), pp. 381–430.

42 Richard M. Ketchum, *The American Heritage Book of the Revolution*, (New York: American Heritage, 1958), p. 220. Alas, the dams that ushered in industrialization would destroy the river fisheries of the Northeast. See Daniel Vickers, "Those Dammed Shad: Would the River Fisheries of New England Have Survived in the Absence of Industrialization?," *The William and Mary Quarterly*, vol. 61, no. 4 (Oct. 2004), pp. 685–712.

43 "From George Washington to Henry Laurens, 23 December 1777," Grizzard Jr. and Hoth, eds., vol. 12, pp. 683–7.

44 "To George Washington from Thomas Wharton, Jr., 17 February 1778," Edward G. Lengel, ed., *The Papers of George Washington, Revolutionary War Series*, vol. 13, pp. 574–6.

45 "From George Washington to Thomas Wharton, Jr., 23 February 1778," Lengel, ed., pp. 651–2.

46 Stanley J. Olsen, "Food Animals of the Continental Army at Valley Forge and Morristown," *American Antiquity*, vol. 29, no. 4 (April 1964), p. 507.

47 "From George Washington to Henry Laurens, 23 December 1777," Grizzard Jr. and Hoth, eds., pp. 683–7.

48 Albigence Waldo, "Valley Forge, 1777–1778. Diary of Surgeon Albigence Waldo, of the Connecticut Line," *The Pennsylvania Magazine of History and Biography*, vol. 21, no. 3 (1897), p. 314.

49 "From George Washington to Major General Nathanael Greene, 12 February 1778," Edward G. Lengel, vol. 13, pp. 514–17.

50 "From Alexander Hamilton to Colonel Henry E. Lutterloh [February 1778]," Syrett, ed., vol. 1, p. 435.

51 "By the end of 1777 lieutenants enrolled 40,000 inhabitants in the militia, organized them in classes, companies, and battalions, all the while supervising the election of officers." See Francis S. Fox, "Pennsylvania's Revolutionary Militia Law: The Statute That Transformed the State," *Pennsylvania History: A Journal of Mid-Atlantic Studies*, vol. 80, no. 2 (Spring 2013), p. 205.

52 Paul David Nelson, "Citizen Soldiers or Regulars: The Views of American General Officers on the Military Establishment, 1775–1781," *Military Affairs*, vol. 43, no. 3 (Oct. 1979), pp. 126–32.

53 "From Alexander Hamilton to George Clinton, 13 February 1778," Syrett, ed., pp. 425–8.

54 "From Alexander Hamilton to James Duane [3 September 1780]," Syrett, ed., pp. 400–18.

55 "From Alexander Hamilton to Lieutenant Colonel John Laurens [12 September 1780]," C. Syrett, ed., vol. 2, pp. 426–8.

3. The Supply Effort, from Grand Forage to Manufacturing

1 J. Franklin Jameson, *American Revolution Considered as a Social Movement* (Princeton: Princeton University Press, 1926), pp. 52–3.

2 William Wiecek, "Somerset: Lord Mansfield and the Legitimacy of Slavery in the Anglo-American World," *University of Chicago Law Review*, vol. 42, no. 1, (Autumn 1974) 86–146; Alfred W. Blumrosen, et al., *Slave Nation: How Slavery United the Colonies and Sparked the American Revolution* (Naperville: Sourcebooks, 2005); Gerald Horne, *The Counter-Revolution of 1776: Slave Resistance and the Origins of the United States of America* (New York: New York University Press, 2014).

3 For a complete history of how the Proclamation Line came to be, see Fred Anderson, *The War That Made America: A Short History of the French and Indian War* (New York: Penguin, 2006).

4 Thomas Paine, *The Works of Thomas Paine: A Hero in the American Revolution*, vol. II (Philadelphia: E. Haskell, 1854), pp. 48–9.

5 Christian Parenti, "The Environment Making State: Territory, Nature, and Value," *Antipode*, vol. 47, no. 4, 2015, pp. 829–48.

6 Gordon S. Wood, *The Radicalism of the American Revolution* (New York: Knopf Doubleday, 2011), pp. 311–12.

7 John Fiske, *The Critical Period of American History, 1783–1789*, (Boston and New York: Houghton, Mifflin and Company, 1888).

8 Richard Buel Jr., *In Irons: Britain's Naval Supremacy and the American Revolutionary Economy* (New Haven: Yale University Press, 1998), p. 7.

9 James T. Adams (1878–1949), *New England in the Republic, 1776–1850* (Gloucester: P. Smith, 1960), pp. 13–14.

10 Jameson, pp. 48–9.

11 C. Stevens Laise, "Interpreting the Colonial Shipyard," *Transactions Society of Naval Architects and Marine Engineers*, vol. 84 (1977), pp. 240–5.

12 Laise, p. 247.

13 Merril D. Smith, ed., *The World of the American Revolution: A Daily Life Encyclopedia* (Santa Barbara: ABC-CLIO, 2015), p. 797.

14 Joseph A. Goldenberg, *Shipbuilding in Colonial America* (Charlottesville: University Press of Virginia, 1976), p. 125. See Jacob M. Price, "A Note on the Value of Colonial Exports of Shipping," *The Journal of Economic History*, vol. 36, no. 3 (Sept. 1976), p. 706. Also see Ralph Davis, *The Rise of the English Shipping Industry in the Seventeenth and Eighteenth Centuries* (London: Macmillan & Co., 1962): "Richard Champion stated in 1774 that nearly a third of British owned ships were American built (2,342 out of 7,694)."

15 Quoted in J. Leander Bishop, *A History of American Manufactures, From 1608 to 1860* (Philadelphia: Edward Young & Co., 1864), p. 90.

16 Buel, pp. 92–3.

17 E. James Ferguson, *The Power of the Purse: A History of American Public Finance, 1776–1790* (Chapel Hill: University of North Carolina Press, 1961), p. 27.

18 Gloria L. Maine, "Inequality in Early America: Evidence From Probate Records of Massachusetts and Maryland," in Robert I. Rotberg, ed., *Social Mobility and Modernization* (Cambridge, MA: MIT Press, 2000), table 1, p. 240.

19 Erna Risch, *Supplying Washington's Army* (Washington: Center of Military History, United States Army, 1981), pp. 425–6.

20 Tench Coxe, *An Examination of Lord Sheffield's Observations on the Commerce of the United States… With two supplementary notes on American Manufacturers* (Philadelphia, Mathew Carey, 1791, London reprint J. Phillips, 1792), p. 42.

21 Wood, p. 248. In a powerful and unique article on the political economy of late-eighteenth-century America, Allan Kulikoff finds "severe recessions during the war years and from 1785 through 1788, followed by recovery and prosperity in the 1790s, but no full return to the average wealth and income of 1774 until after 1800." Wood's point still stands: qualitative transformations, namely increased commercialism, were a byproduct of the war. See Allan Kulikoff, "Such Things Ought Not to Be," in Andrew Shankman, ed., *The World of the Revolutionary American Republic: Land, Labor, and the Conflict for a Continent* (London: Routledge, 2014), p. 134.

22 W. W. Rostow, "The Stages of Economic Growth," *The Economic History Review*, vol. 12, no. 1 (1959), pp. 1–16; also see Lawrence A. Peskin, *Manufacturing Revolution: The Intellectual Origins of Early American Industry* (Baltimore: Johns Hopkins University Press, 2003).

23 Robert K. Wright, Jr., *The Continental Army* (Washington: Center for Military History, United States Army, 1983), pp. 12–23.

24 Thomas Paine, *Common Sense*, third edition (Philadelphia: February 14, 1776).

25 "General Orders, 25 July 1777," Edward G. Lengel, ed., *The Papers of George Washington, Revolutionary War Series*, vol. 10, pp. 402–3.

26 David C. Hsiung, "Food, Fuel, and the New England Environment in the War for Independence, 1775–1776," *New England Quarterly* (December 2007), pp. 616–17.

27 Hsiung, pp. 638 and 645. The armies' ravenous appetites for wood transformed the landscape. As Hsiung writes: "A gazetteer in 1785 observed that Roxbury, a town of about 7,100 acres, had its woods 'very considerably lessened in consequence of the extraordinary demand for the use of the American army encamped in and near the town, in the winter of 1775; there now remains about 550 acres of wood land,' or only about 8 percent of the total area." This in part pushed the area toward "commercial dairy farming" and helped spread the market economy.

28 James A. Henretta, *The Origins of American Capitalism* (Boston: Northeastern University Press, 1991), p. 239.

29 Joseph R. Fischer, *A Well-Executed Failure* (Columbia: University of South Carolina Press, 1997).

30 "From George Washington to Major General John Sullivan, 31 May 1779," Lengel, ed., pp. 716–19.

31 William Wait, "Sullivan's Campaign," *Proceedings of the New York State Historical Association*, vol. 6 (1906), p. 81.

32 Marion Brophy, Wendell Tripp, eds., "Supplies for General Sullivan: The Correspondence of Colonel Charles Stewart, May–September, 1779," *New York History*, vol. 60, no. 3 (July 1979), p. 248.

33 "From Alexander Hamilton to Major General Nathanael Greene [22 May 1779]," Syrett, ed., pp. 51–2.

34 Gerard H. Clarfield, "The Board of War" in *Timothy Pickering and the American Republic* (Pittsburgh: University of Pittsburgh Press, 1980); also, Kenneth Schaffel, "The American Board of War, 1776–1781," *Military Affairs*, vol. 50, no. 4 (Oct. 1986), pp. 185–9; Marion Brophy, Wendell Tripp, eds., "Supplies for General Sullivan: The Correspondence of Colonel Charles Stewart, May–September, 1779," *New York History*, vol. 60, no. 3 (July 1979), p. 248.

35 Quoted in John A. Ruddiman, "'A record in the hands of thousands': Power and Negotiation in the Orderly Books of the Continental Army," *The William and Mary Quarterly*, vol. 67, no. 4 (October 2010), p. 753.

36 John Wright, "Some Notes on the Continental Army," *The William and Mary Quarterly*, vol. 11, no. 2 (April, 1931), pp. 81–105, 93.

37 Wright, p. 94.

38 Bishop, p. 381.

39 Bishop, p. 379.

40 Nile's Principles and Acts of the Revolution, p. 305, quoted in Bishop, p. 394.

41 Bishop, p. 379; quotes on pp. 381, 385.

42 Bishop, p. 606.

43 Solomon K. Smith, "Firearms Manufacturing, Gun Use, and the

Emergence of Gun Culture in Early North America," *49th Parallel*, vol. 34 (Autumn 2014), p. 29.

44 John Ferling, "Myths of the American Revolution," *Smithsonian Magazine*, January 2010. On the class composition, see James Kirby Martin and Mark Lender, *A Respectable Army: The Military Origins of the Republic, 1763–1789* (Arlington Heights: Harlan Division, 1982), pp. 90–1.

45 Henretta, p. 233.

46 Smith, table II, p. 16.

47 Wright, p. 86.

48 Victor S. Clark, (1868–1946), *History of Manufactures in the United States, 1607–1860* (Washington: Carnegie Institution, 1916), p. 220.

49 Bishop, pp. 486–7.

50 Albert Sidney Bolles, *Industrial History of the United States, From the Earliest Settlements to the Present Time* (Norwich: The Henry Bill Publishing Company, 1881), p. 198.

51 Risch, pp. 342–3.

52 Clark, p. 222.

53 "From George Washington to Jonathan Trumbull, Sr., 3 July 1780," *Founders Online*, National Archives.

54 Quoted in Jameson, p. 58.

55 John J. McCusker and Russell R. Menard, *The Economy of British America, 1607–1789* (Chapel Hill: University of North Carolina Press, 1991), p. 79.

56 R. L. Hilldrup, "The Salt Supply of North Carolina During the American Revolution," *The North Carolina Historical Review*, vol. 22, no. 4 (Oct. 1945), p. 393.

57 "From George Washington to Major General Israel Putnam, 22 May 1776," Philander D. Chase, ed., *The Papers of George Washington, Revolutionary War Series*, vol. 4 (Charlottesville: University Press of Virginia, 1991), pp. 371–2.

58 Larry G. Bowman, "The Scarcity of Salt in Virginia during the American Revolution," *The Virginia Magazine of History and Biography*, vol. 77, no. 4 (Oct. 1969), pp. 464–5.

59 Michael S. Adelberg, "'Long in the Hand and Altogether Fruitless': The Pennsylvania Salt Works and Salt-Making on the New Jersey Shore During the American Revolution," *Pennsylvania History: A Journal of Mid-Atlantic Studies*, vol. 80, no. 2 (Spring 2013), p. 217.

60 Hilldrup, p. 409.

61 Adelberg, p. 217.

62 Cathy Matson, "The Revolution, the Constitution, and the Early National Economy," in Stanley Engerman and Robert Gallman, eds., *Cambridge Economic History of the United States: The Colonial Era*, vol. 1 (Cambridge: Cambridge University Press, 1996), p. 369.

63 Buel, p. 74.

64 Risch, pp. 336–7; J. Franklin Jameson, "St. Eustatius in the American

Revolution," *American Historical Review*, vol. 8, no. 4 (July 1903), pp. 683–708.

65 Jameson, pp. 65–6.

66 If the average number of ships built prior to 1776 (a freakishly productive year) was around 400, then it would seem that by midwar, privateers were taking that number or more.

67 "To George Washington from Major General Thomas Mifflin, 13 May 1777," Chase, ed., vol. 9, pp. 413–14.

68 Weeden, p. 782

69 Buel, p. 97.

70 James T. Adams (1878–1949), *New England in the Republic, 1776–1850* (Gloucester: P. Smith, 1926/1960), p. 48.

71 Phillip Hamilton, *The Making and Unmaking of a Revolutionary Family: The Tuckers of Virginia, 1752–1830* (Charlottesville: University of Virginia Press, 2003), p. 38.

72 Buel, pp. 96–106.

4. "The Badness of the Money"

1 John T. Schlebecker, "Agricultural Markets and Marketing in the North, 1774–1777," *Agricultural History*, vol. 50, no. 1, Bicentennial Symposium: Two Centuries of American Agriculture (Jan. 1976), p. 22.

2 Farley Grubb, "State Redemption of the Continental Dollar, 1779–90, *The William and Mary Quarterly*, vol. 69, no. 1 (January 2012), p. 47.

3 E. James Ferguson, *The Power of the Purse: A History of American Public Finance, 1776–1790* (Chapel Hill: University of North Carolina Press, 1961), p. 29.

4 Bennett Baack, "Forging a Nation State: The Continental Congress and the Financing of the War of American Independence," *The Economic History Review*, vol. 54, no. 4 (Nov. 2001), p. 654.

5 John L. Smith Jr., "How Was the Revolutionary War Paid For?" *Journal of the American Revolution*, Feb. 23, 2015. Smith's estimate was "based upon 'Ferguson's estimate of the total cost of the war.'" Edwin J. Perkins, *American Public Finance and Financial Services 1700–1815* (Columbus: Ohio State University Press, 1994), p. 103, table 5.4.

6 Baack, p. 642.

7 Baack, p. 643.

8 "Many in Great Britain and elsewhere believed, that, if Continental paper money could be destroyed, the Americans would be obliged to submit, from lack of funds to maintain their cause. This is why the British Government promoted so extensively the business of

counterfeiting." General Clinton confirmed the policy but also lamented it as a failure in a January 1780 letter. See Albert S. Bolles, *The Financial History of the United States From 1774 to 1789*, 3rd edition (New York: D. Appleton and Co., 1892), pp. 152–3.

9 Robert Middlekauff, *The Glorious Cause: The American Revolution, 1763–1789* (New York: Oxford University Press, 1982), p. 594.

10 Bishop, p. 394.

11 "Valley Forge, 1777–1778, Diary of Surgeon Albigence Waldo, of the Connecticut Line," *The Pennsylvania Magazine of History and Biography*, vol. 21, 1897, p. 308.

12 "Of the Paper Money of America, [1780]," Barbara B. Oberg, ed., *The Papers of Benjamin Franklin*, vol. 34 (New Haven and London: Yale University Press, 1998), pp. 228–32.

13 Oscar Handlin and Mary Handlin, "Revolutionary Economic Policy in Massachusetts," *William and Mary Quarterly*, vol. 4 (1947), pp. 3–26.

14 Quoted in Ferguson, *The Power of the Purse*, p. 58.

15 Bishop, pp. 397–8.

16 "Mifflin to Wadsworth, Oct. 12, 17, 1776," as quoted in Ferguson, p. 58.

17 "To George Washington from Ephraim Blaine, 9 January 1778," Lengel ed., vol. 13, pp. 186–7.

18 Ferguson, p. 64.

19 Woody Holton, *Unruly Americans and the Origins of the Constitution* (New York: Hill and Wang, 2008).

20 John T. Schlebecker, "Agricultural Markets and Marketing in the North, 1774–1777," *Agricultural History*, vol. 50, no. 1 (Jan. 1976), pp. 21–36, 23.

21 E. James Ferguson, "Speculation in the Revolutionary Debt: The Ownership of Public Securities in Maryland, 1790," *The Journal of Economic History*, vol. 14, no. 1 (Winter 1954), p. 38; also see Holton, pp. 38–40; Ferguson, p. 183.

22 Ferguson, p. 60.

23 Ferguson, p. 62.

24 Quoted in John C. Miller, *Alexander Hamilton and the Growth of the New Nation* (New Brunswick: Transaction Publishers, 2004), p. 43.

25 Otto C. Lightner, *The History of Business Depressions* (New York: Northeastern Press, 1922), p. 93.

26 "From Alexander Hamilton to——, [December–March 1779–1780]," Syrett, ed., pp. 236–51. It is not certain to whom this letter was addressed. Only Hamilton's draft remains.

27 *Journal of the Continental Congress*, vol. XVI (Washington: Government Printing Office, 1905), p. 264.

28 Ralph Volney Harlow, "Aspects of Revolutionary Finance, 1775–1783," *The American Historical Review*, vol. 35, no.1 (Oct. 1929), p. 61; Ferguson, p. 51.

29 Buel, p. 144.

30 Ferguson, pp. 36, 40.
31 "From Alexander Hamilton to ———, [December–March 1779–1780]."
32 Quoted in Miller, pp. 43–53.
33 "From Alexander Hamilton to James Duane [3 September 1780]," Syrett, ed., pp. 400–18.
34 "Report Relative to a Provision for the Support of Public Credit [9 January 1790]," Syrett, ed., pp. 65–110.
35 Hamilton made that estimate in 1790 when the new federal government assumed most of the state's debts. As Treasury secretary he tallied "the whole of the debt of the United States" at $54 million; 20 percent of that was owed to foreign powers, mostly France, Spain, and Holland. The still outstanding state debts (that had not been converted to federal bonds) was another "25 millions of dollars, principal and interest." That gives a total of $79 million. To service its debt Hamilton figured the national government would need about $2.2 million annually. "Report Relative to a Provision for the Support of Public Credit [9 January 1790]." For other estimates, see Carey Roberts, "Alexander Hamilton and the 1790s Economy: A Reappraisal," in Douglas Ambrose and Robert W. T. Martin, eds., *The Many Faces of Alexander Hamilton: The Life and Legacy of America's Most Elusive Founding Father* (New York: NYU Press, 2006). Another tabulation holds that when the federal government assumed all the state debts it took on an additional $21.5 million. See, Paul B. Trescott, "Federal-State Financial Relations, 1790–1860," *The Journal of Economic History*, vol. 15, no. 3 (Sep. 1955), pp. 227–45.
36 For a thorough description of this battle and others, see Robert Middlekauff, *The Glorious Cause: The American Revolution, 1763–1789* (New York: Oxford University Press, 2007).

5. Military Mutiny and the Critical Period

1 Harvey Amani Whitfield, *The Problem of Slavery in Early Vermont, 1777–1810* (Montpelier: Vermont Historical Society, 2014). The reality of Vermont's ban was less robust than the letter of the law. As late as the census of 1810, two Vermonters were listed as owning slaves.
2 James Madison quoted in Max Farrand, ed., *Records of the Federal Convention of 1787*, vol. 1 (New Haven: Yale University Press, 1912), pp. 135–6.
3 Harry M. Ward, *George Washington's Enforcers: Policing the Continental Army* (Carbondale: Southern Illinois University Press, 2006), p. xi.
4 "From George Washington to Henry Laurens, 23 December 1777," Grizzard Jr. and Hoth, eds., pp. 683–7.

5   John A. Nagy, *Rebellion in the Ranks: Mutinies of the American Rev-olution* (Yardley, PA.: Westholme Publishing, 2008). Nagy estimates that about 6 percent of recorded courts-martial involved allegations of mutiny, with the largest mutinies happening in the later years of the war.

6   Nagy, pp. 38–9.

7   John K. Alexander, "The Fort Wilson Incident of 1779: A Case Study of the Revolutionary Crowd," *The William and Mary Quarterly*, vol. 31, no. 4 (Oct. 1974), pp. 589–90.

8   Alexander, pp. 606–7.

9   "To John Adams from Henry Laurens, 4 October 1779," Gregg L. Lint, et al., eds., *The Adams Papers*, Papers of John Adams, vol. 8 (Cambridge, MA: Harvard University Press, 1989), pp. 188–91. Despite its date, this letter was written early on the morning of Oct. 5.

10 Carl Van Doren, *Mutiny in January: The Story of a Crisis in the Con-tinental Army Now for the First Time Fully Told from Many Hitherto Unknown or Neglected Sources, both American and British* (New York: The Viking Press, 1943), pp. 22–3.

11 Nagy, *Rebellion in the Ranks*.

12 Robert K. Wright Jr., "Mutiny of the New Jersey Line," Harold E. Selesky, ed., *Encyclopedia of the American Revolution: Library of Military History*, vol. 2 (Detroit: Charles Scribner's Sons, 2006), p. 772.

13 "To George Washington from Anthony Wayne, 2 January 1781," *Founders Online*, National Archives.

14 Nagy.

15 "To George Washington from Israel Shreve, 8 January 1781," *Found-ers Online*, National Archives.

16 Mary A. Y. Gallagher, "Reinterpreting the 'Very Trifling Mutiny' at Philadelphia in June 1783," *The Pennsylvania Magazine of History and Biography*, vol. 119, no. 1/2 (1995), pp. 3–35; Nagy, p. 162.

17 Nagy, p. 170.

18 "To George Washington from Israel Shreve, 20 January 1781," *Found-ers Online*, National Archives.

19 "From George Washington to Israel Shreve, 21 January 1781," *Found-ers Online*, National Archives.

20 Hamilton had lobbied the powerful New York politician James Duane on this matter: "All imposts upon commerce ought to be laid by Con-gress and appropriated to their use, for without certain revenues, a government can have no power; that power, which holds the purse strings absolutely, must rule" ("From Alexander Hamilton to James Duane, [3 September 1780]," Syrett, ed., pp. 400–18).

21 E. James Ferguson, *The Power of the Purse: A History of American Public Finance, 1776–1790* (Chapel Hill: University of North Caro-lina Press, 1961), p. 252.

22 Richard H. Kohn, "The Inside History of the Newburgh Conspiracy:

America and the Coup d'Etat," *The William and Mary Quarterly*, vol. 27, no. 2 (April 1970), p. 190.

23 *Journals of the Continental Congress, 1774–1789, vol. XXIV, 1783 January 1–August 29*, edited from the original records in the Library of Congress by Gaillard Hunt (Washington: Government Printing Office, 1922), pp. 291–3.

24 Kohn quoted in C. Edward Skeen and Richard H. Kohn, "The New-burgh Conspiracy Reconsidered," *The William and Mary Quarterly*, vol. 31, no. 2 (April 1974), p. 275.

25 *Journals of the Continental Congress, vol. XXIV*, pp. 295–6. The entire sequence of communications—the petition, anonymous letters, order to assemble, Washington's response, and his explanatory notes to Congress—are found on pages 290 to 311.

26 "General Orders, 11 March 1783," *Founders Online*, National Archives.

27 "From George Washington to Officers of the Army, 15 March 1783," Jesse Ames Spencer, ed., *Complete History of the United States of America*, vol. 2 (Philadelphia: William T. Aimes, 1882), pp. 174–5.

28 John Fiske, *The Critical Period of American History, 1783–1789* (Boston and New York: Houghton, Mifflin and Company, 1888), p. 111. Fiske's citations are minimal, and this story, which first appears in his book, does not appear in any document in the *Founders Online* collection. However, we do know that Washington received glasses shortly before his Newburgh address, see "From George Washington to David Rittenhouse, 16 February 1783," *Founders Online*, National Archives, last modified June 13, 2018, founders.archives. gov/documents/Washington/99-01-02-10654. [This is an Early Access document from The Papers of George Washington. It is not an author-itative final version.]

29 "From James Madison to Edmund Randolph, 17 June 1783," William T. Hutchinson and William M. E. Rachal, ed., *The Papers of James Madison*, vol. 7 (Chicago: The University of Chicago Press, 1971), pp. 158–62.

30 "From Alexander Hamilton to Major William Jackson [19 June 1783]," Syrett, ed., pp. 397–8.

31 "Continental Congress Report of a Committee Appointed to Confer with the Supreme Executive Council of Pennsylvania on the Mutiny, 24 June 1783," Syrett, ed., pp. 403–7.

32 "Continental Congress Resolutions on Measures to be Taken in Con-sequence of the Pennsylvania Mutiny, 21 June 1783," Syrett, ed., pp. 401–2; "Continental Congress Report on Conference with the Supreme Executive Council of Pennsylvania on the Mutiny, 20 June 1783," Syrett, ed., pp. 399–401.

33 James D. Drake, *The Nation's Nature: How Continental Presump-tions Gave Rise to the United States of America* (Charlottesville: University of Virginia Press, 2011), p. 275.

6. Postwar Depression

1 "From Alexander Hamilton to Marquis de Lafayette [3 November 1782]," Syrett, ed., pp. 191–4.

2 John Fiske, *The Critical Period of American History, 1783–1789* (Boston and New York: Houghton, Mifflin, 1888). Gordon Wood reports that the term "critical period" was used during the 1780s. John Quincy Adams referred to "this critical period" during his commencement address at Harvard in 1787. Quoted in Wood, *Creation of the American Republic* (Charlotte: University of North Carolina Press, 1998), p. 393.

3 Joseph Schumpeter, *Business Cycles: A Theoretical, Historical and Statistical Analysis of the Capitalist Process* (New York: McGraw-Hill Book Company, 1939), p. 222.

4 Peter H. Lindert and Jeffrey G. Williamson, "American Incomes 1774–1860," NBER Working Paper No. 18396 (Sept. 2012), p. 17.

5 Solomon K. Smith, "Firearms Manufacturing, Gun Use, and the Emergence of Gun Culture in Early North America," *49th Parallel*, vol. 34 (Autumn 2014), table II, p. 16.

6 Bishop, p. 290.

7 Quoted in William B. Meyer, "The Making and Unmaking of a Natural Resource: The Salt Industry of Coastal Southeastern Massachusetts," *Massachusetts Historical Review*, vol. 15 (2013), p. 123–50, 125.

8 Bishop, p. 550.

9 Albert S. Bolles, *Industrial History of the United States From the Earliest Settlements to the Present Time* (Norwich, CT and Boston: The Henry Bill Publishing Company, 1881), p. 194.

10 Bolles, p. 198.

11 John H. Flannagan Jr., "Trying Times: Economic Depression in New Hampshire, 1781–1789," Dissertation Ph.D., History, Georgetown University (1972), p. 18.

12 Flannagan, pp. 24, 27.

13 Cathy Matson, "The Revolution, The Constitution, and the Early National Economy," Stanley Engerman and Robert Gallman, eds., *Cambridge Economic History of the United States: The Colonial Era*, vol. 1 (Cambridge: Cambridge University Press, 1996), p. 376.

14 Lorena S. Walsh, "Plantation Management in the Chesapeake, 1620–1820," *The Journal of Economic History*, vol. 49, no. 2 (June 1989), p. 401.

15 Bureau of the Census, Historical Statistics of the United States, Colonial Times to 1957 (Washington: U.S. Government Printing Office, 1960), p. 116, series E1–12.

16 Carey Roberts, "Alexander Hamilton and the 1790s Economy: A Reappraisal," Douglas Ambrose and Robert W. T. Martin, *The Many Faces of Alexander Hamilton: The Life and Legacy of America's Most Elusive Founding Father* (New York: New York University Press, 2006), p. 216.

17 Mary M. Schweitzer, "State-Issued Currency and the Ratification of the U.S. Constitution," *The Journal of Economic History*, vol. 49, no. 2 (June 1989), p. 315.

18 Roberts.

19 "From James Madison to Thomas Jefferson, 20 August 1785," Robert A. Rutland and William M. E. Rachal, eds., *The Papers of James Madison*, vol. 8 (Chicago: The University of Chicago Press, 1973), pp. 344–7.

20 "To Thomas Jefferson from James Madison, 4 December 1786," Julian P. Boyd, ed., *The Papers of Thomas Jefferson*, vol. 10 (Princeton: Princeton University Press, 1954), pp. 574–8.

21 "From George Washington to Edmund Randolph, 19 November 1786," W. W. Abbot, ed., *The Papers of George Washington, Confederation Series*, vol. 4 (Charlottesville: University Press of Virginia, 1995), p. 387.

22 There were, however, scattered pockets of economic recovery. Delaware Valley wheat farming seems to have had relatively healthy postwar growth. The wheat trade was further helped when war broke out in Europe in 1793. "Our object is to feed and theirs to fight," said Secretary of State Thomas Jefferson, adding, "we have only to pray their soldiers may eat a great deal." See Brooke Hunter, "Wheat, War, and the American Economy During the Age of Revolution," *The William and Mary Quarterly*, vol. 62, no. 3 (July 2005), pp. 505–6.

23 Members of the New York Press, *A Brief Popular Account of All the Financial Panics and Commercial Revulsions in the United States, from 1690 to 1857* (New York: J. C. Haney, 1857), p. 2.

24 Matson, p. 372.

25 William Babcock Weeden, *Economic and Social History of New England, 1620–1789* (Boston: Houghton, Mifflin, 1890), p. 818.

26 Victor S. Clark, *History of Manufactures in the United States, 1607–1860* (Washington: Carnegie Institution of Washington, 1916), pp. 228–9.

27 Otto C. Lightner, *The History of Business Depressions* (New York: Northeastern Press, 1922), p. 93.

28 Clark, p. 229.

29 Fiske, p. 140.

30 Woody Holton, *Unruly Americans and the Origins of the Constitution* (New York: Hill and Wang, 2008); Terry Bouton, *Taming Democracy: "The People," the Founders, and the Troubled Ending of the American Revolution* (New York: Oxford University Press, 2009); Jeffrey S. Selinger, *Embracing Dissent: Political Violence and Party Development in the United States* (Philadelphia: University of Pennsylvania Press, 2016).

31 Farley Grubb, "State Redemption of the Continental Dollar, 1779–90," *The William and Mary Quarterly*, vol. 69, no. 1 (Jan. 2012), p. 147.

32 Woody Holton, *Unruly Americans and the Origins of the Constitution* (New York: Hill and Wang, 2008).

33 "Report Relative to a Provision for the Support of Public Credit [9 January 1790]," Syrett, ed., p. 65–110.

34 Woody Holton, "Did Democracy Cause the Recession That Led to the Constitution?," *The Journal of American History*, vol. 92, no. 2 (Sept. 2005), pp. 442–69, 445.

35 Woody Holton, "'From the Labours of Others': The War Bonds Controversy and the Origins of the Constitution in New England," *The William and Mary Quarterly*, vol. 61, no. 2 (April 2004), pp. 271–316.

36 Holton, *Unruly Americans*, p. 136.

37 Holton, *Unruly Americans*, p. 32.

38 Sheldon D. Pollack, *War, Revenue, and State Building: Financing the Development of the American State* (Ithaca: Cornell University Press, 2009), p. 155.

39 Selinger, *Embracing*, p. 31.

40 Holton, *Unruly Americans*, p. 66.

41 Pollack, p. 155.

42 Fiske, *The Critical Period*, pp. 166–7.

43 David B. Robertson, *The Constitution and American Destiny* (New York: Cambridge University Press, 2005), p. 55.

44 E. James Ferguson, *The Power of the Purse: A History of American Public Finance, 1776–1790* (Chapel Hill: University of North Carolina Press, 1961), p. 221.

45 "Report Relative to a Provision for the Support of Public Credit [9 January 1790]," Syrett, ed., pp. 65–110.

46 Christopher Clark, *The Roots of Rural Capitalism: Western Massachusetts, 1780–1860* (Ithaca: Cornell University Press, 1992).

47 E. James Ferguson, "Speculation in the Revolutionary Debt: The Ownership of Public Securities in Maryland, 1790," *The Journal of Economic History*, vol. 14, no. 1 (Winter 1954), p. 38; also Holton, *Unruly Americans*, pp. 39–40.

48 Ferguson, p. 38; also Holton, *Unruly Americans*, pp. 39–40, 112–13.

49 Mary M. Schweitzer, "State-Issued Currency and the Ratification of the U.S. Constitution," *The Journal of Economic History*, vol. 49, no. 2 (June 1989), p. 318.

50 Holton, *Unruly Americans*.

51 Thomas Paine, *Collected Writings* (New York: Library of America, 1995), p. 364.

52 Jefferson seems to have come up with this turn of phrase in 1786 and used it in several letters until 1814. "From Thomas Jefferson to Alexander McCaul, 19 April 1786," Julian P. Boyd, ed., *The Papers of Thomas Jefferson*, vol. 9 (Princeton: Princeton University Press, 1954), pp. 388–90; also "Thomas Jefferson to James Monroe, 16 October 1814," J. Jefferson Looney, ed., *The Papers of Thomas Jefferson, Retirement Series*, vol. 8 (Princeton: Princeton University Press, 2011), pp. 31–3.

53 Adam Smith, *The Wealth of Nations* (New York: Random House, 2000), p. 984.

54 Ferguson, *Power of the Purse*, pp. 245–6.

55 "Abigail Adams to John Adams, 3 January 1784," Richard Alan Ryerson, ed., *The Adams Papers, Adams Family Correspondence*, vol. 5 (Cambridge: Harvard University Press, 1993), p. 2903.

56 "Abigail Adams to John Adams, 3 January 1784."

57 Woody Holton, "Abigail Adams, Bond Speculator," *The William and Mary Quarterly*, vol. 64, no. 4 (Oct. 2007), pp. 821–38.

58 "Abigail Adams to Cotton Tufts, 26 April 1785," Ryerson, ed., pp. 103–9.

59 David Harvey, *The New Imperialism* (New York: Oxford University Press, 2003).

60 Holton, "Abigail Adams, Bond Speculator," pp. 136–7; Chernow, p. 221; Also see William F. Zorow, "New York Tariff Policies, 1775–1789," *New York History*, vol. 37, no. 1 (Jan. 1956), pp. 40–63. Zorow argues that historians overemphasize the damage and danger of the New York tariff yet offers proof that the tariff was high and was leveled against sister states, in particular New Jersey and Connecticut.

61 Fiske, p. 53.

62 John C. Miller, *Alexander Hamilton and the Growth of the New Nation* (New Brunswick: Transaction Publishers, 2004; Originally published 1959 by Harper and Brothers), p. 135.

63 Fiske, pp. 146–7.

64 Quoted in Westel Woodbury Willoughby, *The Rights and Duties of American Citizenship* (New York: American Book Company, 1898), p. 128.

7. Challenging the Weak State

1 Julian P. Boyd, "Connecticut's Experiment in Expansion: The Susquehannah Company, 1753–1803," *Journal of Economic and Business History*, vol. 27 (1931), pp. 38–69.

2 Paul B. Moyer, *Wild Yankees: The Struggle for Independence Along Pennsylvania's Revolutionary Frontier* (Ithaca: Cornell University Press, 2009), p. 2.

3 Moyer, p. 29; James Truslow Adams (1878–1949), *New England in The Republic, 1776–1850* (Gloucester: P. Smith, 1960), p. 111; Oscar J. Harvey, *Wilkes-Barré (the "Diamond city") Luzerne County, Pennsylvania; its history, its natural resources, its industries, 1769–1906* (Wilkes-Barré: The Committee on souvenir and program, 1906), p. 31.

4 *Wilkes-Barré (the "Diamond city") Luzerne County, Pennsylvania; its history, its natural resources, its industries, 1769–1906.* (Wilkes-Barré: The Committee on Souvenir and Program, 1906), pp. 18–40.

5 Paul B. Moyer, "'A dangerous Combination of Villains': Pennsylvania's

Wild Yankees and the Social Context of Agrarian Resistance in Early America," *Pennsylvania History: A Journal of Mid-Atlantic Studies*, vol. 73, no. 1 (2006), pp. 41 and 42.

6 Fiske, p. 48. For details on flood, see Moyer, *Wild Yankees*, pp. 58–9.
7 Kathryn Shively Meier, "Devoted to Hardships, Danger, and Devastation: the Landscape of Indian and White Violence in Wyoming Valley, Pennsylvania, 1753–1800," in Bruce E. Stewart, ed., *Blood in the Hills: A History of Violence in Appalachia* (Lexington: University Press of Kentucky, 2011), p. 67.
8 Moyer, p. 56.
9 Moyer, p. 33.
10 Moyer.
11 Moyer, p. 59.
12 Terry Bouton, *Taming Democracy: "The People," the Founders, and the Troubled Ending of the American Revolution* (New York: Oxford University Press, 2009), pp. 164–5.
13 Julian P. Boyd, "Attempts to Form New States in New York and Pennsylvania in 1786–1796," *Quarterly Journal of the New York State Historical Association*, vol. 12, no. 3 (July 1, 1931), pp. 257–70.
14 Moyer, p. 65.
15 Willard Sterne Randall, *Ethan Allen: His Life and Times* (New York: W. W. Norton, 2012).
16 Randall, p. 495.
17 Kevin T. Barksdale, *The Lost State of Franklin: America's First Secession* (Lexington: The University Press of Kentucky, 2015), p. 18.
18 Barksdale, p. 53.
19 Barksdale, Chapter 6.
20 Peter F. Copeland, "Lord Dunmore's Ethiopian Regiment," *Military Collector & Historian*, vol. 58, no. 4 (Winter 2006), pp. 208–15.
21 Copeland, p. 215; also see James W. St. G. Walker, "Blacks as American Loyalists: The Slaves' War for Independence," *Historical Reflections*, vol. 2, no. 1 (Summer 1975), pp. 51–67
22 Cassandra Pybus, "Jefferson's Faulty Math: The Question of Slave Defections in the American Revolution," *The William and Mary Quarterly*, vol. 62, no. 2 (April 2005), p. 264.
23 Tim Lockley and David Doddington, "Maroon and Slave Communities in South Carolina Before 1865," *The South Carolina Historical Magazine*, vol. 113, no. 2 (April 2012), p. 128.
24 Lockley and Doddington, p. 132; *Gazette of the State of Georgia*, October 19, 1786, quoted in Lockley and Doddington, p. 145.
25 Sylviane A. Diouf, *Slavery's Exiles: The Story of the American Maroons* (New York: New York University Press, 2014), p. 194.
26 On this particular Savannah area group, see Chapter 3 in Timothy J. Lockley, *Maroon Communities in South Carolina: A Documentary Record* (Columbia: University of South Carolina Press, 2009); also Chapter 7 in Diouf.

27 Diouf, pp. 189–90.

28 Cited in Diouf, p. 194. This sobriquet was not often used but it kindled concern by linking the fugitives to the menace of the British.

29 "Thomas Pinckney to Georgia Gov. George Matthews, April 2, 1787," reprinted in Lockley, p. 56.

30 Chapter 7 in Diouf.

31 "McGillivary to O'Neill, January 1, 1784," quoted in Daniel S. Dupree, *Alabama's Frontiers and the Rise of the South* (Bloomington: Indiana University Press, 2018), p. 136.

32 Dupree.

33 Quoted in Dupree, p. 139.

34 Cited in Jeffrey Ostler, "To Extirpate the Indians": An Indigenous Consciousness of Genocide in the Ohio Valley and Lower Great Lakes, 1750s–1810," *The William and Mary Quarterly*, vol. 72, no. 4 (Oct. 2015), p. 604.

35 Ostler, p. 606.

36 Ostler, p. 603.

37 Ostler, p. 604.

38 Robert Worster, *The American Military Frontiers: The United States Army in the West, 1783–1900* (Albuquerque: University of New Mexico Press, 2009), p. 3.

39 "From Alexander Hamilton to George Clinton, 3 October 1783," Syrett, ed., pp. 464–9.

40 Colin G. Calloway, *The American Revolution in Indian Country: Crisis and Diversity in Native American Communities* (New York: Cambridge University Press, 1995), p. 272.

41 Sarah E. Miller, "'Foolish Young Men' and the Contested Ohio Country, 1783–1795," in Charles Beatty-Medina, Melissa Rinehart, eds., *Contested Territories: Native Americans and Non-Natives in the Lower Great Lakes, 1700–1850* (East Lansing: Michigan State University Press, 2012), p. 35.

42 "From Alexander Hamilton to George Clinton, 3 October 1783," Syrett, ed., pp. 464–9.

43 Lisa Brooks, *The Common Pot: The Recovery of Native Space in the Northeast* (Minneapolis: University of Minnesota Press, 2008), p. 106–7.

44 "From James Madison to Edmund Pendleton, 12 September 1780," William T. Hutchinson and William M. E. Rachal, ed., *The Papers of James Madison*, vol. 2 (Chicago: The University of Chicago Press, 1962), pp. 80–3.

45 Quoted in Miller, p. 37.

46 "Enclosure, 15 June 1789," Dorothy Twohig, ed., *The Papers of George Washington, Presidential Series*, vol. 2 (Charlottesville: University Press of Virginia, 1987), pp. 490–5.

47 "Virginia Delegates to Benjamin Harrison, 8 September 1783," Hutchinson and Rachal, ed., pp. 300–3.

48 "Benjamin Harrison to Virginia Delegates, 19 September 1783," Hutchinson and Rachal, ed., pp. 349–50.

49 "From George Washington to Jacob Read, 3 November 1784," W. W. Abbot, ed., *The Papers of George Washington, Confederation Series*, vol. 2 (Charlottesville: University Press of Virginia, 1920, pp. 118–23.

50 "From George Washington to Henry Knox, 23 September 1783," *Founders Online*, National Archives.

51 Collin G. Callaway, *The Victory With No Name: The Native American Defeat of the First American Army* (Oxford: Oxford University Press, 2015), p. 19.

52 Quoted in Callaway, p. 42.

53 "Rousting the Squatters: Ensign Armstrong's Report on Destroying Squatters' Cabins, 1785," in Emily Foster, ed., *The Ohio Frontier: An Anthology of Early Writings* (Lexington: University Press of Kentucky, 2000).

54 "Speech of the United Indian Nations, November 28, 1786," Peter Kratzke, ed., *The American Revolution, 1754–1805*, (Ipswich, MA: Salem Press, 2013), p. 655.

55 Patrick Henry quoted in Charles G. Talbert, "Kentucky Invades Ohio—1786," *The Register of the Kentucky Historical Society*, vol. 54, no. 188 (July 1956), p. 205.

56 Quoted in Colin G. Calloway, *The Shawnees and the War for America* (New York: Penguin, 2007), p. 83.

57 Charles G. Talbert, "Kentucky Invades Ohio—1786," *The Register of the Kentucky Historical Society*, vol. 54, no. 188 (July 1956), p. 209.

58 Talbert, p. 209. For other accounts of Moluntha's murder, see Chapter 5 in Gregory Evans Dowd, *A Spirited Resistance: The North American Indian Struggle for Unity, 1745–1815* (Baltimore: Johns Hopkins University Press, 1992); also, John Sugden, *Blue Jacket: Warrior of the Shawnees* (Lincoln: University of Nebraska Press, 2000); two accounts of the murder are given in Charles McKnight (1826–1881), *Our Western Border: Its Life, Combats, Adventures, Forays, Massacres, Captivities, Scouts, Red Chiefs, Pioneer Women, One Hundred Years Ago*, (Philadelphia: J. C. McCurdy & Co., 1875).

59 Population estimate from Lowell H. Harrison, *Kentucky's Road to Statehood* (Lexington: The University Press of Kentucky, 2015), p. 24; quote from James D. Drake, *The Nation's Nature: How Continental Presumptions Gave Rise to the United States of America* (Charlottesville: University of Virginia Press, 2011), p. 272.

60 "From George Washington to the United States Senate and House of Representatives, 10 August 1789," Twohig, ed., p. 413.

61 Callaway, *Victory with No Name*.

8. Shays's Rebellion

1 See Chapter 2 in Michael J. Klarman, *The Framers' Coup: The Making of the United States Constitution* (New York: Oxford University Press, 2016).

2 Holton, p. 66.

3 Holton, p. 65.

4 Alan Taylor, "The Hungry Year: 1789 on the Northern Border of Revolutionary America," in Alessa Johns, ed., *Dreadful Visitations: Confronting Natural Catastrophe in the Age of Enlightenment* (New York: Routledge, 1999), pp. 146, 155–6.

5 Benjamin Franklin, "Meteorological Imaginations and Conjectures (Paper Read 1784)," *Memoirs of the Literary and Philosophical Society of Manchester*, 2nd ed. (1789), pp. 373–7.

6 Taylor, pp. 146, 155–6; Alexandra Witze, Jeff Kanipe, *Island on Fire: The Extraordinary Story of a Forgotten Volcano That Changed the World* (New York: Pegasus Books, 2016).

7 Thorvaldur Thordarson and Stephen Self, "Atmospheric and environmental effects of the 1783–1784 Laki eruption: A review and reassessment," *Journal of Geophysical Research*, vol. 108, no. D1 (2003).

8 While this was good for corn it was bad for the commercial staple tobacco. See "To Thomas Jefferson from James Madison, 4 December 1786," Boyd, ed., pp. 574–8.

9 Sidney Perley, *Historic Storms of New England* (Salem: Salem Press Publishing Co., 1891), p. 119.

10 Perley.

11 Leonard L. Richards, *Shays's Rebellion: The American Revolution's Final Battle* (Philadelphia: University of Pennsylvania Press, 2003), p. 75.

12 Quoted in Daniel P. Szatmary, *Shays' Rebellion: The Making of an Agrarian Insurgency* (Amherst: University of Massachusetts Press, 1980), p. 33.

13 Richards, p. 54.

14 Klarman, p. 87.

15 Richards, p. 8.

16 On "Regulator" movements, see Richard Maxwell Brown, *The South Carolina Regulators* (Cambridge: Harvard University Press, 1963); Marjoleine Kars, *Breaking Loose Together: The Regulator Rebellion in Pre-Revolutionary North Carolina* (Chapel Hill: The University of North Carolina Press, 2002).

17 C. O. Parmenter, *History of Pelham, Mass., 1738–1898* (Amherst: Carpenter & Morehouse, 1898), p. 373.

18 Richards. As Holton points out, the first attempt to shut a court was in early June in Bristol County in southeastern Massachusetts.

See Introduction and Chapter 1 in Holton's *Unruly Americans*; and Klarman, chapter 2.

19 Richards, p. 90.

20 Richards, Chapter 1.

21 Szatmary, pp. 78–9; Holton, p. 149; "Charles Storer to John Adams, 26 Sep. 1786," *The Adams Papers*, vol. 18, Gregg L. Lint, et al., eds. (Cambridge, MA: Harvard University Press, 2016), pp. 466–7.

22 "To George Washington from Benjamin Lincoln," Abbot, ed., vol. 4, pp. 418–36.

23 *Federalist* 6 online at https://avalon.law.yale.edu/subject_menus/fed. asp.

24 "To George Washington from Henry Lee, Jr., 1 October 1786," Abbot, ed., pp. 281–2.

25 "Abigail Adams to Thomas Jefferson, 29 January 1787," C. James Taylor, et al., eds., pp. 455–7.

26 "Abigail Adams to Thomas Jefferson, 29 January 1787."

27 "[October 1786]," Robert Taylor, et al., eds., pp. 106–20.

28 "From Thomas Jefferson to David Hartley, 2 July 1787," Boyd, ed., pp. 525–6.

29 "To James Madison from William Grayson, 22 November 1786," Robert A. Rutland and William M. E. Rachal, eds., *The Papers of James Madison*, vol. 9 (Chicago: The University of Chicago Press, 1975), pp. 173–5.

30 "To George Washington from Benjamin Lincoln," Abbot, ed., pp. 418–36.

31 *Daily Advertiser* March 8, 1787, cited in footnote 4 of "Abigail Adams to Mary Smith Cranch, 28 April 1787," at Founders Online, National Archives.

32 Szatmary, p. 91.

33 Szatmary, p. 113.

34 Willard Sterne Randall, *Ethan Allen: His Life and Times* (New York: W. W. Norton & Company 2012), p. 520.

35 Quoted in Richards, p. 120.

36 Randall, p. 521.

37 See Chapter 15 in Randall.

38 See Chapter 11, Chilton Williamson, *Vermont in Quandary: 1763–1825* (Montpelier: Vermont Historical Society, 1949).

39 "New York Assembly, Remarks on an Act Acknowledging the Independence of Vermont [28 March 1787]," Syett, ed., pp. 126–41.

9. The Constitution as Reaction to Crisis

1 Max Farrand, *The Records of the Federal Convention of 1787*, three volumes (New Haven: Yale University Press, 1911); Michael

J. Klarman, *The Framers' Coup: The Making of the United States Constitution* (New York: Oxford University Press, 2016). On the mechanics of the meeting, see Chapter 1 in Robert A. Dahl, *How Democratic Is the American Constitution?* (New Haven: Yale University Press, 2003). On ratification see, Pauline Maier, *Ratification: The People Debate the Constitution, 1787–1788* (New York: Simon and Schuster, 2010).

2 James Madison was famous for writing detailed unofficial notes. In recent years, Mary Sarah Bilder has shown that Madison's notes were also bowdlerized multiple times before publication in 1836. See Bilder, *Madison's Hand: Revising the Constitutional Convention* (Cambridge, MA: Harvard University Press, 2015). For a popular discussion of the book, see Fred Barbash, "How James Madison doctored the story of the Constitutional Convention of 1787," *Washington Post*, Nov. 18, 2015. So numerous were Madison's revisions, Bilder argues, that the published version of his notes is less an account written as the action unfolded than a dissembling palimpsest that projects backward Madison's later Jeffersonian Republican version of himself. Seeking to appear the States' Rights Democrat, he cast Federalists like Hamilton as autocrats. In reality, all the framers were elitists and autocratic. They all supported property qualifications for voting and holding office. Madison was in many ways the driving force behind the Constitution and thus quite the federalist. At the convention he proposed that the national legislature have the power to overturn state laws. After ratification Madison did a political about-face. Partial notes from other delegates also survive. Only in 1911 were all these collected and published together in Farrand, ed.

3 George A. Steiner, *Government's Role in Economic Life* (New York: McGraw-Hill, 1953), p. 91.

4 James Madison, "*Federalist* Number 51, [6 February] 1788," Rutland, et al., eds., *The Papers of James Madison*, vol. 10, pp. 476–80.

5 On deeper traditions of the Constitution, see Daniel Lazare, *The Frozen Republic: How the Constitution Is Paralyzing Democracy* (New York: Harcourt Brace, 1996), p. 38.

6 Joel Richard Paul, *Without Precedent: Chief Justice John Marshall and His Times* (New York: Riverhead Books, 2018), especially, pp. 252–60.

7 Lazare, p. 43.

8 Martin Diamond, "Democracy and The Federalist: A Reconsideration of the Framers' Intent," *American Political Science Review* vol. 53, no. 1 (March 1959).

9 Michael Parenti, *Democracy for the Few* (New York: St. Martin's Press, 1988). See Chapter 4 for more details.

10 The traditional view was that most states' constitutions were copies of their old colonial charters, "with no change except to substitute the sovereignty of the people for that of the king." William C. Morey,

"The First State Constitutions," *The Annals of the American Academy of Political and Social Science*, vol. 4 (Sep. 1893), pp. 1–32: 19.

11　David Waldstreicher, "Anti-Foundational Founders: Did Post-Structuralism Fail the Historians, or Did the Historians Fail Post-Structuralism?," *American Quarterly*, vol. 53, no. 2 (June 2001), p. 342.

12　*Federalist*, No. 6.

13　"Conjectures about the New Constitution [17–30 September 1787]," Syrett, ed., pp. 275–7.

14　"Federalist No. 85, [28 May 1788]," Syrett, ed., pp. 714–21.

15　John Lynch, *Simon Bolívar: A Life* (New Haven: Yale University Press, 2006); Janet Burke and Ted Humphrey, eds., *Nineteenth-Century Nation Building and the Latin American Intellectual Tradition: A Reader* (Indianapolis: Hackett, 2007); Matthew Brown, ed., *Simon Bolívar: The Bolivarian Revolution* (New York: Verso, 2007); Marie Arana, *Bolivar: American Liberator* (New York: Simon and Shuster, 2013); Joshua Simon, "Simon Bolívar's Republican Imperialism: Another Ideology of the American Revolution," *History of Political Thought,* vol. 33, no. 2 (Summer 2012), pp. 280–304.

16　"James Madison's Version [of Hamilton's Convention Speech] [18 June 1787]," Syrett, ed., pp. 187–95.

17　"Madison's Version," p. 113

18　"Madison's Version," p. 119.

19　"Madison's Version," p. 117.

20　For excellent discussions of slavery and development, see Gavin Wright, *Slavery and American Economic Development* (Baton Rouge: Louisiana State University Press, 2013); John Majewski, *Modernizing a Slave Economy: The Economic Vision of the Confederate Nation* (Chapel Hill: University of North Carolina Press, 2009); Majewski, *A House Dividing: Economic Development in Pennsylvania and Virginia Before the Civil War* (New York: Cambridge University Press, 2000).

21　Harvey Amani Whitfield, *The Problem of Slavery in Early Vermont, 1777–1810* (Montpelier: Vermont Historical Society, 2014). Alas, the reality of Vermont's ban was less robust than the letter of the law. As late as the census of 1810 two Vermonters were listed as owning slaves. Ethan Allen seems to have had a slave, and one of his daughters moved to Alabama.

22　James Madison quoted in Farrand, ed., vol.1, p. 135.

23　John Rutledge quoted in Farrand, p. 364.

24　David Waldstreicher, *Slavery's Constitution: From Revolution to Ratification* (New York: Hill and Wang, 2009), pp. 17, 114. Also: Paul Finkelman, "Slavery and the Constitutional Convention: Making a Covenant with Death" in *Beyond Confederation: Origins of the Constitution and American National Identity,* eds. Richard Beeman, Stephen Botein, and Edward C. Carter II (1987), pp. 195–217.

25　James Oakes, "'The Compromising Expedient': Justifying a Proslavery

Constitution," *Cardozo Law Review*, vol. 17, no. 6 (1996), p. 2023.

26 Kenneth Morgan, "A Slaveowners' Constitution," *Reviews in American History*, vol. 39, no. 2, (June 2011), pp. 254–60.

27 The original pre-amendment Constitution mentions Native Americans only twice. Ned Blackhawk, "American Indians and the Study of U.S. History," in Eric Foner and Lisa McGirr, eds., *American History Now* (Philadelphia: Temple University Press, 2011).

28 Charles Beard, *An Economic Interpretation of the Constitution* (New York: Mcmillan, 1913) p. 100.

29 Jason W. Moore, *Capitalism in the Web of Life: Ecology and the Accumulation of Capital* (New York: Verso, 2015); Christian Parenti, "The Environment Making State: Territory, Nature, and Value," *Antipode*, vol. 47, no. 4 (Sept. 2015), pp. 829–48.

30 "Federalist No. 1, [27 October 1787]," Syrett, ed., pp. 301–6.

31 Vladimir Lenin, *"Left-Wing" Communism: An Infantile Disorder* (USSR: Progress Publishers, 1964), p. 51.

32 "Federalist No. 6 [14 November 1787]," Syrett, ed., pp. 309–17.

33 "Federalist No. 8 [20 November 1787]," Syrett, ed., pp. 326–32.

34 *Federalist* No. 8.

35 *Federalist* No. 11.

36 "The Federalist No. 84 [28 May 1788]," Syrett, ed., pp. 702–14.

37 Pauline Maier, *Ratification: The People Debate the Constitution, 1787–1788* (New York: Simon & Schuster, 2011).

38 Maier.

10. A Dirigiste Interpretation of the Constitution

1 Michael J. Klarman, *The Framers' Coup: The Making of the United States Constitution* (New York: Oxford University Press, 2016).

2 Beard, p. 169.

3 "No State shall enter into any Treaty, Alliance, or Confederation; grant Letters of Marque and Reprisal; coin Money; emit Bills of Credit; make any Thing but gold and silver Coin a Tender in Payment of Debts; pass any Bill of Attainder, ex post facto Law, or Law impairing the Obligation of Contracts, or grant any Title of Nobility."

4 Ann Markusen, Peter Hall, Scott Campbell, and Sabina Deitrick, *The Rise of the Gunbelt: The Military Remapping of Industrial America*, (New York: Oxford University Press, 1991).

5 Leander Bishop, *American Manufacturing From 1608 to 1860, Volume 1* (Philadelphia: Edward Young and Company, 1868), p. 495; Robert B. Gordon, "Who Turned the Mechanical Ideal Into Mechanical Reality?," *Technology and Culture*, vol. 29, no. 4 (Oct. 1988), pp. 744–8.

6 Fred L. Block and Matthew R. Keller, eds., *State of Innovation: The*

U.S. Government's Role in Technology Development (Boulder: Paradigm Publishers, 2011), p. 4.

7   "From George Washington to the United States Senate and House of Representatives, 8 January 1790," Dorothy Twohig, ed., pp. 543–9.

8   Gaillard Hunt and James Brown Scott, eds., *James Madison, The Debates in the Federal Convention of 1787 Which Framed the Constitution of the United States of America* (New York: Oxford University Press, 1920), pp. 563–4.

9   "Alexander Hamilton's Final Version of the Report on the Subject of Manufactures [5 December 1791]," Syrett, ed., pp. 230–340.

10 James Oakes, *Freedom National: The Destruction of Slavery in the United States, 1861–1865*, (New York: W.W. Norton and Company, 2013).

11 For an overview of colonial-era business corporations chartered by colonies, see Simeon E. Baldwin, "American Business Corporations before 1789," *The American Historical Review*, vol. 8, no. 3 (April 1903), pp. 449–65. Baldwin found that during "the days of colonial government there were in all but six of these of strictly American origin or character. They came in this order: (1) The New York Company "for Settleing a Fishery in these parts," 1675; (2) The Free Society of Traders, in Pennsylvania, 1682; (3) The New London Society United for Trade and Commerce, in Connecticut, 1732; (4) The Union Wharf Company in New Haven, 1760; (5) The Philadelphia Contributionship for the insuring of Houses from Loss by Fire, 1768; (6) The Proprietors of Boston Pier, or the Long Wharf in the Town of Boston in New England, 1772." Also see Jason Kaufman, "Corporate Law and the Sovereignty of States," *American Sociological Review*, vol. 73, no. 3 (June 2008), pp. 402–25.

12 Merritt Roe Smith, *Harpers Ferry Armory and the New Technology: The Challenge of Change* (Ithaca: Cornell University Press, 1977); Merritt Roe Smith, "Army Ordnance and the 'American System' of Manufacturing, 1815–1861," in Smith, ed., *Military Enterprise and Technological Change: Perspectives on the American Experience* (Cambridge, MA: MIT Press, 1985), pp. 39–86. For more on naval power and commerce, see Matthew Karp, *This Vast Southern Empire: Slaveholders at the Helm of American Foreign Policy* (Cambridge, MA: Harvard University Press, 2016).

13 *Federalist* No. 24.

14 W. D. Adler and A. J. Polsky, "Building the New American Nation: Economic Development, Public Goods, and the Early U.S. Army," *Political Science Quarterly*, vol. 125 (2010), p. 88.

15 Smith, *Harpers Ferry Armory and the New Technology*, p. 28. Starting in 1808, the federal government spent more than $200,000 per year to arm and equip the state militias, thus pulling the state's military units closer to the federal government.

16 Peter Linebaugh, *The Magna Carta Manifesto: Liberties and Commons*

for All (Berkeley: University of California Press, 2008), p. 30.

17 Jonathan Nitzan and Shimshon Bichler, *Capital as Power: A Study of Order and Creorder* (New York: Routledge, 2009), p. 313.

18 Mario Schmidt, "Why Wampum Is More Money Than Scholars Think," *Suomen Antropologi: Journal of the Finnish Anthropological Society*, vol. 39, no. 2 (2014), pp. 20–38.

19 Andro Linklater, *Measuring America: How the United States Was Shaped by the Greatest Land Sale in History* (New York: Plume, 2002), p. 67.

20 "VII. Final State of the Report on Weights and Measures [4 July 1790]," Boyd, ed., pp. 650–74.

21 Arthur H. Frazier, *United States Standards of Weights and Measures, Their Creation and Creators* (Washington: Smithsonian Institution Press, 1978). In 1799, the Fifth Congress passed an act ordering the surveyor of each port of entry to "from time to time examine and try the weights and measures, and other instruments used in ascertaining the duties on imports with standards to be provided by each collector at public expense for that purpose" (*Statutes at Large: 5th Congress*, Sess. III, CH. 22, 1799, p. 643).

22 In 1821, Secretary of State John Quincy Adams submitted to Congress a long and rather philosophical report on the subject of measurement, or "the instruments used by man for the comparison of quantities and proportions of things." For Adams these were an integral component of human society, almost a binding element. Adams wrote that his goals were "uniformity, permanency, universality; one standard to be the same for all persons and all purposes, and to continue the same forever." This, however, required "powers which no legislator has hitherto been found to possess." Secretary of State John Quincy Adams, "Weights and Measures," Communicated to the Senate, February 2, 1821, 16th Congress, No. 503, 2d Session, *American State Papers: Documents, Legislative and Executive, of the Congress of the United States*, vol. 2 (Washington: Gales and Seaton, 1834), p. 656.

23 Karl Polanyi, *The Great Transformation: The Political and Economic Origins of Our Time* (Boston: Beacon Press, 1945, 2001), pp. 66, 145.

11. Public Debt as Central Power

1 On their combined purposes, see William Appleman Williams, "The Age of Mercantilism: An Interpretation of the American Political Economy, 1763 to 1828," *The William and Mary Quarterly*, vol. 15, no. 4 (Oct. 1958), pp. 419–37.

2 "Report Relative to a Provision for the Support of Public Credit [9 January 1790]," Syrett, ed., pp. 65–110. "Final Version of the Second

Report on the Further Provision Necessary for Establishing Public Credit (Report on a National Bank), 13 December 1790," *The Papers of Alexander Hamilton*, vol. 7 (New York: Columbia University Press, 1963), pp. 305–42; and "Report on the Establishment of a Mint," pp. 570–607.

3 "Report Relative to a Provision for the Support of Public Credit [9 January 1790]." Also see John C. Miller, *Alexander Hamilton and the Growth of the New Nation* (New Brunswick: Transaction Publishers, 2004), p. 230.

4 Most Southern states, except for South Carolina, had been particularly sloppy in their record keeping; see E. James Ferguson, *The Power of the Purse: A History of American Public Finance, 1776–1790* (Chapel Hill: University of North Carolina Press, 1961), pp. 206–7; Hamilton's request for information on these accounts is found in "Treasury Department Circular to the Governors of the States, 26 September 1789," Syrett, ed., pp. 411–12.

5 Ferguson explained the circular logic as follows: "Virginia's case stands out clearly and is typical of the Carolinas and, to a lesser extent, Maryland. Virginians were overloaded with both state and federal certificates. When the state got around to paying debts after the war, it did not distinguish between the two kinds of certificates; the people insisted that both be accepted for taxes. The county courts liquidated, i.e., examined and adjusted to specie value, all certificates or other claims. The people who presented them got state notes in exchange. These notes were rapidly absorbed by taxes, which included a special 'certificate tax,' estimated to return $546,000 annually to the state treasury. From 1782 through 1785 it appears that Virginia redeemed $3,250,000 in certificates and was then able to discontinue the special tax. The state thus 'paid' claims which otherwise would have survived to become part of the public debt." Ferguson, p. 182.

6 The Bank of England began with a royal charter of incorporation that allowed it to sell £1.5 million worth of stock. It managed to raise £1.2 million in private capital, all of which was loaned to the government. The borrowing government, in turn, agreed to pay the lenders a hefty, tax-free, 8 percent annual interest, plus an annual management fee of £4,000. The Bank also had the right to accept deposits and issue bank notes, essentially paper currency. Investors trusted that the government would service its debt because it had tax revenues and the coercive powers to insure their steady flow. W. Marston Acres, *The Bank of England From Within: 1694–1900* (London: Oxford University Printing Press, 1931), p. 8; also see Chapter 7, "Banking Evolution in England" in Richard S. Grossman, *Unsettled Account: The Evolution of Banking in the Industrialized World since 1800* (Princeton: Princeton University Press, 2010); John Clapham, *The Bank of England* (Cambridge: Cambridge University Press, 1944); Halley Goodman, "The Formation of the Bank of England: A Response to Changing

Political and Economic Climate, 1694," *Penn History Review*, vol. 17, no. 1 (Fall 2009).

7 Douglass C. North and Barry R. Weingast, "Constitutions and Commitment: The Evolution of Institutions Governing Public Choice in Seventeenth-Century England," *The Journal of Economic History*, vol. 49, no. 4 (1989), pp. 803–32; Barry R. Weingast, "The Political Foundations of Democracy and the Rule of Law," *The American Political Science Review*, vol. 91, No. 2 (June 1997), pp. 245–63.

8 Steven Pincus, *1688: The First Modern Revolution* (New Haven: Yale University Press, 2009).

9 Chernow, p. 347. Chernow's footnote is unclear as regards the source on Angelica Schuyler Church sending *Wealth of Nations*. But she did write to Hamilton: "I shall send by the first ships every well written book that I can procure on the subject of finance. I cannot help being diverted at the avidity I express to whatever relates to this subject. It is a new source of amusement or rather of *interest*." See "To Alexander Hamilton from Angelica Church, 4 February 1790," Syrett, ed., p. 245.

10 Adam Smith, "Book V: On the Revenue of the Sovereign or Commonwealth, Chapter III: On Public Debts," *An Inquiry into the Nature and Causes of The Wealth of Nations* (New York: Random House, 1937).

11 "Report Relative to a Provision for the Support of Public Credit [9 January 1790]," Syrett, ed., pp. 65–110.

12 Necker quoted Donald F. Swanson and Andrew P. Trout, "Alexander Hamilton, 'the Celebrated Mr. Neckar,' and Public Credit," *The William and Mary Quarterly*, vol. 47, no. 3 (July 1990), p. 425.

13 "Report Relative to a Provision for the Support of Public Credit [9 January 1790]."

14 Holton, *Unruly Americans*; Holton, "Abigail Adams, Bond Speculator," *The William and Mary Quarterly*, Third Series, vol. 64, no. 4 (Oct. 2007), pp. 821–38.

15 John R. Nelson Jr., *Liberty and Property: Political Economy and Policymaking in the New Nation, 1789–1812* (Baltimore: Johns Hopkins University Press, 1987), quoted in Max M. Edling and Mark D. Kaplanoff, "Alexander Hamilton's Fiscal Reform: Transforming the Structure of Taxation in the Early Republic," *The William and Mary Quarterly*, Third Series, vol. 61, no. 4 (Oct. 2004), p. 717.

16 Leonard L. Richards, *Shays's Rebellion: The American Revolution's Final Battle* (Philadelphia: University of Pennsylvania Press, 2016), p. 8; Richards, p. 75.

17 Ferguson, pp. 295–6.

18 Ferguson, p. 292.

19 "From Alexander Hamilton to George Washington, 10 September 1790," Syrett, ed., pp. 31–2.

20 "Report Relative to a Provision for the Support of Public Credit [9 January 1790]."

21 James Oakes, *The Ruling Race: The History of American Slaveholders* (New York: W.W. Norton, 1998), p. 26; also Sharon Ann Murphy, "Banking on Slavery in the Antebellum South," paper at the Yale University Economic History Workshop, May 1, 2017.

22 A good summary of this moment is offered here: "Madison's Election to the First Federal Congress, October 1788–February 1789 (Editorial Note)," Rutland and Hobson, eds., pp. 301–4.

23 Ferguson, p. 297.

24 Thomas Jefferson quoted in John C Miller, *Alexander Hamilton and the Growth of the New Nation* (New Brunswick: Transaction Publishers, 1959), pp. 250–2.

25 Norman K. Risjord, "The Compromise of 1790: New Evidence on the Dinner Table Bargain," *The William and Mary Quarterly*, vol. 33, no. 2 (April 1976), pp. 309–14.

26 John C Miller, *Alexander Hamilton and the Growth of the New Nation* (New Brunswick: Transaction Publishers, 1959), p. 250.

27 Webster quoted in Richard Sylla, "Experimental Federalism: The Economics of American Government, 1789–1914," Chapter 12 in Stanley L. Engerma and Robert E. Gallman, eds., *The Cambridge Economic History of United States, Volume 2: The Long Nineteenth Century* (Cambridge: Cambridge University Press, 2000), p. 499.

12. The Bank Uniting Sword and Purse

1 "Second Report on the Further Provision Necessary for Establishing Public Credit (Report on a National Bank), 13 December 1790," Syrett, ed., pp. 305–42. Quotations in section all drawn from the Report.

2 David J. Cowen, "The First Bank of the United States and the Securities Market Crash of 1792," *The Journal of Economic History*, vol. 60, no. 4 (Dec. 2000), p. 1042.

3 Max M. Edling and Mark D. Kaplanoff, "Alexander Hamilton's Fiscal Reform: Transforming the Structure of Taxation in the Early Republic," *The William and Mary Quarterly*, vol. 61, no. 4 (Oct. 2004), pp. 713–44.

4 The eight states they studied were New Hampshire, Massachusetts, Rhode Island, Connecticut, New York, New Jersey, Pennsylvania, and Delaware. Edling and Kaplanoff, p. 731.

5 Edling and Kaplanoff, p. 731. It is worth noting that in some localities, like New Jersey, propertied women had the vote. Property-owning women in New Jersey were finally disenfranchised in 1807. "After the Revolution most states specifically disfranchised women, even when property holders, though Rhode Island, Connecticut, and Delaware did not; only New Jersey explicitly enfranchised 'all inhabitants' who

could meet the residence and property qualification." See Donald Rat-
cliff, "The Right to Vote and the Rise of Democracy, 1787–1828,"
Journal of the Early Republic, vol. 33, no. 2 (Summer 2013), p. 229.
Before and during the Revolutionary War, propertied, taxpaying
single women in Virginia also had the right to vote, though they rarely
used it. When Lee Corbin, sister of Richard Henry Lee, inherited her
deceased husband's property and became a taxpayer, she wrote to
her brother, then a member of the Continental Congress, to complain
that taxation without representation was unfair. He responded that
women had "as legal a right to vote as any other person," and if they
failed to vote this was due to custom not to law. See Linda Grant De
Pauw, "Women and the Law: The Colonial Period," *Human Rights*,
vol. 6, no. 2 (Winter 1977), p. 112. Also see, Judith Apter Klinghoffer
and Lois Elkis, "'The Petticoat Electors': Women's Suffrage in New
Jersey, 1776–1807," *Journal of the Early Republic*, vol. 12, no. 2
(Summer 1992), pp. 159–93.

6 Douglas A. Irwin, "Revenue or Reciprocity? Founding Feuds over
Early U.S. Trade Policy," in Douglas Irwin and Richard Sylla, eds.,
Founding Choices: American Economic Policy in the 1790s (Chicago:
University of Chicago Press, 2010), p. 101.

13. The *Report*

1 In 1889 Henry Cabot Lodge wrote that Hamilton "admired and
quoted but ... did not follow" Smith. Lodge, *Alexander Hamilton*
(Boston: Houghton Mifflin Company, 1898), p. 108.

2 Alice Amsden, *Asia's Next Giant: South Korea and Late Industrialization* (Oxford: Oxford University Press, 1989), p. 3.

3 Ian Patrick Austin, *Common Foundations of American and East Asian
Modernisation: From Alexander Hamilton to Junichreo Koizumi*,
(Singapore: Select Books, 2009).

4 Raymond Williams gave this etymology: "Capitalism as a word
describing a particular economic system began to appear in English
from eC19 [the early nineteenth century], and almost simultaneously
in French and German. Capitalist as a noun is a little older; Arthur
Young used it, in his journal of *Travels in France* (1792), but relatively
loosely: 'moneyed men, or capitalists'. Coleridge used it in the developed sense—'capitalists ... having labour at demand'—in *Tabletalk*
(1823)." Williams, *Keywords: A Vocabulary of Culture and Society*,
Revised Edition (New York: Oxford University Press, 1976), p. 50.

5 Michael Hudson, *America's Protectionist Takeoff, 1815–1914* (ISLET-
Verlag, 2010), p. vii; Fred L. Block, *The Vampire State: And Other
Myths and Fallacies About the U.S. Economy* (New York: New Press,
1997); Block and Matthew R. Keller, *State of Innovation: The U.S.*

Government's Role in Technology Development (New York: Routledge, 2011); Mariana Mazzucato, *The Entrepreneurial State: Debunking Public vs. Private Sector Myths* (New York: Anthem, 2013).

6 Ha-Joon Chang, *Bad Samaritans: The Myth of Free Trade and the Secret History of Capitalism* (New York: Bloomsbury Press, 2002), p. 50.

7 "Alexander Hamilton's Final Version of the Report on the Subject of Manufactures, [5 December 1791]," Syrett, ed., vol. 10, pp. 230–340. Hereafter *Report on the Subject of Manufactures.*

8 That is how Hamilton paraphrased the Physiocratic position. In *Wealth of Nations* Smith put it this way: "It is the work of nature which remains after deducting or compensating every thing which can be regarded as the work of man. It is seldom less than a fourth, and frequently more than a third of the whole produce. No equal quantity of productive labour employed in manufactures can ever occasion so great a reproduction. In them nature does nothing; man does all; and the reproduction must always be in proportion to the strength of the agents that occasion it." See Adam Smith, *An Inquiry into the Nature and Causes of the Wealth of Nations*, ed. I. R. McCulloch, vol. II (Edinburgh 1828), p. 147. David Ricardo was able to see "nature" in a broader context: "Does nature nothing for man in manufactures? Are the powers of wind and water, which move our machinery, and assist navigation, nothing? The pressure of the atmosphere and the elasticity of steam, which enable us to work the most stupendous engines—are they not the gifts of nature? to say nothing of the effects of the matter of heat in softening and melting metals, of the decomposition of the atmosphere in the process of dyeing and fermentation. There is not a manufacture which can be mentioned, in which nature does not give her assistance to man, and give it too, generously and gratuitously." See, David Ricardo, *On the Principles of Political Economy, and Taxation*, 2nd edition (1819), note to pp. 61–2.

9 Smith, *Wealth of Nations*, Book I, p. 449.

10 James Madison quoted in Farrand, ed., p. 135.

11 John Rutledge quoted in Farrand, ed., p. 364.

12 David McCullough, *John Adams* (New York: Simon & Schuster, 2001).

13 Jefferson owned about 600 people during his lifetime. Annette Gordon-Reed, *The Hemingses of Monticello: An American Family* (New York: W. W. Norton & Company, 2008). On the nail manufacture see Stephen B. Hodin, "The Mechanisms of Monticello: Saving Labor in Jefferson's America," *Journal of the Early Republic*, vol. 26, no. 3 (Fall 2006), p. 384.

14 Edward G. Bourne, "Alexander Hamilton and Adam Smith," *The Quarterly Journal of Economics*, vol. 8, no. 3 (April 1894), pp. 328–44.

15 For a comparison of the views of Coxe and Hamilton, see Harold Hutcheson, *Tench Coxe: A Study in American Economic Development* (New York: DaCapo Press, 1969), pp. 99–102. Mention of Hamilton's

essay on Smith is found in Clinton Rossiter, *Alexander Hamilton and the Constitution* (New York: Harcourt, Brace, 1964), pp. 119, 130.

16 Samuel Fleischacker, "Adam Smith's Reception Among the American Founders, 1776–1790," *The William and Mary Quarterly*, vol. 59, no. 4 (Oct. 2002), pp. 897–924: 898. For more on Hamilton's relationship to Smith, see Edward G. Bourne, "Alexander Hamilton and Adam Smith," *The Quarterly Journal of Economics*, vol. 8, no. 3 (April 1894), pp. 328–44.

17 Jason W. Moore, *Capitalism in the Web of Life: Ecology and the Accumulation of Capital* (New York: Verso, 2015).

18 *Report on the Subject of Manufactures*.

19 For a superb history of climate denial-ideology, see Naomi Oreskes and Erik M. Conway, *Merchants of Doubt: How a Handful of Scientists Obscured the Truth on Issues from Tobacco Smoke to Global Warming*, (New York: Bloomsbury, 2011).

20 *Report on the Subject of Manufactures*.

21 Raymond Williams missed this first use of the word.

22 *Report on the Subject of Manufactures*.

23 For a classic and lucid description of the process, see Karl Marx and Friedrich Engels, *The Communist Manifesto* (London: Penguin, 1967 [1848]); also see David Harvey, *The Condition of Postmodernity* (Malden, MA: Blackwell, 1990).

24 *Report on the Subject of Manufactures*.

25 *Report on the Subject of Manufactures*.

26 John R. Nelson Jr., "Alexander Hamilton and American Manufacturing: A Reexamination," *The Journal of American History*, vol. 65, no. 4 (March 1979), pp. 971–95; also see Andrew Shankman, "'A New Thing on Earth': Alexander Hamilton, Pro-Manufacturing Republicans, and the Democratization of American Political Economy," *Journal of the Early Republic*, vol. 23, no. 3 (Autumn 2003), p. 327.

27 Quoted in Ugo Rabbeno, *The American Commercial Policy, Three Historical Essays* (London: Macmillan and Co., 1895), p. 139.

28 Doron Ben-Atar, "Alexander Hamilton's Alternative: Technology Piracy and the Report on Manufactures," *The William and Mary Quarterly*, vol. 52, no. 3 (July 1995), pp. 389–414; Jacob E. Cooke "Tench Coxe, Alexander Hamilton, and the Encouragement of American Manufactures," *The William and Mary Quarterly*, vol. 32, no. 3 (July 1975), pp. 369–92.

29 *Report on the Subject of Manufactures*, p. 43. On early state-level quality control, see Victor S. Clark, *History of Manufactures in the United States, 1607–1860* (Washington: 1916), p. 263.

30 These shibboleths of mainstream economics have their origins. The idea of the "free rider problem" emerges out of torts regarding people literally riding for free on trains and then suing the railroads after problems occurred. The concept is then taken up as a metaphor in labor policy discussions around the problem of compulsory versus

voluntary dues-paying, as in: "The reluctance of workers to pay union dues after their immediate demands have been met. The 'free rider' is a well-known problem of the American union." Sumner H. Slichter, "The Taft-Hartley Act," *The Quarterly Journal of Economics,* vol. 63, no. 1 (Feb. 1949), pp. 1–31:2. By the sixties, the concept had been absorbed into public choice economics. See James M. Buchanan, "What Should Economists Do?," *Southern Economic Journal,* vol. 30, no. 3 (Jan. 1964), pp. 213–22. The "prisoner's dilemma" goes back to the work of the atomic strategist Thomas C. Schelling. See Thomas C. Schelling, "The Strategy of Conflict Prospectus for a Reorientation of Game Theory," *The Journal of Conflict Resolution,* vol. 2, no. 3 (Sept. 1958), pp. 203–64.

31 "Bill of Exchange," *Encyclopædia Britannica,* vol. 3 (Cambridge: Cambridge University Press, 1911), p. 940.

32 In the third draft of the *Report,* where Hamilton introduced this quote, he wrote and crossed out "(Smith W of Nations 1 vol. P 219)." According to *Founders Online,* "The edition from which H is quoting is *An Inquiry into the Nature and Causes of the Wealth of Nations.* By Adam Smith, LL.D. and F.R.S. Formerly Professor of Moral Philosophy in the University of Glasgow. In Three Volumes. vol. I (Dublin: Printed for Messrs. Whitestone, Chamberlaine, W. Watson, Potts, S. Watson, Hoey, Williams, W. Colles, Wilson, Armitage, Walker, Moncrieffe, Jenkin, Gilbert, Cross, Mills, Hallhead, Faulkner, Hillary, and J. Colles. 1776). References which Hamilton made to Smith, however, in other documents in the Hamilton Papers, Library of Congress, do not coincide with the pagination of this edition of *The Wealth of Nations.*" See note 100 in "Alexander Hamilton's Third Draft of the Report on the Subject of Manufactures, 1791," Syrett, ed., vol. 10, pp. 64–124.

33 Ugo Rabbeno, *The American Commercial Policy, Three Historical Essays* (London: Macmillan and Co., 1895), p. 137.

34 Rabbeno, p. 139.

35 Rabbeno, p. 137.

36 Chalmers A. Johnson, *MITI and the Japanese Miracle* (Stanford: Stanford University Press, 1982).

14. Small-Government Apocalypse

1 "Thomas Jefferson's Memorandum of Conversations with Washington, 1 March 1792," Robert F. Haggard and Mark A. Mastromarino, eds., *The Papers of George Washington, Presidential Series,* vol. 10, (Charlottesville: University of Virginia Press, 2002), pp. 5–10.

2 "From James Madison to Henry Lee, 1 January 1792," Rutland and Mason, ed., *The Papers of James Madison,* vol. 14, pp. 179–81.

3 She did, however, worry about runaway speculation but deemed it

"an Evil that will cure itself in Time." "Abigail Adams to Mary Smith Cranch, 25–29 March 1792," Taylor, et al., eds., *The Adams Papers, Adams Family Correspondence*, vol. 9, pp. 273–4.

4   John C. Miller, *Alexander Hamilton and the Growth of the New Nation* (New Brunswick: Transaction Publishers, 1959), p. 298.

5   Chernow, Chapter 33.

6   Lawrence A. Peskin, *Manufacturing Revolution: The Intellectual Origins of Early American Industry* (Baltimore: Johns Hopkins University Press, 2010), see Chapter 5.

7   Cathy Matson, "Mathew Carey's Learning Experience: Commerce, Manufacturing, and the Panic of 1819," *Early American Studies*, vol. 11, no. 3 (2013), pp. 455–85.

8   Tench Coxe, "A Communication from the Pennsylvania Society for the Encouragement of Manufactures and the Useful Arts" (Philadelphia: Printed for the Society by Samuel Ackerman, 1804), p. 4.

9   Coxe seems to have attempted a relaunch in 1801; see "A Communication from the Pennsylvania Society for the Encouragement of Manufactures and the Useful Arts" (Philadelphia: Printed for the Society by Samuel Ackerman, 1804).

10   Robert S. Fitton, *The Arkwrights: Spinners of Fortune* (Manchester: Manchester University Press, 1989), p. 81. "To Alexander Hamilton from Thomas Marshall, 19 July 1791," Syrett, ed., pp. 556–7.

11   On sums invested, see: "Acts of the Sixteenth General Assembly of the State of New Jersey, October 25th 1791" (Burlington, NJ: Isaac Neale, 1791), p. 731. For details on members/owners, see Daniel Pace, "The Society for Establishing Useful Manufactures: Class and Political Economy in the Early Republic" (2015), Seton Hall University Dissertations and Theses (ETDs). 2108.

12   Peskin, pp. 116–17.

13   Robert F. Jones, "Economic Opportunism and the Constitution in New York State: The Example of William Duer," *New York History*, vol. 68, no. 4 (Oct. 1, 1987), pp. 357–75; Robert F. Jones, "William Duer and the Business of Government in the Era of the American Revolution," *The William and Mary Quarterly*, vol. 32, no. 3 (July 1975), pp. 393–416.

14   Robert F. Jones, "William Duer," p. 411.

15   Hunter Research, "Factories Below the Falls: Paterson's Allied Textile Printing Site in Historic Context," Report for the New Jersey Department of Environmental Protection Division of Parks and Forestry, September 2010, DPMC #P1047-00, Chapter 5, p. 19.

16   "From Thomas Jefferson to Thomas Mann Randolph, Jr., 30 May 1790," Boyd, ed., pp. 448–50. Jefferson owned the third edition of Smith's book.

17   "Thomas Jefferson to James Monroe, 16 October 1814," J. Jefferson Looney, ed., *The Papers of Thomas Jefferson, Retirement Series*, vol. 8 (Princeton: Princeton University Press, 2011), pp. 31–3.

18 "Thomas Jefferson to William H. Crawford, 20 June 1816," Looney, ed., pp. 173–6.

19 "II. First Annual Message to Congress, 8 December 1801," Barbara B. Oberg, ed., *The Papers of Thomas Jefferson*, vol. 36 (Princeton: Princeton University Press, 2009), pp. 58–67; also see Frank Bourgin, *The Great Challenge: The Myth of Laissez-Faire in the Earlier Republic* (New York: Harper & Row/Perennial Library, 1989), p. 133.

20 Robert M. S. McDonald, "The (Federalist?) Presidency of Thomas Jefferson," in Francis D. Cogliano, ed., *A Companion to Thomas Jefferson* (London: Blackwell Publishing, 2012).

21 Harvey Chalmers, *The Birth of the Erie Canal* (New York: Bookman Associates, 1960), p. 94.

22 Richard Sylla, "Experimental Federalism: The Economics of American Government, 1789–1914," in Stanley L. Engerma and Robert E. Gallman, eds., *The Cambridge Economic History of United States*, vol. 2 (Cambridge: Cambridge University Press, 2000), p. 518.

23 "From Thomas Jefferson to Albert Gallatin, 13 October 1802," Barbara B. Oberg, ed., *The Papers of Thomas Jefferson*, vol. 38, *1 July–12 November 1802* (Princeton: Princeton University Press, 2011), pp. 486–8.

24 John Joseph Wallis, "The Other Foundings: Federalism and the Constitutional Structure of American Government," in Douglas Irwin and Richard Sylla, eds., *Founding Choices: American Economic Policy in the 1790s* (Chicago: University of Chicago Press, 2010), p. 194. For a hostile but revealing review, see Andrew Shankman's "Founding Choices: American Economic Policy in the 1790s by Douglas A. Irwin and Richard Sylla," *The Business History Review*, vol. 86, no. 3 (Autumn 2012), pp. 595–7.

25 Alan Taylor, *The Civil War of 1812: American Citizens, British Subjects, Irish Rebels, and Indian Allies* (New York: Alfred A. Knopf, 2010).

26 Francis B. Heitman, *Historical Register and Dictionary of the United States Army, From Its Organization, September 29, 1789, to March 2, 1903*, vol. II (Washington: Government Printing Office, 1903), pp. 568–9; for the Navy's numbers, see "An Act making appropriations for the Navy of the United States, for the year one thousand eight hundred and one" (2 Stat. 122 [March 3, 1801]); "An Act making an appropriation for the support of the Navy of the United States, for the year one thousand eight hundred and two" (2 Stat. description begins The Public Statutes at Large of the United States of America, II (Boston, 1850). description ends 178–9 [May 1, 1802]).

27 Gordon S. Wood, *Empire of Liberty* (Oxford: Oxford University Press, 2009), p. 702.

28 John K. Mahon, *History of the Militia and the National Guard* (New York: Macmillan, 1983), p. 66.

29 Mahon, p. 66.

30 George Robert Gleig, *A Narrative of The Campaigns of the British Army at Washington and New Orleans* (London: John Murray, 1821), pp. 130–1.

31 Gleig, pp. 132–6.

32 Gleig, pp. 132–3.

33 Gleig, pp. 134–5.

34 Quoted in Charles J. Ingersoll, *Historical Sketch of the Second War between the United States of America and Great Britain* (Philadelphia: Lea and Blanchard, 1845–9), p. 185.

35 Ingersoll, p. 189.

36 Alan Taylor, *The Internal Enemy: Slavery and War in Virginia, 1772–1832* (New York: W. W. Norton, 2013), p. 302.

37 Gleig, pp. 132–6.

38 Gerald Horne, *The Counter-Revolution of 1776: Slave Resistance and the Origins of the United States of America* (New York: NYU Press, 2014).

39 Horne.

15. The *Report*'s Long Impact

1 Quoted in Douglas A. Irwin, "The Aftermath of Hamilton's 'Report on Manufactures,'" *The Journal of Economic History*, vol. 64, no. 3 (Sept. 2004), pp. 800–1.

2 Michael Lind, *A Land of Promise: An Economic History of the United States* (New York: Harper Collins, 2012), p. 15.

3 For details, see Richard Sylla, "Experimental Federalism: The Economics of American Government, 1789–1914," in Stanley L. Engerman and Robert E. Gallman, eds., *The Cambridge Economic History of the United States, vol. II* (New York: Cambridge University Press, 2000); Alasdair Roberts, *America's First Great Depression: Economic Crisis and Political Disorder After the Panic of 1837* (Ithaca: Cornell University Press, 2013).

4 George Rogers Taylor, *The Transportation Revolution 1815–1860* (New York: M.E. Sharp, 1951), p. 301.

5 Andrew Shankman, "Introduction: Conflict for a Continent," *The World of the Revolutionary American Republic: Land, Labor, and the Conflict for a Continent* (London: Routledge, 2014), p. 10.

6 Stephen Aron, *How the West Was Lost: The Transformation of Kentucky from Daniel Boone to Henry Clay* (Baltimore: Johns Hopkins University Press, 1999).

7 Ha-Joon Chang, "Kicking Away the Ladder," *Post-Autistic Economics Review*, no. 15, Sept. 4, 2002.

8 Daniel Raymond, *Thoughts on Political Economy in Two Parts* (Baltimore: Fielding Lucas Jr., 1820), pp. v–vi.

9   Quoted in Michael Perelman, "Henry Carey's Political-Ecological Economics: An Introduction," *Organization & Environment*, vol. 12, no. 3 (Sept. 1999), p. 283.

10 Andrew Shankman, "Capitalism, Slavery, and the New Epoch: Mathew Carey's 1819," in Seth Rockman and Sven Beckert, eds., *Slavery's Capitalism: A New History of American Economic Development* (Philadelphia: University of Pennsylvania Press, 2016), pp. 243–61.

11 Mathew Carey, *The Olive Branch: Or, Faults on Both Sides, Federal and Democratic. A Serious Appeal on the Necessity of Mutual Forgiveness and Harmony* (Philadelphia: M. Carey and Son, 1818).

12 Perelman, "Henry Carey's Economics," pp. 280–1.

13 "Marx to Weydemeyer, March 5, 1852," *Marx and Engels: Collected Works*, vol. 39 (London: Lawrence & Wishart, 2011), p. 58. For further discussion of Marx and Carey, see Perelman, 1987, p. 24. Interestingly, Marx put this in a letter to Joseph Weydemeyer, a German socialist and veteran of the failed revolutions of 1848 who moved to St. Louis in 1851. When the U.S. Civil War began, Weydemeyer joined the Union Army and fought as an officer in the western theater. It was in the West, under Grant and Sherman, that the Union began to develop its economically oriented strategy of Hard War, which targeted the South's economic base as opposed to just its armies. In other words, Missouri's German "Red Republicans" likely had something to do with the shift toward making economically aggressive war upon the Confederacy's mode of production, rather than just its armies. See, Andrew Zimmerman, "From the Rhine to the Mississippi: Property, Democracy, and Socialism in the American Civil War," *The Journal of the Civil War Era*, vol. 5, no. 1 (Mar 2015), pp. 3–37.

14 Perelman, pp. 280–1.

15 After the Meiji Restoration, Japan sought to industrialize and modernize in the face of military and economic threats from Western powers, including the U.S., and borrowed heavily from American political economy. Taken up with ardor, the Hamiltonian tradition—protecting and building national markets with tariffs, subsidizing infant industries directly with subsidies, recruiting and developing skilled labor, creating a coherent and effective credit system, building infrastructure and communication networks, creating a research infrastructure, and all of this at state expense—drove forward a crash program of industrialization beginning in the 1870s.

16 William Otto Henderson, *Friedrich List, Economist and Visionary, 1789–1846* (Totowa, NJ: Frank Cass, 1983), p. 150.

17 Maurice G. Baxter, *Henry Clay and the American System* (Lexington: University Press of Kentucky, 2015), pp. 108–9.

18 Richard R. John, *Spreading the News: The American Postal System From Franklin to Morse* (Cambridge, MA: Harvard University Press, 1998).

19 John Lawrence Larson, *Internal Improvement: National Public Works*

and the Promise of Popular Government in the Early United States (Chapel Hill: University of North Carolina Press, 2001), p. 46.

20 William Taylor Barry, "Report of the Postmaster General, November 24, 1829," (Washington: Department of Post Office, 1829), p. 43. Also: *The United States Postal Service: An American History, 1775–2006* (Washington: Government Relations, United States Postal Service, 2012). Three quarters of all federal civil servants were postal employees. Before long the Post Office would become the largest single piece of the central government, surpassing even the federal military. In other words, for much of early American history, the Post Office was the single largest employer in the country, public or private.

21 Report of the Postmaster General, p. 43.

22 Alexis de Tocqueville, *Democracy in America* (New York: Harper Perennial, 1966), footnote 6, p. 303.

23 Tocqueville, p. 303.

24 Tocqueville, p. 554.

25 John Majewski, Christopher Baer, and Daniel B. Klein, "Responding to Relative Decline: The Plank Road Boom of Antebellum New York," *The Journal of Economic History*, vol. 53, no. 1 (March 1993), pp. 106–22.

26 Richard R. John, *Spreading the News: The American Postal System From Franklin to Morris* (Cambridge, MA: Harvard University Press, 1995), p. 39. Books and all other parcels were not even allowed to be shipped through the post until the middle nineteenth century.

27 John, p. 4.

28 John, p. 221.

29 Christian Parenti, "The Environment Making State: Territory, Nature, and Value," *Antipode*, vol. 47, no. 4 (2015), pp. 829–48.

30 John Bell Rae, "Federal Land Grants in Aid of Canals," *The Journal of Economic History*, vol. 4, no. 2 (Nov. 1944), p. 167.

31 In his classic *Oriental Despotism*, Karl Wittfogel described water's political imperatives: "No operational necessity compels [a farmer] to manipulate either soil or plants in cooperation with many others. But the bulkiness of all except the smallest sources of water supply creates a technical task which is solved either by mass labor or not at all." See Wittfogel, *Oriental Despotism: A Comparative Study of Total Power* (New Haven: Yale University Press, 1957), p. 15. Murray J. Leaf, in "Irrigation and Authority in Rajasthan," *Ethnology*, vol. 31, no. 2 (April 1992), pp. 115–32, explained: "The need to control corvee labor and competition between societies requires ever larger works, larger works require heavier corvees of labor, heavier corvees require higher levels of integration and co-ordination and therefore large permanent systems ultimately require permanent specialized bureaucracies who will decide how many people are needed for what, and where. These must be 'vertically' organized." In other words, the argument behind the idea of hydraulic despotism or the Asiatic mode of

production: large-scale canal irrigation systems seem to require mass organization, and that seems to require a centralized powerful state. For an interesting and surprisingly sympathetic discussion of Wittfogel's ideas in transit from left to right, see Neil Smith, "Rehabilitating a Renegade?: The Geography and Politics of Karl August Wittfogel," *Dialectical Anthropology*, vol. 12, no. 1 (1987), pp. 127–36.

32 Craig R. Hanyan, "China and the Erie Canal," *The Business History Review*, vol. 35, no. 4 (Winter 1961), pp. 558–66.

33 George Leonard Staunton, *An Authentic Account of an Embassy from the King of Great Britain to the Emperor of China* (London: 1797), vol. II, p. 403; cited in Hanyan, p. 562.

34 "Notes on the Erie Canal," *Bulletin of the Business Historical Society*, vol. 6, no. 5 (Nov. 1932), p. 6.

35 David Hosack, *Memoir of DeWitt Clinton* (New York: J. Seymour, 1829), p. 347.

36 Gerard Koepple, *Bond of Union: Building the Erie Canal and the American Empire* (New York: Da Capo Press, 2009), p. 93.

37 Hanyan, p. 566.

38 Ulysses Prentiss Hedrick, *A History of Agriculture in the State of New York* (Albany: New York State Agricultural Society, 1933), pp. 243–4.

39 Hedrick, pp. 243–4.

40 Daniel Walker Howe, *What Hath God Wrought, the Transformation of America, 1815 to 1848* (Oxford: Oxford University Press 2007), p. 118.

41 Howe, p. 5.

42 Adriaen van der Donck, Charles T. Gehring, William A. Starna, and Diederik Willem Goedhuys, et al., *A Description of New Netherland* (Lincoln: University of Nebraska Press, 2008), p. 21.

43 On the Hessian fly, see Alan Taylor, "'The Hungry Year': 1789 on the Northern Border of Revolutionary America," in Alessa Johns, ed., *Dreadful Visitations: Confronting Natural Catastrophe in the Age of Enlightenment* (New York: Routledge, 1999).

44 Thomas S. Wermuth, "New York Farmers and the Market Revolution: Economic Behavior in the Mid-Hudson Valley, 1780–1830," *Journal of Social History*, vol. 32, no. 1 (Fall 1998), p. 188.

45 Wermuth, pp. 119–20.

46 *The United States Postal Service: An American History, 1775–2006*.

47 Todd Shallat, *Structures in the Stream: Water, Science, and the Rise of the U.S. Army Corps of Engineers* (Austin: University of Texas Press, 2010), p. 147.

48 Robert Gudmestad, *Steamboats and the Rise of the Cotton Kingdom* (Baton Rouge: Louisiana State University Press, 2011), p. 118; also see Walter Johnson, *River of Dark Dreams: Slavery and Empire in the Cotton Kingdom* (Cambridge, MA: Harvard University Press, 2013), pp. 87–91.

49 Henry Shreve quoted in Ari Kelman, "Forests and Other River Perils"

in Craig E. Colten, *Transforming New Orleans & Its Environs: Centuries of Change* (Pittsburgh: University of Pittsburgh Press, 2000), p. 60.

50 Karl Marx, *Capital: A Critique of Political Economy*, vol. 2 (New York: Penguin, Reprint edition, 1992).

51 David Maldwyn Ellis, "Railroad Land Grant Rates, 1850–1945," *The Journal of Land & Public Utility Economics*, vol. 21, no. 3 (Aug. 1945), p. 207.

52 "A New Fight Erupts Over Land Grants," *Business Week*, Sept. 16, 1972, p. 35; see also the statement by Senator Fred Harris, *Congressional Record*, CXVIII, no. 146, Sept. 19, 1972; Michael Lind, *Land of Promise: An Economic History of the United States* (New York: Harper Collins, 2012); Michael Perelman, *Railroading Economics: The Creation of the Free Market Mythology* (New York: Monthly Review Press, 2006).

53 Heywood Fleisig, "The Central Pacific Railroad and the Railroad Land Grant Controversy," *The Journal of Economic History*, vol. 35, no. 3 (Sept. 1975), pp. 552–66, 563.

54 Richard J. Orsi, "'The Octopus' Reconsidered: The Southern Pacific and Agricultural Modernization in California, 1865–1915," *California Historical Quarterly*, vol. 54, no. 3 (Fall 1975), pp. 199, 212.

55 Edna Monch Parker, "The Southern Pacific Railroad and Settlement in Southern California," *Pacific Historical Review*, vol. 6, no. 2 (June 1937), pp. 103–19.

56 Thomas A. Clinch, "The Northern Pacific Railroad and Montana's Mineral Lands," *Pacific Historical Review*, vol. 34, no. 3 (Aug. 1965), p. 325.

57 Richard A. Walker, *The Conquest of Bread: 150 Years of Agribusiness in California* (New York: The New Press, 2004), p. 86.

58 See Chapter 14 in James McPherson, *Battle Cry of Freedom* (New York: Oxford University Press, 2003).

59 Blake Bell, "Homestead National Monument of America and the 150th Anniversary of the Homestead Act," *Western Historical Quarterly*, vol. 43, no. 1 (Spring 2012), pp. 72–8.

60 McPherson, p. 451.

61 J. Bartlett Brebner, "Laissez Faire and State Intervention in Nineteenth-Century Britain," *The Journal of Economic History*, vol. 8, no. S1 (January 1948), pp. 59–73.

62 Emma Griffin, "Why Was Britain First?: The Industrial Revolution in Global Context," Chapter 8 in *Short History of the British Industrial Revolution* (Basingstoke: Palgrave Macmillan, 2010). Napoleon's so-called "Continental System," announced from occupied Berlin, imposed de facto protectionism in the form of a trade embargo upon Britain. In occupied western Germany, local manufacturing picked up pace accordingly.

63 Imanuel Geiss, *The Question of German Unification: 1806–1996* (New York: Routledge, 2013), pp. 32–4; Andre Wakefield, "Books,

Bureaus, and the Historiography of Cameralism," *European Journal of Law and Economics*, vol. 19, no. 3 (May 2005), pp. 311–20; Cheryl Schonhardt-Bailey, "Parties and Interests in the 'Marriage of Iron and Rye,'" *British Journal of Political Science*, vol. 28, no. 2 (April 1998), pp. 291–332.

64 J. A. Aho, quoted in W. R. Lee, "Economic Development and the State in Nineteenth-Century Germany," *The Economic History Review*, New Series, vol. 41, no. 3 (Aug. 1988), p. 358.

65 Cheryl Schonhardt-Bailey, "Parties and Interests in the 'Marriage of Iron and Rye,'" *British Journal of Political Science*, vol. 28, no. 2 (April 1998), pp. 291–332.

66 Oscar Eckenstein, K. Richard Oscar Bertling, W. Robinson, *Modern railway practice: a treatise on the modern methods of the construction and working of German railways. Approved by the Prussian minister of public works, the Bavarian minister of communications, and the railway authorities of other German states* (Originally published by Ministerium der Offentlichen Arbeiten; English publication by R. Hobbing: London, 1914), p. 25.

67 Martin Kitchen, *The Political Economy of Germany, 1815–1914* (Montreal: McGill–Queen's University Press, 1978); Alexander Gerschenkron, *Bread and Democracy in Germany* (Ithaca: Cornell University Press, 1989). Also Chapter 8 in Emma Griffin, *A Short History of the British Industrial Revolution* (Basingstoke: Palgrave Macmillan, 2010).

68 Arthur Walworth, *Black Ships Off Japan: The Story of Commodore Perry's Expedition* (New York: Alfred A. Knopf, 1946).

69 See in Ronald E. Dolan and Robert L. Worden, *Japan: A Country Study* (Washington: Government Printing Office, 1990), pp. 36–50; Also, Chapter One, Chuhei Sugiyama, *The Origins of Economic Thought in Modern Japan* (New York: Taylor and Francis, 1994).

70 Wakayama Norikazu quoted in Sugiyama, p. 8.

71 Sugiyama, pp. 9–12.

72 C. Mosk, *Competition and Cooperation in Japanese Labour Markets* (New York: Springer, 1995), p. 35.

73 Ronald E. Dolan and Robert L. Worden, *Japan: A Country Study* (Washington: Government Printing Office, 1990), pp. 36–50; Tom Nicholas, "Hybrid Innovation in Meiji, Japan," *International Economic Review*, vol. 54, no. 2 (May 2013), pp. 575–600.

74 Mark Ravina, *To Stand with the Nations of the World: Japan's Meiji Restoration in World History* (New York: Oxford University Press, 2017); also see Chapter 1 in S. C. M. Paine, *The Japanese Empire: Grand Strategy from the Meiji Restoration to the Pacific War* (New York: Cambridge University Press, 2017); Carl Mosk, "Japan, Industrialization and Economic Growth," EH.Net Encyclopedia, edited by Robert Whaples, Jan. 18, 2004.

Index